DDoS Attacks

Evolution, Detection, Prevention, Reaction, and Tolerance

DDoS Attacks

Evolution, Detection, Prevention, Reaction, and Tolerance

Dhruba Kumar Bhattacharyya
Jugal Kumar Kalita

CRC Press
Taylor & Francis Group
Boca Raton London New York

CRC Press is an imprint of the
Taylor & Francis Group, an **informa** business

CRC Press
Taylor & Francis Group
6000 Broken Sound Parkway NW, Suite 300
Boca Raton, FL 33487-2742

Printed on acid-free paper
Version Date: 20160308

International Standard Book Number-13: 978-1-4987-2964-2 (Hardback)

Visit the Taylor & Francis Web site at
http://www.taylorandfrancis.com

and the CRC Press Web site at
http://www.crcpress.com

Contents

List of Figures

List of Tables

Preface

Rapid technological advances have made the Internet ubiquitous around the globe. Access speeds and reliability of access are always improving, and as a result, diverse services provided on the Internet are greatly impacting every aspect of our day-to-day lives. Using these services, people routinely depend on the Internet to share confidential and valuable personal and professional information. Because smooth functioning of society depends highly on the Internet, individuals with bad intentions routinely exploit inherent weaknesses of the Internet to paralyze targeted services all over the net. With increasing incidences of network attacks, detecting such unwelcome intrusions has become an important research area. Among all the threats for which network defenders need to watch out, Distributed Denial-of-Service (DDoS) attacks are among the most common and most devastating. In this attack, people with malice use tools that are frequently available on the net to disrupt Websites, databases or enterprise networks by first gathering information on their weaknesses and later exploiting them. DDoS is a coordinated attack, launched using a large number of compromised hosts. A DDoS attack is considered high-rate when it generates a large number of packets or extremely high-volume traffic within a very short time, say a fraction of a minute, to disrupt service. An attack is referred to as a low-rate attack, if it is mounted over minutes or hours. To counter DDoS attacks, several significant defense mechanisms have been developed.

This book discusses the evolution of DDoS attacks, how to detect a DDoS attack when one is mounted, how to prevent such attacks from taking place, and how to react when a DDoS attack is in progress with the goal of possibly tolerating the attack and doing the best under the circumstances without failing completely. It introduces types of DDoS attacks, characteristics that they demonstrate, reasons why such attacks can take place, what aspects of the network infrastructure are usual targets, and how these attacks are actually launched. The book elaborates upon the emerging botnet technology, current trends in the evolution and use of this technology, and the role of this technology in facilitating the launching of DDoS attacks, and challenges in countering the role of botnets in the proliferation of DDoS attacks. The book introduces statistical and machine learning methods applied in the detection and prevention of DDoS attacks in order to provide a clear understanding of the state of the art. It presents DDoS reaction and tolerance mechanisms with a view to studying their effectiveness in protecting network resources without compromising the quality of services. Further, the book includes a discussion of a large number of available tools and systems for launching DDoS attacks of various types and for monitoring the behavior of the attack types. The book also provides a discussion on how to develop a custom testbed that can be used to perform experiments such as attack launching, monitoring of network traffic, detection of attacks, as well as for testing strategies for prevention, reaction and mitigation. Finally, the reader will be exposed to additional current issues and challenges that need to be overcome to provide even better defense against DDoS attacks.

Dhruba Kumar Bhattacharyya
Jugal Kumar Kalita

MATLAB® and Simulink are registered trademarks of The MathWorks, Inc. For product information, please contact:
The MathWorks, Inc.
3 Apple Hill Drive
Natick, MA 01760–2098 USA
Tel: 508–647–7000
Fax: 508–647–7001
Email: info@mathworks.com
Web: www.mathworks.com

Acknowledgments

This humble work would not have been possible without the constant support, encouragement and constructive criticism of a large number of academicians, scientists and professionals. We are grateful to the panel of reviewers for their constructive suggestions and critical evaluation. Special thanks and sincere appreciation are due to Prof Sukumar Nandi of IITG, Prof R K Agrawal of JNU, Prof S K Gupta of IITD, Dr P N R Rao of DeitY and our dedicated faculty members and research group members: Prof N Sarma, Prof U Sarma, Prof S M Hazarika, Dr Sanjib Deka, Dr M H Bhuyan, Mr Debojit Boro, Mr Nazrul Hoque, Mr R C Baishya, Mr Hasin A Ahmed, Mr Hirak J Kashyap and Mr R K Deka. The constant support and cooperation received from our colleagues and students during the period of writing this book is sincerely acknowledged.

Dhruba Kumar Bhattacharyya
Jugal Kumar Kalita

Authors

 **Dhruba Kumar Bhattacharyya** received his Ph.D. degree from Tezpur University in 1999 in cryptography and error-control coding. He is a professor in Computer Science and Engineering at Tezpur University. Professor Bhattacharyya's research areas include network security, data mining and bioinformatics. He has published more than 200 research articles in leading international journals and peer-reviewed conference proceedings. Dr. Bhattacharyya has authored three technical reference books and edited eight technical volumes. Under his guidance, thirteen students have received their Ph.D. degrees in the areas of machine learning, bioinformatics and network security. He is Chief Investigator of several major research grants, including the Centre of Excellence, Tezpur University of Ministry of HRD, Government of India under Frontier Areas of Science and Technology and Centre for Advanced Computing, Tezpur University funded by Ministry of IT, Government of India. He is on the editorial board of several international journals and has also been associated with several international conferences. More details about Dr. Bhattacharyya can be found at http://agnigarh.tezu.ernet.in/~dkb/index.html.

 **Jugal Kumar Kalita** teaches computer science at the University of Colorado, Colorado Springs. He received his M.S. and Ph.D. degrees in computer and information science from the University of Pennsylvania in Philadelphia in 1988 and 1990, respectively. Prior to that he received an M.Sc. from the University of Saskatchewan in Saskatoon, Canada, in 1984 and a B.Tech. from the Indian Institute of Technology, Kharagpur, in 1982. His expertise is in the areas of artificial intelligence and machine learning, and the application of techniques in machine learning to network security, natural language processing

and bioinformatics. He has published 150 papers in journals and refer-
eed conferences. He is the author of a book on Perl titled *On Perl: Perl
for Students and Professionals*. He is also a co-author of a book titled
Network Anomaly Detection: A Machine Learning Perspective with
Dr. Dhruba K Bhattacharyya. He received the Chancellor's Award at
the University of Colorado, Colorado Springs, in 2011, in recognition
of lifelong excellence in teaching, research and service. More details
about Dr. Kalita can be found at http://www.cs.uccs.edu/~kalita.

Chapter 1

Introduction

Rapid technological advances in accuracy, speed, and reliability of the modern Internet infrastructure have made significant impacts on our daily lives. With the proliferation of Web-enabled applications, the flow of valuable and confidential information is growing across public as well as private networks. Networks are designed to share assets and resources efficiently among network users, and Web-enabled applications play a vital role in our day-to-day personal and professional lives. In recent years, the Internet has provided a global computational and communication environment by interconnecting billions of computers. In addition, the integration of the Internet with wireless and mobile technologies is ushering in an impressive wave of modern devices and applications on these devices. Figure 1.1 shows the statistics of Internet users in the world up to the year 2014.

People depend on the Internet to share confidential and valuable personal and professional information with other network users. On the other hand, because of general high reliance on the Internet, some people also exploit the weaknesses of the Internet to paralyze targeted segments of it. A common example of such weaknesses of the Internet is mismatch of speeds between core and edge routers. Another major weakness of the Internet arises due to inappropriate configurations of routers. Such weaknesses often cause a networked system to become a target of attacks, which are launched to gain unlawful access to valuable and confidential information or damage private or professional resources. Although, a good number of firewall and cryptographic systems have been developed in recent years, these are not free of limitations. Defense mechanisms that identify intrusions as they

1

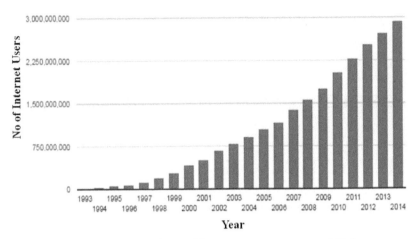

Figure 1.1: Number of Internet users up to 2014.

happen or are about to happen, provide another way to defend networked systems from any attack. In spite of tremendous efforts made by defenders, zero-day and other complex attacks are being launched almost every day. Among all the threats for which network defenders need to watch out, denial-of-service (DoS) attacks are considered the most common and often the most devastating ones.

1.1   Anomalies in Networks

Attacks in a network are also called anomalies in network traffic. Generally, anomalies or attacks are network events that deviate from the normal, expected or usual behavior, and are suspect from a security perspective. Such anomalies in a network may be due to two basic types of reasons [243]: performance-related and security-related. Because many individual entities are put together to form a computer network to contribute toward providing complex communication services, things may go wrong with any of the interacting entities. A performance-related anomaly may occur due to malfunction of network devices, e.g., because of a router misconfiguration. On the other hand, security-related anomalies occur due to malicious attempts or activities to disrupt normal functioning of the network. Anomalies caused due to security-related reasons may be of six distinct types [24]: infection, explosion, probe, cheating, traverse and concurrency. An *in-*

fection attempts to tamper with a system to install malicious files or executables such as viruses or worms to infect the target system. The second category, i.e., *explosion anomalies* attempt to cause overflow in the target system with bugs. A commonly known example of this category of anomalies is buffer overflow. A *probe* attempts to gather information to identify the vulnerabilities of systems. Nmap is a common example of a utility to perform probe. The fourth category, i.e., *cheating*, attempts to use fake or abnormal addresses for sources or destinations for information requests. A common example of cheating is spoofing of IP addresses or MAC addresses. A *traverse* attack attempts to compromise the target system by matching possible key pieces of information required to protect the system. Two common examples of traverse attempts are brute force attacks and dictionary attacks. The fifth category is more serious and attempts to victimize a system or a service by sending mass requests beyond the capacity of the system or the service. A common example of this category is the *Distributed Denial-of-Service attack*. In addition to these, almost every day new attacks are being created and many do not belong to any of these categories. Most newer attacks attempt to infect a target system by exploiting undiscovered weaknesses or bugs in the system.

1.2 Distributed Denial-of-Service (DDoS) Attacks

DDoS is a coordinated attack, launched using a large number of compromised hosts. At an initial stage, the attacker identifies the vulnerabilities in one or more networks for installation of malware programs in multiple machines to control them from a remote location. At a later stage, the attacker exploits these compromised hosts to send attack packets to the target machine(s), which is (are) usually outside the original network of infected hosts, without the knowledge of these compromised hosts. Depending on the intensity of attack packets and the number of hosts used to attack, commensurate damage occurs in the victim network. If the attacker can exploit a large number of compromised hosts, a network or a Web server may be disrupted within a short time. Some common examples of DDoS attacks are *fraggle*, *smurf* and *SYN flooding*. DDoS attack statistics up to the year 2014

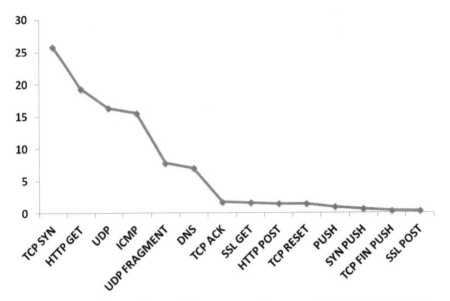

Figure 1.2: DDoS attack statistics up to the year 2014 (DDoS attack percentage is shown on the y-axis)

are shown in Figure 1.2. It can be seen in the figure that among the commonly used DDoS attacks shown on the x-axis, TCP SYN, HTTP GET, UDP, and ICMP flooding are most frequently used.

1.3   Causes of DDoS Attacks

DDoS attacks are catastrophic and can bring down a server or network very quickly. Generally, a DDoS attacker forms (or hires) a network with compromised hosts to launch DDoS attacks. The attacker takes advantage of these compromised hosts to gather security related information. Eight prominent reasons for DDoS attacks are the following: (i) High interdependencies exist in Internet security. (ii) Internet resources are limited. (iii) Many unwittingly compromised hosts, puppeteered by one or more dangerous masters, conspire against a few targeted servers or hosts. (iv) Intelligence and resources that may be used to thwart impending attacks are not usually collected. (v) Simple and straightforward routing principles are used on the Internet. (vi) There are mismatches in design and speeds between core and edge networks are commonplace. (vii) Network management is frequently slack. (viii) The common and useful practice of sharing resources has its drawbacks.

1.4   Targets of DDoS Attacks

Generally a DDoS attacker aims to attack any of the following targets:

(i) Routers
(ii) Links
(iii) Firewalls and defense systems,
(iv) Victim's infrastructure
(v) Victim's OS
(vi) Current communications
(vii) Victim's applications.

1.5   Launching of DDoS Attacks

There are four basic steps in launching a DDoS attack. (a) *Selection of agents.* The master attacker chooses the agents that will perform the attack. Based on the nature of vulnerabilities present, some machines are compromised to use as agents. Attackers victimize these machines, which may have abundant resources, so that a powerful attack stream can be generated. In the early years, the attackers attempted to acquire control of these machines manually. However, with the development of advanced security attack tool(s), it has become easier to identify these machines automatically and instantly. (b) *Compromise.* The attacker exploits security holes and vulnerabilities of the agent machines and plants the attack code. The attacker also takes necessary steps to protect the planted code from identification and deactivation. In the direct DDoS attack strategy, the compromised nodes, aka agents or zombies situated between the attacker and the victim, are unwitting accomplice hosts recruited from among a large number of unprotected hosts on the Internet with high-bandwidth connectivity. The DDoS attack strategy is usually more complex due to inclusion of an intermediate layer of nodes between the zombies and victim(s). It further complicates the traceback of the path from the victim to the attackers mostly due to (i) the complexity in untangling the traceback information because of the involvement of multiple machines, and/or (ii) having to retrace the connection back via a large number of distributed routers or servers.

Unless a sophisticated defense mechanism is used, it is usually difficult for the users and owners of the compromised agents to realize that they have become a part of a DDoS attack system. (c) *Communication*. The attacker communicates with any number of handlers to identify which agents are up and running, when to schedule attacks, or when to upgrade agents. Such communication among the attackers and handlers can be via various protocols such as ICMP, TCP, or UDP. Based on the configuration of the attack network, agents can communicate with a single handler or multiple handlers. (d) *Attack*. The master attacker initiates the attack. The victim, the duration of the attack, as well as special features of the attack such as the type, the length of TTL (time-to-live), and port numbers can be adjusted. The attackers use available bandwidth and each sends a huge number of packets to the target host or network to immediately overwhelm the resources.

1.6   Current Trends in Botnet Technology

A *botnet* is defined as a large group of malware-infected machines, referred to as *zombies*, which are controlled by a malicious entity, referred to as the *botmaster*. The botmaster is used to control the zombies remotely and to instruct them through commands to perform malicious activities. Bots are controlled using a botnet architecture and a command-and-control system, which may be based on P2P, IRC, HTTP or DNS. People with malice can use botnets to commit cyber crimes such as launching DoS attacks, sending spam mail or stealing personal and valuable data such as login IDs and passwords for mail accounts or bank credentials. It is common knowledge that a majority of email traffic is spam and most of the messages are sent through botnets.

1.7   Machine Learning in DDoS Attack Handling

The coordinated nature of DDoS attacks with variable packet intensity involving a large number of compromised nodes demands a cost-effective detection mechanism, which can distill the voluminous anomalous traffic from normal traffic in real time or near real time with a minimum number of false alarm(s). In such a detection mechanism, the following components play major roles.

1.7.1   Traffic Attributes and User-Parameter Selection

To make a defense system cost-effective, the number of network traffic attributes selected for analysis of captured and preprocessed traffic data should be as low as possible. The most influential attributes to take part in the anomaly detection process can be identified using appropriate attribute selection or ranking methods. In practice, most DDoS defense systems have been found to operate successfully using only 2 to 3 traffic attributes.

A most desirable quality of a network or application defense system is low dependency on user parameters (if not totally independent of such parameters), apart from other qualities such as cost effectiveness, easy implementability, reliability, robustness, scalability, high accuracy and low collateral damage. Most practical defense systems are heavily dependent on multiple user parameters, and the performance of these systems is highly sensitive to these parameters. On the other hand, due to rapid technological advancement, significant changes routinely occur in a network's operating environment or scenario. As a result, the parameter values valid for network scenario 1, may not be effective for scenario 2. Thus, development of appropriate heuristic methods to support selection of the proper values for these parameters can alleviate this problem of parameter selection.

1.7.2   Selection of Metrics or Measures

Generally, central to a machine learning method for traffic analysis, is the use of a similarity or dissimilarity (distance) metric or measure. Sometimes, such metrics or measures are integral to the machine learning method. For example, in ROCK [93] clustering, the concept of a "link" is integral to the method. On the other hand, many other methods are not bound to a specific measure. For example, in k-means [251] clustering, the proximity measure can be Manhattan, Euclidean, or Cosine distance or even others. However, the performance of the method may be dependent on the measure used. Hence, depending on the situation, and the type and nature of data selected for analysis, a careful selection of the metric or measure can help improve the accuracy of clustering or classification significantly.

1.7.3   Analysis of Data

In the recent past, spurred by the evolution of new DDoS attack tools, several novel and practical machine learning approaches have been used for DDoS attack detection and prevention. The relevance and effectiveness of such methods are mostly based on their performance in terms of classification accuracy and execution time. These approaches belong to four basic categories, viz., statistical, knowledge-based, soft computing-based, and other data mining and machine learning approaches [24].

Statistical techniques fit a statistical model to the given data and then apply a statistical inference test on an unseen instance to determine if it can be explained by this model. In knowledge-based methods, predefined rules or patterns of attack are checked against connection events to test their legitimacy. Soft computing techniques apply problem-solving technologies such as fuzzy logic, probabilistic reasoning, neural networks and genetic algorithms. Machine learning or data mining techniques include clustering, classification, and association rule mining. Clustering is a technique that is also known as unsupervised classification. It does not need to be trained with a training dataset and the strength of clustering lies within the algorithm itself. Hence, it is very popular. Classifiers such as SVM [149], [51] and HMM [24] are also used in many detection approaches. An association mining technique works using a support-confidence framework and typically it comprises two steps, i.e., frequent itemset generation and rule generation. It finds the frequent itemsets by computing the frequency of occurrences of the itemsets in a database of transactions individually as well as in association. Once frequent itemsets are found, rule generation becomes trivial. A detailed discussion on these three basic data mining techniques are given in [24].

1.7.4   Mode of Detection

A DDoS defense system can operate in a centralized or in a distributed mode depending on the deployment of its modules. In a centralized DDoS defense system, all modules comprising the system are deployed at the same location, whereas the modules of a distributed DDoS defense system are usually deployed at different places and they attempt to identify attacks quickly at multiple places with additional resources in a coordinated manner. With limited resources, a centralized defense system is usually unable to identify all classes of DDoS attacks in real time. Especially, when the attack intensity grows very rapidly, it is almost impossible for such systems deployed at the victim end to counter the flooding, and often such systems themselves become victimized by attackers.

On the other hand, distributed defense systems are usually more powerful with sufficient resources to counter high-rate as well as low-rate DDoS attacks. Due to the ability to inspect network traffic at several places on edge networks as well as the cooperative approach they take, such a system can identify anomalous traffic quickly.

1.7.5 Generation of Alarm Information and Reaction

After the preprocessed traffic data has been analyzed with appropriate machine learning techniques, the next step is to decide whether a packet is to be identified as anomalous or normal. If it is found anomalous with reference to the value of a user threshold, the system needs to decide on the information to generate along with some alarm for subsequent action. To react with proper action to block of such an attack type now and also in the future, the generation of the alarm with adequate explanatory information (e.g., protocol or source IP) is important. Most mitigation strategies are based on a dynamically updated black list of IPs and thus anomaly identification should help the generation of such a list.

1.8 DDoS Defense

Building adequate defense against DDoS attacks is a non-trivial problem for the network administrator as well as the network security researcher. If attackers have high skill levels, existing defense may not be able to handle all types of new DDoS attacks in near real time. Many real-time DDoS attack detection methods have been published in the literature. But there is still no defense mechanism that can handle all classes of DDoS attacks in real time, let alone doing so with low computational overhead. Since a DDoS attacker uses a large number of compromised nodes to flood the network instantly, early detection of an attacker's preparatory activities is essential so that the attack can be mitigated immediately. It is also expected that the detection system should not be a cause of high collateral damage. Thus, detecting attacks without affecting legitimate traffic when there are a large

number of distributed attack sources, IPs are spoofed, and attack rates
are dynamic, is definitely a big challenge. The six major problems to
be addressed by a DDoS defense system are: (i) handling of dynamic
rate attacks, (ii) identification of spoofed IP addresses, (iii) handling
a large number of attack sources, (iv) ensuring minimum degradation
on legitimate services, (v) creating a minimum number of false alarms,
and (vi) doing all this using a generic threshold setting for parameter
values.

1.9 Modules of a DDoS Defense System

A generic DDoS defense system is composed of three modules, viz.,
monitoring, detection and reaction. Network *monitoring* collects information regarding the network used by the target as well for nodes that
can be used to launch the attack. On the other hand, traffic analysis allows the defender to see services being used on a network and to
compare against activities that should be seen. This allows one to identify unauthorized services within a network. In order to perform basic
network monitoring, one needs to collect information on the traffic at
various points within the network. A *detection* module produces reports to a management station. Some detection modules may attempt
to stop an intrusion attempt but this is neither required nor expected.
An intrusion detection module is primarily focused on identifying possible incidents, logging information about them and reporting attempts.
A detection module can be used for various purposes such as identifying problems with security policies, documenting existing threats
and deterring individuals from violating security policies. A detection
module gathers and analyzes information from various sources within a
computer or a network to identify possible security breaches, which include both intrusions and misuse. A *reaction* module follows a two-step
process. The first set of procedures constitutes the passive component,
involving inspection of the systems configuration files to detect inadvisable settings, inspection of the password files to detect inadvisable
passwords, and inspection of other system areas to detect policy violations. The second set of procedures constitutes the active component.
Here, mechanisms are set in place to react to known methods of attack and to generate system responses. Intrusion Detection Systems
(IDSs) can respond to suspicious events in several ways, which include
displaying an alert, logging the event, or even paging an administrator.

1.10 Types of DDoS Defense Systems

With the rapid emergence of external and internal threats to networks and resources, system administrators and defenders must think about security all the time. As a result, researchers have looked at a variety of approaches to confront DDoS attacks in a network.

1.10.1 Based on Approach

Based on the approach used to confront intrusions, intrusion defense systems can be categorized into four types: DDoS detection, DDoS prevention, DDoS response, and DDoS tolerance.

1.10.1.1 DDoS Detection

A DDoS detection system is an application to monitor a network or system for non-conforming or malicious activities or policy violations. If it detects any such activities, it alerts the system or network administrator. A detection system uses a set of techniques to detect suspicious activities either at the network or at the host levels.

1.10.1.2 DDoS Prevention

A DDoS prevention system is an "upgraded" version of a DDoS detection system because both monitor network traffic and/or system activities for malicious instances. The main difference is that intrusion prevention systems are able to actively block intrusions that are detected. An intrusion prevention system can take actions such as sending an alarm, dropping malicious packets, resetting the connection and/or blocking traffic from the offending IP addresses.

1.10.1.3 DDoS Response

A DDoS response system, by contrast, continuously monitors system health based on alerts generated by a DDoS detection system, so that malicious or unauthorized activities can be handled effectively by applying appropriate countermeasures to prevent problems from worsening and to return the system to a healthy mode. A notification system generates alerts when an attack is detected. An alert can contain information such as attack description, time of attack, source IP, and user accounts used to attack. A DDoS response system automatically executes an appropriate set of response actions based on the type of attack.

1.10.1.4   DDoS Tolerance

A DDoS tolerance system takes a fault-tolerant design approach to defend network resources against DDoS attacks. Abandoning the conventional aim of preventing all intrusions, intrusion tolerance instead uses mechanisms that prevent intrusions from leading to complete system failure so that the system can still function at a reduced, but reasonable level.

1.10.2   Based on Nature of Control

In this section, we discuss types of defense systems based on the control structure used to counter attack traffic. There are three locations where the processes used to control detection and prevention can be situated. These are centralized, hierarchical and distributed.

1.10.2.1   Centralized DDoS Defense

In this type of defense system, each detection element produces alerts locally. The generated alerts are sent to a central server that plays the role of a correlation handler and analyzes them. Using centralized control, an accurate detection decision can be made based on all available alert information. The main drawback of this approach is that the central unit is a single point of failure; any failure in the central server leads to the collapse of the whole process of correlation. In addition, the central unit should be able to handle the high volume of data which it may receive from the local detection elements in a short amount of time.

1.10.2.2   Hierarchical DDoS Defense

Such a system is divided into several small groups based on similar features such as geography, administrative control, and use of similar software platforms. Such a defense system works as a detection element at the lowest level, while at a higher level it is furnished with both a detection element and a correlation handler, and it correlates alerts from both its own level and lower levels. The correlated alerts are then passed to a higher level for further analysis. This approach is more scalable than the centralized approach, but still suffers from the vulnerability of the central unit. Besides, the higher-level nodes have higher-level abstraction of the input, which limits detection coverage.

1.10.2.3 Distributed DDoS Defense

In distributed DDoS defense, there is no centralized coordinator to process the information; it is a fully autonomous system with distributed management control. All participating detection and prevention systems have their own components communicating with each other. A major advantage of such a system is that the network entities do not have complete information of the network topology, and as a result, it is possible to have a scalable design since there is no central entity responsible for doing all the correlation work. Local alarm correlation is simpler in this structure. However, two major disadvantages of the approach are that (a) information on all alerts is not available during decision making, and as a result, accuracy may be low; (b) the alert information usually has a single feature (like an IP address), which is too narrow to detect large-scale attacks.

1.10.3 Based on Defense Infrastructure

In this section, we discuss various defense systems that are developed based on the infrastructure used. These are two basic types, viz., host-based and network-based.

1.10.3.1 Host-Based DDoS Defense

In this architecture, data is analyzed by individual computers that serve as hosts. The network architecture used is agent based, which means that a software agent resides on each of the hosts in the system. Thus, a host-based DDoS Detection and Prevention System processes data that originate on the individual computers themselves, such as event and kernel logs. Such a system can also monitor which program accesses which resources and may flag anomalous usage. Such a system also monitors the state of the system and makes sure that everything makes sense, which is necessary for the use of anomaly filters.

1.10.3.2   Network-Based DDoS Defense

A network-based DDoS defense system examines data exchanged among computers. Such systems are supposed to be capable of monitoring and collecting system audit trails in real time as well as on a scheduled basis, thus distributing both CPU utilization and network overhead and providing a flexible means of security administration. A network-based DDoS defense system captures network traffic from the wire as it travels to a host. This can be analyzed for a particular signature or for unusual or abnormal behaviors. Several sensors are used to sniff packets on the network; these are computer systems designed to monitor network traffic. If any suspicious or anomalous behavior occurs, it triggers an alarm and passes the message to the central computer system or an administrator, in addition to generating an appropriate automatic response.

1.10.4   Based on Defense Location

A DDoS defense system can be deployed in three possible locations: victim end, intermediate, and source end. Each has its own advantages and disadvantages.

1.10.4.1   Victim-End DDoS Defense

Victim-end DDoS detection methods are generally employed in the routers of a network that may potentially become the victim of a DDoS attack. This includes any network worth much these days, especially those belonging to large company, non-profit or government networks. The detection software stores information about known intrusion signatures or profiles of normal behavior. This information is updated by the processing elements as new knowledge becomes available. The stored intrusion signatures (or references or profiles) and also procedures for other critical events such as false alarms are updated. The processing element in a detection engine frequently stores intermediate results in what is called *configuration data*. Detecting attacks at the victim end is relatively easy because a DDoS attack at the victim is indicated by higher resource consumption all of a sudden, and the detection mechanism looks for abnormal rise in such consumption. However, an important and obvious disadvantage is that these approaches detect the attack only after it reaches the victim and detecting an attack when legitimate clients have already been affected is pyrrhic victory.

1.10.4.2   Source-End DDoS Defense

A source-end DDoS defense system attempts to prevent congestion not only on the victim side, but also in the whole intermediate network. The main difficulty with this approach is in its implementation. This is because during these attacks, sources are widely distributed and a single source is likely to behave almost as normal traffic. Another crucial problem is the practical difficulty of deploying a system at the source end without prescient knowledge of where an attack may originate from millions of small or big networks on the Internet, dispersed around the globe. In addition, if there is a rogue network, why would it allow outsiders to place detection mechanisms on it or why would it monitor itself on behalf of others?

1.10.4.3   Intermediate Network DDoS Defense

The intermediate network DDoS defense system tries to strike a balance between detection accuracy and attack bandwidth consumption, which are the major issues in the previous two approaches, i.e., source-end and victim-end defense. Such schemes apply rate limits on connections passing by a router after comparing with stored normal profiles. The main difficulty with this approach is deployability. To achieve full detection accuracy, all routers on the Internet will have to employ this detection scheme, because unavailability of this scheme in only a few routers may cause failure to the entire detection and traceback processes. Thus, full practical implementation of this scheme is unattainable because it requires re-configuring all routers on the Internet.

1.10.5   Based on Technique Used

Many techniques have been developed to detect and prevent intrusion. We categorize them as misuse detection and anomaly detection.

1.10.5.1   Misuse Detection

In misuse detection, we characterize abnormal system behavior first and then define any other behavior as normal. In other words, anything we do not know is considered normal. For example, one could develop patterns for attacks such as pulsing, increasing, constant rate or subgroup DDoS attacks, and try to identify whether any traffic pattern conforms to any of these patterns. Thus, misuse detection systems

attempt to detect only known attacks based on predefined characteristics. However, a novel and effective attack may take place using
unexpected patterns of traffic and it will be missed. As a result, the
accuracy of such IDSs depends solely on how well the knowledge of attack information has been captured, preprocessed and fed to the IDS's
detection engine. However, well-crafted expert knowledge of known
attacks can enable misuse detection-based IDSs to perform accurately
with low false positives.

1.10.5.2 Anomaly Detection

These techniques are based on first establishing the normal behavior of
a subject, e.g., a user or a system. Any action that significantly deviates
from the normal behavior is considered intrusive. If we can establish a
normal activity profile for a system, we can flag all system states that
vary significantly from established profile. Anomaly-based techniques
try to detect the complement of bad behavior whereas misuse-based
detection tries to recognize known bad behavior. The main advantage
of anomaly detection is that it can detect unknown attacks.

1.11   DDoS Tools and Systems

In recent years, a large number of tools for DDoS attack launching as
well as for network defense have been developed. These tools can be
used to capture, to visualize, to analyze and to detect various attack
types with multiple objectives. Some commonly used detection, capturing and analysis tools include LOIC, HOIC, Wireshark, Gulp and
Ntop. These tools support capturing live network traffic, preprocessing raw traffic, selection of relevant features, analysis of vulnerabilities,
visualization of traffic over a subset of selected traffic attributes and
actual detection of attacks.

People with malice may use attack tools to disrupt a network for
many different purposes. Attackers generally target Websites or
databases as well as enterprise networks by gathering information on
their weaknesses. Typically, for a chosen class of attacks, the attackers
explore and use relevant tools to launch the attack. A large number of
defense tools also have been made available by various network security research groups as well as private security professionals to counter
attacks mounted using attack tools. The available tools have different
purposes, capabilities and interfaces. We categorize existing tools into

two major categories: tools for attackers and tools for network defenders. In this book, we discuss a taxonomy of the tools used for attack generation as well as attack detection.

1.12 DDoS Defense Evaluation

There is a critical need for a common evaluation methodology for Distributed Denial-of-Service (DDoS) defenses, to enable independent evaluation and comparison. An evaluation or assessment of quality or accuracy of a system, mechanism or method is usually a snapshot in time. With the passage of time after a system is initially built, the environment changes and new vulnerabilities arise, and accordingly, the evaluation must be performed again after updates and possible parameter tuning. Many performance metrics have been proposed to assess the effectiveness, cost and security of defense systems. However, it is worth mentioning that the information obtained during one round of evaluation plays a significant role in subsequent evaluations as well as in the final end product that results.

1.13 Prior Work

In the past decade, several similar and relevant books have been published.

The ones we have found are listed below.

(i) *Internet Denial-of-Service: Attack and Defense Mechanisms* by Jelena Mirkovic, Sven Dietrich, David Dittrich and Peter Reiher, published by Prentice Hall, 2005.

(ii) *An Investigation into the Detection and Mitigation of Denial-of-Service (DoS) Attacks: Critical Information Infrastructure Protection* by S.V. Raghavan (Ed), E Dawson (Ed), published by Springer, 2011.

(iii) *Network Security and DDoS: Cooperative Defense against DDoS attack Using GOSSIP protocol* by Imran Sohail, Sikandar Hayat, published by Lambert Academic Publishing, June, 2010.

(iv) *An Introduction to DDoS Attacks and Defense Mechanisms: An Analyst's Handbook* by B. B. Gupta, published by Lambert Academic Publishing, December, 2011.

(v) *A Defense Framework Against Denial-of-service in Computer Networks* by Sherif Khattab, published by ProQuest, 2008.

(vi) *A Novel Distributed Denial-of-service Detection Algorithm* by Brett Tsudama, published by California Polytechnic State University, 2004.

(vii) *A Defense Framework for Flooding-based DDoS Attacks* by Yonghua You, published by Queen's University, Canada, 2007.

(viii) *Practical Packet Analysis: Using Wireshark to Solve Real-World Network Problems* by Chris Sanders, published by No Starch Press, Second Edition, 2011.

(ix) *Network Flow Analysis* by Michael W. Lucas, published by No Starch Press, July, 2010.

In (i), the authors present how DoS attacks are waged and how to improve a network's resilience to such attacks. The authors describe several measures and laws involved and their implications, and the kinds of damage they can cause. Some real examples of DoS attacks are discussed from the view-points of the attacker, victim, and unwitting accomplices. This book discusses only DoS attacks. In (ii), the authors provide insights into the complexity of the DoS and DDoS problem to be solved as well as the breadth of research being conducted on various facets of the DoS/DDoS problem. Some areas covered are understanding DDoS behavior in real-time at high-packet rates; management of Web services during a DDoS attack; creating conducive environments for DDoS prevention through provable authentication protocols; identification of vulnerabilities specific to DDoS in emerging technologies; and the process of sustaining a legal, regulatory, and policy focus with international cooperation. In (iii), the authors show the effectiveness of an algorithm using OmNet++ Ver. 4.0 simulation in detecting DDoS attacks. The authors also show how the nodes can be protected from such an attack using the GOSSIP protocol. In (iv), the author discusses how DDoS attacks are prepared and executed, how to think about DDoS from a defense perspective, and how to provide for computer and network defenses. The book also presents a suite of actions that can be taken before, during and after an attack. In (v), three resource-efficient dodging-based DoS defense algorithms are discussed. Honeybees combine channel hopping and error-correcting codes to achieve bandwidth-efficient and energy-efficient mitigation of jamming in multi-radio networks. In roaming honeypots, dodging enables the camouflaging of honeypots or trap machines as real servers, making it hard for attackers to locate and avoid traps. Furthermore, shuffling requests among servers opens up windows of opportunity, during which legitimate requests are serviced. Live baiting efficiently identifies service-level DoS attackers by employing results from group-testing theory, discovering defective members in a population using a minimum number of tests. The cost and benefit of the dodging algorithms are analyzed theoretically, in simulation, and using prototype experiments. In (vi), the applicability of implementing ratio-based SYN flood detection (RSD) on a network processor is explored, and results are presented. In (vii), the authors introduce and describe a distance-based distributed DDoS defense framework which defends against attacks by coordinating between the distance-based DDoS defense systems at the source end and the victim end. In (viii), the author discusses network protocols in various contexts, including a large number of new scenarios. It teaches how to make sense of PCAP data. The book also includes a separate section on troubleshooting slow networks and packet analysis for security to help understand how modern exploits and malware behave at the packet level. Finally, in (ix), the author shows how to use open source software to build a flow-based network awareness system. The author also discusses the use of network analysis and auditing to address problems and improve network reliability. Unlike most of these DDoS security books, we focus on the following.

(a) DDoS attacks|types, characteristics, causes, targets and how they are launched.

(b) Botnet technology|evolution, trends and challenges.

(c) Statistical and machine learning approaches applied in the detection and prevention of DDoS attacks in order to provide a clear understanding of the state of the art.

(d) DDoS reaction and tolerance mechanisms to study their effectiveness in protecting network resources without compromising the quality of services.

(e) Practical use of a large number of tools and systems for launching DDoS attacks of various types and for monitoring the behavior of the attack types.

(f) Practical knowledge of developing a custom testbed for attack launching, monitoring, detection, prevention, reaction and mitigation.

1.14   Contribution of This Book

The following are the major contributions of this book.

(a) An in-depth discussion on botnet technology, its evolution, trends and challenges botnet technology presents in countering DDoS attacks.

(b) A systematic presentation of various statistical, machine learning, know-ledge-based and soft computing methods for DDoS detection, prevention, reaction and tolerance in networks and clouds.

(c) Discussion of a large number of practical tools and systems that are used by malicious actors to launch DDoS attacks of various types and also tools and systems used by defenders for monitoring and mitigating such attacks. We also discuss how researchers can develop a custom testbed to experiment and understand how malicious actors launch attacks so that defenders can monitor, detect, prevent and mitigate such attacks.

(d) A list of important unresolved issues and research challenges.

1.15   Organization of This Book

This book discusses distributed denial-of-service (DDoS) attacks in networks, the evolution of such attacks, and methods for DDoS detection, prevention, reaction and tolerance. To clearly understand how attacks are launched by malicious actors, we discuss how such launches are performed in the context of a private network from the perspective of an attacker. Such experiments should be performed by students, researchers and professionals in a restricted context so that things do not get out of hand but at the same time they can get insights into the minds of attackers as well as the techniques used for better prevention and mitigation. This book also discusses a large number of DDoS defense mechanisms and systems developed using statistical and machine learning techniques. To understand the effectiveness of such a method or a system, we also discuss performance metrics that can be used in a real-life as well as in a simulation environment.

In Chapter 1, we provide an introduction to anomalies in networks, why anomalies come into existence, the targets anomalies aim to attack and recent trends in anomaly generation. This chapter also introduces various types of DDoS defense systems to protect network resources. Chapter 2 delves deeper into various issues related to design of modern networks, followed by discussion of vulnerabilities that may affect the performance and security of a modern network. Chapter 3 discusses DDoS attacks, strategies adopted by attackers and a taxonomy of DDoS attacks. This chapter discusses characteristics, models and architectures of botnet technology used to launch various DDoS attacks at various scales. In Chapter 4, we discuss how to develop a custom experimental testbed and a DDoS attack tool to (i) launch both high-rate and low-rate DDoS attacks, (ii) monitor and analyze network traffic, and (iii) visualize the traffic patterns graphically to support building DDoS defense. Chapter 5 presents an overview of a DDoS defense system that has been developed, followed by an in-depth discussion of various DDoS defense approaches, the nature of control among the participants in DDoS defense, defense architectures, deployment of these systems on the network, and the underlying mathematical as well as algorithmic techniques used. In Chapter 6, we discuss several popular and highly cited (as per Google Scholar) DDoS defense systems. This chapter also discusses performance metrics that can be used to evaluate a DDoS defense system. Chapter 7 concludes the book with a discussion of research issues and challenges in this evolving field of network security research.

Chapter 2

DDoS, Machine Learning, Measures

The Internet impacts greatly upon every aspect of our lives, and hence is a critical resource for everyone. Any disruption or unavailability of this resource may lead to serious impacts at various levels of our society. As the dependency on the Internet keeps on growing at an exponential rate, the threats to the availability of network resources have also been increasing rapidly. Threats which aim to overcrowd networked computer systems or resources and consequently make unavailable legitimate services are typically referred to as Denial-of-Service (DoS) attacks [6]. When such a threat is activated through a large group of compromised machines, called zombies or bots, which send coordinated traffic to the victim, in an attempt to exhaust the network resources such as CPU, memory or link bandwidth of the victim, we refer to it as Distributed Denial-of-Service (DDoS) flooding attack. Currently, the DDoS flooding attack is generally considered the strongest weapon of choice by intruders who want to block availability of Internet services by overwhelming a network with unsolicited traffic. The ever-increasing lethality of DDoS attacks pose a serious concern to network health and as a result, has spurred sustained research in finding effective and efficient methods to handle these attacks. In a DDoS attack, the victim can range from a single Web server to the Internet connection to an entire university or an entire city or even an entire country. In most cases, the users of the compromised machines that participate in an attack are unaware of the fact.

The easy accessibility of a large number of attack tools floating in the public domain is a major cause for networks or organizations frequently coming under DDoS attacks. One can easily set up and use these tools to launch attacks by sending unsolicited traffic to the victim from distributed armies of bots or compromised computers on the Internet [6]. This unsolicited traffic is enough to paralyze the victim so that it no longer functions or provides service to legitimate users by consuming all of its resources and network bandwidth. Since the consequences of such attacks may leave a victim losing millions of dollars and many customers, both industry and academia are continuously working on finding new and improving existing defense mechanisms to counter DDoS flooding attacks. However, parallel with the continuous efforts made by defenders, attackers are also improving their skills to launch attacks at varied scales and levels of craftiness to keep themselves always one step ahead to evade detection mechanisms. In addition, the pregnable architecture of the Internet is another major cause, allowing the attacker to easily spoof the source IP (SIP) addresses of attack packets, thus making it more difficult to detect the attack. Further, the detection of malicious traffic becomes even harder, if its size and pattern are similar to those of legitimate traffic, making malicious traffic unobtrusive. As a result, the following are the major issues that need to be addressed when developing a solution to counter DDoS attacks.

(a) Resources of any Internet host are limited, and they can be easily exhausted by a sufficiently large number of user requests.

(b) If an attacker is able to acquire more resources than the resources of a victim before mounting an attack, the DDoS attack is likely to be successful.

(c) Intelligence and resources are often not collocated. Typically, the intelligence needed for service guarantees is located at end hosts, but high-bandwidth pathways required for large throughput are usually situated in the intermediate network. Attackers attempt to exploit abundant resources present in unwitting parts of the network to launch a successful flooding attack.

(d) Compromised hosts, which may be handlers or masters, are capable of controlling a large number of agents by sneaking in special programs that run on the agents.

(e) Attack daemon agents or zombie hosts are commonly external to the victim's own network, making it difficult to deliver efficient counter responses from the victim. They are external to the network of the attacker and can renounce liability if the attack is successfully traced back.

(f) Internet security is highly interdependent among the many players that reside on it. No matter how secure a victim's system may be, whether or not this system will be a DDoS victim depends on what is brewing in the rest of the global Internet.

2.1 Issues in Internet Design

The Internet was originally designed to provide a scalable and open networking and resource sharing environment among academics and research professionals [6]. However, with the ever-increasing growth of the Internet in the past two decades, security threats have also been growing exponentially. In this section we discuss the design issues of modern networks, the ones that have given rise to the growth of most DDoS attacks.

2.1.1 Complex Edge but Simple Core

According to [209], end-to-end protocol design should rely on maintenance of state outside the network, i.e., at the end points, so that the state can only be destroyed when the end points themselves break. Such a principle will lead to a simple Internet architecture with complex edges but a simple network layer [40]. However, with such a simple interconnection network, one cannot expect an intermediate router to be equipped with all the necessary functionality to counter illegitimate traffic. It will not be practical, if we engage a router in processing packets rather than routing them. Further, to provide support for DDoS detection and prevention, if the intermediate network router is loaded with a significantly high amount of additional work, it will definitely lead to performance degradation, which is not desirable!

2.1.2 Link Bandwidth Mismatch between Core and Edge

The modern Internet has a provision for maintaining varied link bandwidth between core and edge networks. To accommodate heavy traffic either as a receiver or as a sender, core networks are provisioned with high link bandwidth, whereas an edge network is provisioned with low link bandwidth because it supports a smaller number of end users. However, in a situation where a large number of sources attempt to communicate with a single destination, such a high-bandwidth core link may overwhelm a low-bandwidth edge link, and may cause a denial-of-service situation.

2.1.3   Routing Principles

The present Internet architecture aims to provide the best possible services and manage to survive even under the worst of conditions. It can perform multi-path routing to support continued communication even when gateways or routers fail. Thus, it can help bypass failed portions of the network and choose alternative paths to forward traffic. Consequently, such provisions also allow attackers to send spoofed attack traffic. Since packets from the same source can be routed through multiple paths, on detection of a potential attack, it becomes difficult to trace back to the origin of attack accurately.

2.1.4   Lack of Centralized Network Management

The distributed management approach of the Internet, i.e., the lack of a centralized mechanism for management of Internet resources: is another major design issue. The Internet was designed and can be viewed as an interconnection of a large number of smaller-sized enterprise networks, aiming to provide global access to each end user. Although such an approach has helped the Internet grow fast, it has also enabled users with malign intentions to access resources easily to create denial-of-services by blocking them using a coordinated approach. Even if we develop several DDoS defense solutions for multiple locations, due to lack of a centralized management authority, global deployment and effective control of attacks is a major issue.

2.1.5   Sharing of Reserved Resources across Data Centers

As stated earlier, IP networks were designed to provide the best possible packet-switched services by allowing users to share all resources. Due to such a sharing of resources, the service provided to one user may be affected by improper behavior of another user. A user with malign intentions can easily disturb other legitimate users by unnecessarily occupying most of the shared resources. Such inter-user dependencies on the Internet are considered one of the major causes of most DoS and DDoS attacks.

2.2 DDoS Attacks and Their Types

Using client/server technology, a perpetrator can multiply the effectiveness of the DoS attack significantly by harnessing the resources of multiple unwitting accomplice computers, which serve as attack platforms. Generally, a DDoS attack is considered more damaging than a DoS attack and it usually takes more planning and diligence to mount a DDoS attack. A DDoS attacker generally follows four steps. In *step* 1, the attacker scans the whole network to find and recruit vulnerable host(s). The vulnerable hosts are then compromised for exploitation by the attacker using malware or backdoor programs in *step* 2. In *step* 3, the attacker infects the compromised hosts to create a base for effective launching of the attack. Finally, the attack is launched using the compromised hosts in *step* 4. Figure 2.1 shows how the typical DDoS attack works.

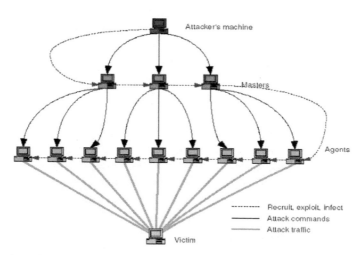

Figure 2.1: DDoS strategy: Recruiting, exploiting, infecting, and attacking.

2.2.1 Agent-Handler and IRC-Based DDoS Attack Generation

Sprecht and Lee [226] discuss the pros and cons of two types of architectures, viz., (i) the agent-handler and (ii) the Internet relay chat (IRC). In (i), the three main role players, i.e., clients, handlers, and agents are organized as in Figure 2.2(a). To initiate an attack, the attacker establishes communication with the client to interact with the rest of agent system. The attacker installs malicious software throughout the Internet and these installations are used as handlers. Such handlers are used by the clients to exchange messages with the agents. The compromised systems are used to host instances of the agent software and ultimately to execute the attack. Interestingly, the existence of such malicious software as well as the communication between the client and the agents are not known to the owners and the users of the systems. In (ii), for communication between the client and the agents, an IRC channel is used, as shown in Figure 2.2(b). The agents communicate through IRC ports, making it difficult for the defender to trace DDoS command packets.

2.2.2 Types of DDoS Attacks

DDoS attacks are classified by various researchers in different ways following different criteria. The following subsections present DDoS attack types based on OSI layers, approaches used to launch attacks, volume of traffic generated, and based on attack rate dynamics. Various types of DDoS attacks are also discussed in more detail in [101], [170].

2.2.2.1 Layer-Specific DDoS Attacks

Based on Open Systems Interconnection (OSI) layers, whose services are used to carry out attacks, DDoS attacks can be classified into two categories, i.e., application layer DDoS and transport and network layer DDoS. In an *application layer* attack, the attacker uses layer 7, i.e., application layer protocols such as HTTP and HTTPS, to send traffic to the victim. Such traffic normally carries CPU-intensive queries to the server and makes it busy forever. The volume of traffic needed to put a server down is comparatively lower than that of the other type, i.e., a network layer attack. The traffic in an application layer attack is indistinguishable from legitimate traffic, making it very difficult to detect. A detailed description of application layer DDoS attacks can

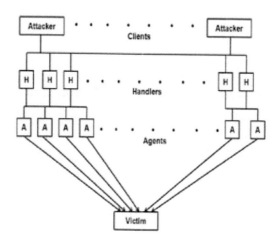

(a) Agent handler architecture

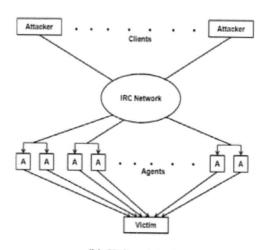

(b) IRC architecture

Figure 2.2: Agent handler and IRC architectures.

be found in [63]. In a *network or transport layer* attack, the attacker tries to exhaust resources such as the bandwidth of the links which carry traffic to the victim, or the memory of devices such as routers, switches, and firewalls. To achieve this objective, the zombies send huge amounts of traffic in layers 3 and 4 to the victim. Such an attack is normally large in volume ranging from a few Mbps to several hundreds of Gbps. Different network layer protocols such as Internet Control Message Protocol (ICMP), User Datagram Protocol (UDP) and Transmission Control Protocol (TCP) are used in such an attack.

The most commonly used network layer DDoS attacks are TCP SYN flooding [46], ICMP echo [39], UDP flooding [45], DNS amplification [252], and NTP [96], [197].

2.2.2.2 Direct and Reflector-Based DDoS Attacks

In a DDoS attack, it is not always the zombies that send attack traffic to the victim. Servers running UDP-based services are often used by attackers to carry out massive DDoS attacks. Such servers are used as reflectors by the attacker. Based on the nature of the attacking machines, DDoS attacks are classified into two categories, viz., *direct* and *reflector-based*. In a *direct* attack, the attacker uses zombies directly to launch DDoS attacks of various types. In contrast, in a *reflection or amplification* attack, many innocent intermediate nodes, known as reflectors, are used to generate an attack. The attacker sends requests to the reflector servers by spoofing the source IP as if it were the victim's IP. As a result, these servers reply to the victim by sending messages whose volume is normally many times larger than the original request message size. Hence, this type of DDoS attack is also called an *amplification attack*. The attacker uses this technique to amplify the attack traffic up to several hundred times. DNS amplification attacks and NTP attacks are examples of reflection-based DDoS attacks (DRDoS). Figures 2.3 and 2.4 present schematic views of direct and indirect DDoS attacks. A detailed description of how reflection attacks with different UDP services and amplification factors can be used to amplify attack traffic can be found in [6].

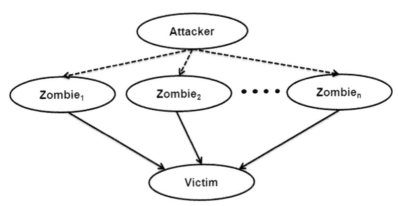

Figure 2.3: Direct DDoS attack.

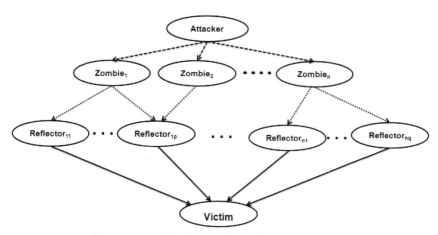

Figure 2.4: Reflector-based DDoS attack.

2.2.2.3 Direct and Indirect DDoS Attacks

One can also classify DDoS attacks based on whether the attack traffic is sent to the victim directly or through intermediaries. In a *direct attack*, the attacker sends the attack traffic directly to the victim using a large number of compromised machines. In contrast, in an *indirect attack*, the attacker, instead of attacking the victim directly, attacks the links and other services that are important for the victim to remain functional. Link-flooding attacks such as *crossfire* [129] and *coremelt* [235] are examples of indirect DDoS attacks.

2.2.2.4 High-Rate and Low-Rate DDoS Attacks

DDoS attacks can also be classified based on the volume of attack traffic, as *low* and *high*. In a low-rate DDoS attack, the attacker usually performs the attack by sending attack traffic at a low rate matching the legitimate traffic profile. For example, in case of an application layer attack, the attacker tries to exhaust the victim's processing resources by sending it CPU-intensive queries. Similarly, in a *shrew* attack [53], [64], the volume of the attack traffic is comparatively low. In a high-rate DDoS attack, the attacker sends a huge volume of attack traffic toward the victim. It is the most common type of DDoS attack. High-rate traffic, sometimes called a flash crowd [52], is often mistaken for a DDoS flooding attack, resulting in dropping of legitimate user requests. However, as pointed out in [64], a flash crowd can be distinguished from malicious traffic by observing the rate of introduction of new IP addresses over a sequence of time intervals. In a flash crowd, new IP addresses are introduced suddenly, resembling a flooding attack, but the rate of introduction of new IP addresses drops after some time, though the high request rate from legitimate users may persist.

2.2.2.5   Attack Types Based on Rate Dynamics

In addition to the classification mentioned above, DDoS attacks can be classified based on other traffic characteristics, such as the dynamics of the attack traffic rate. Mirkovic et al. [167] classify DDoS attacks based on attack rate dynamics into four categories.

(a) *Constant rate attack*: The attack rate reaches its maximum within a very short period of time. All zombies, after receiving a command from an attacker, start sending attack traffic at a constant rate. This type of attack creates a sudden packet flood at the victim end.

(b) *Increasing rate attack*: Instead of attacking the victim with full force instantly, the attacker gradually increases the traffic intensity toward the attacker. An increasing rate attack approach is adopted by the attacker to understand the victim's response to attack traffic, so that the attacker can attempt to evade the victim's detection mechanisms.

(c) *Pulsing attack*: In this type of attack, the attacker activates a group of bots periodically to send attack traffic to the victim. Such a mechanism is used to remain undetected by a detection mechanism. *Shrew 52* is an example of a pulsing rate DDoS attack, sending short synchronized bursts of traffic to disrupt TCP connections on the same link, by exploiting a weakness in the TCP retransmission timeout mechanism.

(d) *Subgroup attack*: As in the case of a pulsing rate attack, here also the attacker sends pulses of attack traffic to the victim. However, the zombies are divided into groups and these groups are activated and deactivated in different combinations. Such a subgroup attack approach is used by the attacker to remain disguised and carry on the attack for a longer period of time [169].

Figure 2.5 shows these four different attack types.

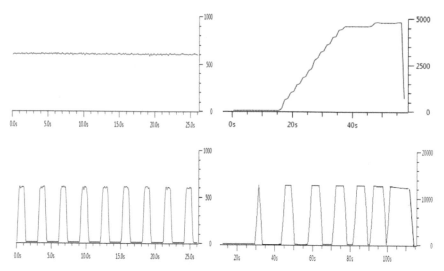

Figure 2.5: Constant-rate, increasing, pulsing, and sub-group attacks.

2.3 DDoS Attack Targets

The target of a DDoS attack can range from a single Web server to the Internet connection to an entire university or an entire city or even an entire country [130]. Typically, a DDoS attacker chooses any of four common targets on the victim network, as stated below.

2.3.1 On Infrastructure

Many DDoS attackers aim to paralyze a networked system by targeting its underlying infrastructure. Such infrastructure may range from the smallest wireless access point to a large public key infrastructure spread out over the entire globe or a global domain name system (DNS). The larger the coverage of the infrastructure, the greater the impact of DDoS attacks.

2.3.2 On Link

A very common target of DDoS attacks is the link. An attacker can launch a DDoS attack successfully by sending a large amount of coordinated traffic to exhaust the link completely. As a consequence, many legitimate packets may be dropped.

2.3.3   On Router

IP routers are often targets of DDoS attacks. A common approach to launch a DDoS attack on a router is to overwhelm the routing table by populating it with a very large number of routes, causing the CPU power to be insufficient or the router's memory to run out. Many attackers also take advantage of the weaknesses of routing protocols to launch such attacks.

2.3.4   On OS

The operating system (OS) can play an important role in protecting resources from an application DDoS attack. As a result, many attackers target the OS itself. If such an attack can be launched successfully, it may cause serious damage to all applications running on the OS.

2.3.5   On Defense Mechanism

The target of DDoS attacks can be the defense system itself. The firewall and the DDoS detection mechanism are often targeted by DDoS attackers. Firewalls, which can be stateful or stateless, can be targeted to exhaust the resources by sending a large volume of traffic, which may lead the firewall to maintain excessive states and finally may lead to it run out of memory. However, in case of a defense mechanism, the impact or consequence of a DDoS attack will be different. For example, the mechanism may fail to perform correctly, and as a consequence, may lead to the generation of a large number of false alarms.

2.4   Current Trends in DDoS Attacks

DDoS attacks have been rampant for more than a decade. With every passing day, the availability of the sophisticated tools and other resources to perform a DDoS attack is becoming more plentiful. As a result, the frequency and the power in terms of complexity and volume of DDoS attacks are increasing. Arbor Networks *Worldwide Infrastructure Security Report*, Volume X [4] reports that the volume of DDoS attacks has increased hundreds of times over the last few years. Figure 2.6 shows the increase in DDoS attack volume over the last few years. From the same report, a few observations are summarized below to help assess current DDoS attack trends.

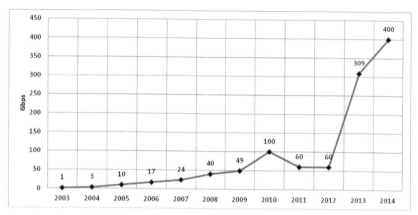

Figure 2.6: Current trends in DDoS attacks.

(a) A key factor causing increased attack trends up to several hundred Gbps-sized DDoS attacks, is the use of reflection and amplification.

(b) The use of multi-vector DDoS attacks, where a combination of different attack policies are used to evade the detection mechanism of the victim, is another reason. One of the most commonly seen multi-vector attacks in recent times is a SYN flood attack comprising of two types of SYN packets— first, regular SYN packets and second, large SYN (more than 250 bytes) packets. The advantage of this combination is that it can exhaust the victims CPU as well as network bandwidth.

(c) Application-layer DDoS attacks such as HTTP flooding contribute another common serious security threat. These attacks are low-rate attacks and are difficult to easily distinguish from legitimate traffic.

(d) DDoS attack frequency has been increasing while attack durations are getting shorter. Figure 2.7 shows the distribution of the number of DDoS attacks experienced per month across the Internet and the distribution of attack durations.

The Incapsulas Q2 2015 DDoS Global Threat Landscape Report [1] underscores the same facts about current trend in DDoS attacks. An up-and-coming pervasive network scenario called the Internet of Things (IoT), whose basic idea is to interconnect electronic objects with diverse

---
[1] https://www.incapsula.com

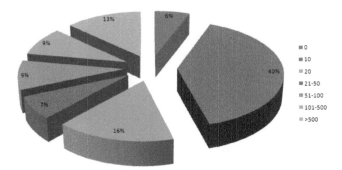

Figure 2.7: DDoS attack frequency.

capabilities and in diverse locations, such as home security systems, TVs, medical devices, GPS and smart watches, sensors, handheld devices, weather observations, control valves at power plants, door locks in prisons, traffic signals, and embedded systems to facilitate greater connectivity among the things in this world, is expected to bring in more opportunities to create mischief for the DDoS attackers. IoT will drastically increase the population of IP-enabled devices on the Internet, most of which will be equipped with light security mechanisms, [2] opening up a new range of candidate devices for the attackers to recruit as zombies [17].

2.5 Strength of DDoS Attackers

Recent statistics on occurrences of DDoS attacks (see Figures 2.7 and 2.8), show that attack frequency is increasing from year to year. Below, we enumerate some important features of current DDoS attackers, which tell us that it is not straightforward to entirely eliminate DDoS attacks from the Internet.

(a) The attacker can spoof the source IP address inscribed in the attack packets, which gives the attacker two crucial advantages: first, the attacker can hide its identity; second, the attacker can use this mechanism to amplify the attack traffic hundreds of times as in the case of DRDoS attacks.

(b) The attackers can arbitrarily change values of fields in layer 3, 4 and 7 protocol headers. For example, in a TCP SYN flooding

---

[2]http://www.cio.com.au/article/570160/3- reasons-wary-internet-things/

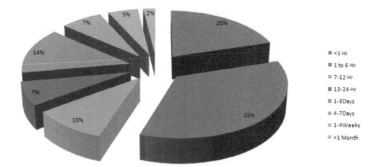

Figure 2.8: Statistics of attack durations.

attack, the attacker can alter fields like the SIP and TTL of the IP layer header as well as set and reset TCP flags in the transport layer header.

(c) The attacker can change the attack rate, the secret cabal of attacking bots, and even the identity of the victim dynamically and at will. The attacker can also mix multiple attack vectors, even across layers, as in the case of a multivector DDoS attack, making defense more difficult.

(d) The attack traffic can be made completely indistinguishable from the legitimate traffic in terms of content. For example, in a HTTP GET or POST flooding attack [273], the attacker sends a huge number of seemingly legitimate HTTP GET or HTTP POST requests to the victim.

2.6 Desired Characteristics of DDoS Defense System

The primary goal of the defending side of a DDoS attack is to keep the victim alive and reachable by legitimate users even if the victim is under a DDoS attack. Thus, an appeal to DDoS defense has to have the following characteristics.

(a) *Real-time Performance*: A defense system should be able to detect an ongoing, and possibly impending attack before the attack paralyzes the victim with its overwhelming malicious traffic.

(b) *Scalability*: Since the attack rates of today's DDoS attacks are hundreds of Gbps, both the time and space complexities of the detection mechanism play important roles in the scalability of the defense system.

(c) *Maintaining QoS*: A major obstacle in defending against a DDoS attack is that the attack traffic, especially in the case of a low-rate DDoS attack, is indistinguishable from legitimate traffic in content. Hence, just detecting an attack is not enough to protect the victim; special mechanisms are needed to separate legitimate traffic from attack traffic with high confidence, so that the QoS to legitimate users can be maintained.

(d) *Source Identification*: A DDoS attack defense system should be robust against IP spoofing. It should have a suitable mechanism such as traceback or pushback to locate the attack sources.

2.7   Recent DDoS Attacks

Large networked server sites like Google and Facebook are equipped with huge pools of computing and storage resources. Such giant sites with ample resources can usually mitigate the impact of DDoS attacks in real-time but may still be in trouble on rare occasions. However, other Web entities like networks of government sites, news sites, technical repositories, gaming servers are often successfully attacked and put down. Below, we report a few recent DDoS attacks that were successfully launched.

(a) *Against Dutch Government sites*: On February 10, 2015 the sites of the federal government were subject to a massive DDoS attack and the sites were down for 10 hours.[3] Other sites hosted on the same network were also affected by the attack.

(b) *Against the National Security Agency (NSA) of the United States*: On October 25, 2013, the NSA site was attacked and was fully paralyzed for an extended period of time.[4] The attack was suspected

---

[3]http://www.pcworld.com/article/2883092/ddosattack-takes-dutch-government-sitesoffline-for-10-hours.html

[4]http://www.ibtimes.com/nsa-website-down-following-apparent-ddos-attack-possiblyanonymous-or-foreign-government-1442452

to be performed by the loosely associated international network of activists and hacktivists called *Anonymous*.[5]

(c) *Against Github*: On March 24, 2015, Github, a code repository hosting service that is widely used by software developers around the world to manage source code, was under a massive DDoS attack.[6] The attack was reported to continue for 24 hours with partial success. The attacker used TCP layer 7 to mount the attack.

(d) *Against thousands of French websites*: During the second week of January 2015, more than 19,000 Websites ranging from those of military regiments to pizza shops were under minor DDoS attacks. This was an unusual and peculiar attack.[7]

The above mentioned incidents indicate the urgent need to put together serious efforts by each country to counter and mitigate possible threats caused by DDoS attacks.

2.8 Machine Learning Background

Machine learning is a broad, inter-disciplinary area of research which includes the study of techniques that computers can use to learn from data. Problems which can be solved using computers can be divided into two basic categories. For category 1 problems, human experts have adequate knowledge and expertise to develop algorithms, write code, and implement. Of course, category 1 problems can be non-trivial and complex. In contrast, the category 2 problems are also non-trivial and complex, but ones for which straightforward coding skills are not enough to find appropriate solutions. Machine learning aims to address questions for category 2 problems with a high degree of cost effectiveness in terms of accuracy and resources, by learning patterns from data.

To explain the role of machine learning, let us take an example research question from microarray data analysis in computational biology. What are those rare genes not participating in any of the groups

---

[5]https://en.wikipedia.org/wiki/Anonymous

[6]http://thehackernews.com/2015/03/github-hit-by-massive-ddos-attack-from 27.html

[7]http://money.cnn.com/2015/01/15/technology/security/french-websites-hacked/

of co-expressed gene patterns in a given yeast dataset? If prior knowledge is not provided or available to solve such a problem, a machine learning researcher will focus on developing an unsupervised learning (discussed in detail in Section 2.8.1) mechanism with the primary objective of achieving high accuracy and efficiency. To find the solution, one may use a data mining approach such as an efficient clustering or outlier mining technique with an appropriate proximity measure to support the unsupervised learning mechanism. A biologist might collaborate with a statistician to test hypotheses and to validate the solutions provided by the machine learning technique.

Machine learning researchers have classified the task of learning in different ways following different criteria. One common approach for classification distinguishes between *analytical* and *empirical* learning. In analytical learning, the learner does not require any external input, whereas, in empirical learning, some form of external knowledge or experience is a must. In analytical learning, the learning program can achieve improved performance by analyzing and solving various instances of the problem repeatedly over time, and by remembering the past outcomes. In contrast, in empirical learning, the learning program can improve its performance only by using external experience or knowledge.

2.8.1   Supervised and Unsupervised Machine Learning

The most common way of classifying machine learning methods is to separate them into *supervised* and *unsupervised* learning. In supervised learning, the method needs prior knowledge in the form of labeled instances or examples given by "domain experts," which are used by the method in classifying or assigning a label to a new instance or an object. In unsupervised learning, the method analyzes and attempts to learn from data without any prior knowledge, human intervention or supervision.

Thus, a supervised learning method typically builds a prediction model for normal or known attack classes based on prior knowledge and attempts to assign class labels to an input test instance with reference to the learned prediction model. To assign a class label, a typical approach is to compare the test instance (e.g., by computing similarity or dissimilarity) with the reference model(s) to decide the class to which the instance belongs. So, a supervised learning method is highly dependent on the prior knowledge or labeled traffic. But if the knowledge is inadequate or inaccurate, it may lead to a high level of false alarms. In the past two decades, a large number of supervised learning methods have been introduced for DDoS detection. We discuss some prominent supervised learning methods in *Chapter 5* and analyze pros and cons.

In contrast, the unsupervised learning methods are mostly dependent on certain assumptions. For example, while addressing the problems of network anomaly detection, some machine learning researchers assume that (i) anomalous or attack traffic has high intra-class similarity and (ii) attack traffic is statistically different from normal traffic. So, if these assumptions are not true for a given network scenario, such methods will suffer from a large number of false alarms. In *Chapter 5*, we discuss several prominent DDoS detection methods developed using the unsupervised learning approach. It will be worthwhile to mention that a common feature of both these types of learning methods is the dependency on a proximity measure for effective comparison of a test instance to decide whether it belongs to a pre-defined class or a pre-assumed group. So, selection of an appropriate measure for effective comparison is an important task to achieve good performance. The performance of most supervised and unsupervised machine learning methods may suffer if an inappropriate proximity measure is used, one that fails to capture the essence of a real-life application mostly due to (i) high dimensionality of the data, (ii) selection of an inappropriate subset of attributes to describe data instances, and (iii) dependency on multiple sensitive input parameters during comparison and analysis.

Next, we introduce a set of popular proximity measures that have been used commonly by machine learning researchers for DDoS defense.

2.8.2 Measures: Similarity and Dissimilarity

As discussed in the previous section, the performance of identifying the class label of a test instance in a *supervised learning* method or deciding the belongingness of a test instance to any of a pre-assumed set of unlabeled groups of instances in an *unsupervised learning* method, is highly influenced by the selection of a proximity measure. Proximity is a measurement of similarity or dissimilarity between a pair of objects or instances. A proximity value measures *similarity* if the larger the value for a pair of objects, the closer or more alike the objects are. Examples of similarities are cooccurences, interactions, statistical correlations, associations, social relations, and reciprocals of distances. A proximity value measures *dissimilarity* if the smaller the value for a pair of objects, the closer or more alike we think they are. Examples of dissimilarity measures are distances, differences, and reciprocals of similarities. The proximity from object P to Q is the same as proximity from object Q to P. In other words, proximity follows the property of symmetricity.

Mathematically, the similarity between a pair of instances, i.e., say $S(P,Q)$ is a numeric quantity that represents the strength of closeness between the instances, possibly considering two subsets of attributes of the instances. In contrast, dissimilarity or distance between a pair of objects, i.e., say $D(P,Q)$ is a quantitative measure or value of how apart or distant the objects are. So, if $S(P,Q)$ represents the normalized similarity between a pair of instances (P,Q) and $D(P,Q)$ represents the normalized dissimilarity between (P,Q), then $D(P,Q) = 1 - S(P,Q)$.

So, for two identical instances, the similarity becomes 1 whereas the dissimilarity or distance becomes 0. Mathematicians, statisticians, and machine learning researchers have introduced a large number of similarity and dissimilarity measures to help answer research questions in various domains. Keeping in view the difficulty of selecting an appropriate measure for network anomaly detection with high detection accuracy, we introduce some commonly used measures [29], [138], [37], [192], [48], [128], [28], [22], [133], [8], [153] in DDoS detection under the categories of dissimilarity measures, correlation measures, divergence measures, and information metrics. We also present results of some empirical studies for the benefit of researchers and professionals.

2.8.2.1   Dissimilarity Measures

In this section, we introduce four well-known distance measures commonly used by network security researchers.

(a) *Manhattan or L_1 Distance:* The Manhattan distance between two points, P and Q, each with n dimensions, is calculated as

$$d_1(P,Q) = ||P - Q||_1 = \sum_{i=1}^{n} |p_i - q_i|$$

where P and Q are vectors $P = (p_1, p_2, \ldots, p_n)$ and $Q = (q_1, q_2, \ldots, q_n)$. The Manhattan distance is always greater than or equal to zero. The measurement is zero for identical points and high for points that show little similarity.

(b) *Euclidean or L_2 Distance:* The Euclidean distance between two points, P and Q, with n dimensions is calculated as

$$d(P,Q) = \sqrt{\sum_{i=1}^{n}(p_i - q_i)^2}$$

.

The Euclidean distance is always greater than or equal to zero. The measurement is zero for identical points and high for points that show little similarity.

(c) *Cosine Measure:* Given two vectors of attributes, P and Q, the Cosine measure, $cos(\theta)$, is represented using a dot product and magnitude calculation as

$$cos(\theta) = \frac{P.Q}{||P||||Q||} = \frac{\sum_{i=1}^{n} P_i \times Q_i}{\sqrt{\sum_{i=1}^{n}(P_i)^2} \times \sqrt{\sum_{i=1}^{n}(Q_i)^2}}$$

.

(d) *Hamming Distance:* Hamming distance calculates the number of positions at which the corresponding symbols of two equal-length strings are different. This measure is faster than most other measures. For example, two strings $P(101001)$ and $Q(101101)$ are different by one symbol, and hence the Hamming distance of P and Q is 1. Similarly, Hamming distance between strings *angel* and *demon* is 5.

2.8.2.2   Correlation Measures

In this section, we present five established correlation and residue measures. These are Pearson correlation [28], [143], Spearmen Rank Correlation [61], Kendall correlation [133], shifting-and-scaling correlation [8], and Normalized Mean Residue Similarity (NMRS) [158] measure. We also analyze their effectiveness in distinguishing two objects or instances, where one object may be a transformation variant of the other.

(a) *Pearson Correlation:* The correlation between two sets of data is a measure of how well they are related. The most common measure of correlation in statistics is the Pearson Correlation [28], [143]. The full name is the Pearson Product Moment Correlation or PPMC. It computes if there exists a linear relationship between two sets of data. The sample Pearson r is calculated as follows:

$$r_{pq} = \frac{cov_{pq}}{\sigma_p \sigma_q}, \tag{2.1}$$

where cov_{pq} is defined as

$$cov_{pq} = \sum_{i=1}^{N} \frac{(p_i - P')(q_i - Q')}{N - 1}.$$

In the above, we have variables P and Q for which we have N paired observations. P' and Q' are the mean values for P and Q, respectively. The value of Pearson r is a standardized covariance, and ranges from -1, indicating a perfect negative linear relationship, to $+1$, indicating a perfect positive relationship. A value of zero suggests no linear association, but does not mean two variables are independent, an extremely important point to remember.

(b) *Spearman Rank Correlation:* Spearman rank correlation [61] is a non-parametric test that is used to test the association between two ranked variables, or one ranked variable and one measurement variable. It was developed by Spearman, and thus it is called the Spearman rank correlation. The Spearman rank correlation test does not make any assumptions about the distribution of the data and is appropriate when the variables are measured on a scale that is at least ordinal and scores on one variable are related to the other variable.

The following formula is used to calculate the Spearman rank correlation:

$$\rho = 1 - \frac{6 \sum d_i^2}{n(n^2 - 1)}, \tag{2.2}$$

where ρ is Spearman rank correlation, d_i is the difference between the ranks of corresponding values p_i and q_i, and n is the number of values in each data variable.

(c) *Kendall's correlation:* The Kendall rank correlation [133] is also a non-parametric test that measures the strength of dependence between two variables. If we consider two samples, P and Q, where each sample size is n, we know that the total number of possible pairings between P and Q is $n(n-1)/2$. The following formula is used to calculate the value of Kendall's rank correlation:

$$\tau = \frac{(n_c - n_d)}{\frac{1}{2}n(n-1)}, \tag{2.3}$$

where n_c is the number of concordant values and n_d is the number of discordant values.

(d) *Shifting-and-scaling correlation:* This measure, also referred to as the *SSSim* measure, is a robust correlation measure that can handle shifting, scaling, absolute, and shifting-and-scaling correlations between a pair of objects. SSSim was introduced to detect gene pairs with high correlation in gene expression data [8]. It is robust to noisy expression values because this measure uses the idea of local means computed using consecutive values within small running windows. Some basic definitions used in this measure are given below.

   (i) *Local mean:* The local mean of an object P_i for a condition $c_j \in C$ is the mean of the values $P_i(c_{j-1})$, $P_i(c_j)$ and $P_i(c_{j+1})$ for $j \neq 1$ and $j \neq n$ and n is the total number of conditions. If $j = 1$, local mean = mean$[\ P_i(c_j), P_i(c_{j+1})]$. If $j = n$, local mean = mean$[\ P_i(c_{j-1}), P_i(c_j)]$.

   (ii) *Baseline condition pair:* This is a pair of conditions or attributes that is used as the reference condition or attribute pair. The ratio between differences with other condition (attribute) pairs and this pair is used in the computation of SSSim score.

Let $P_1 = \{p_1, p_2, p_3, p_4, \ldots, p_n\}$, $P_2 = \{q_1, q_2, q_3, q_4, \ldots, q_n\}$ exhibit shifting-and-scaling patterns and the first and second conditions be baseline condition pairs for $1 \leq k \leq (n-1)$. Then we have [272]:

$$\frac{p_{k+1} - p_k}{p_2 - q_1} = \frac{q_{k+1} - q_k}{q_2 - q_1}. \tag{2.4}$$

Based on this equation, the SSSim measure [8] was proposed. If (P_1, P_2) is a pair of objects, then SSSim of (P_1, P_2) is given as

$$SSSim(P_1, P_2) = 1 - \frac{\sum\limits_{i=2}^{n-1} \frac{|\frac{p_{i+1}-p_i}{p_2-p_1} - \frac{q_{i+1}-q_i}{q_2-q_1}|}{2*max(|lmean_i - \frac{p_{i+1}-p_i}{p_2-p_1}|, |lmean_i - \frac{q_{i+1}-q_i}{q_2-q_1}|)}}{n-2},$$

(2.5)

where $lmean_i = mean(\frac{a_{i+1}-a_i}{a_2-a_1}, \frac{b_{i+1}-b_i}{b_2-b_1}, \frac{a_{i+2}-a_{i+1}}{a_2-a_1}, \frac{b_{i+2}-b_{i+1}}{b_2-b_1})$, if $i = 2$

$mean(\frac{a_i-a_{i-1}}{a_2-a_1}, \frac{b_i-b_{i-1}}{b_2-b_1}, \frac{a_{i+1}-a_i}{a_2-a_1}, \frac{b_{i+1}-b_i}{b_2-b_1})$, if $i = n-1$

$mean(\frac{a_i-a_{i-1}}{a_2-a_1}, \frac{b_i-b_{i-1}}{b_2-b_1}, \frac{a_{i+1}-a_i}{a_2-a_1}, \frac{b_{i+1}-b_i}{b_2-b_1}, \frac{a_{i+2}-a_{i+1}}{a_2-a_1}, \frac{b_{i+2}-b_{i+1}}{b_2-b_1})$, otherwise.

The range for the SSSim score for any gene expression pair is $[0, 1]$ and there is no need for normalization. If the value of the SSSim score is 1, the objects perfectly exhibit shifting-and-scaling correlation. The measure introduces the local mean, i.e., $lmean_i$, of an object for a condition or attribute instead of the mean of all expressions in order to make it robust to noisy values.

(e) *Normalized Mean Residue Similarity*: NMRS [158] is a correlation measure which can distinguish shifted patterns (with a value 1) from a shifted and anti-correlated pattern (with a value 0) between two given objects.

The NMRS between a pair of objects P $= \{a_1, a_2, a_3 \ldots a_n\}$ and Q $= \{b_1, b_2, b_3 \ldots b_n\}$ is defined as

$$NMRS(P, Q) = 1 - \frac{\sum\limits_{i=1}^{p} |a_i - a_{mean} - b_i + bmean|}{2 \times max(\sum\limits_{i=1}^{p} |a_i - a_{mean}|, \sum\limits_{i=1}^{p} |b_i - b_{mean}|)},$$

(2.6)

where a_{mean} is the mean of all the elements of object P_1;
$a_{mean} = \{a_1 + a_2 + a_3 + \ldots + a_n\} / n$;
b_{mean} is the mean of all the elements of object Q_1;
$b_{mean} = \{b_1 + b_2 + b_3 + \ldots + b_n\} / n$

2.8.2.3   *f*-Divergence Measures

In this section, we introduce four *f*-divergence measures. These are *K-L*-divergence, Hellinger distance, Total Variation Distance (TVD), and α-divergence, and are useful in faster anomaly detection.

(a) *K-L Divergence:* The *K-L divergence* D_f of a probability distribution Q from another distribution P is an asymmetric measure of difference that quantifies the information lost when Q is used to approximate P. The K-L divergence measure can be defined as follows:

$$D_f(P||Q) = \sum_{i=1}^{n} p_i \, log_2(\frac{p_i}{q_i})$$

Thus, the above equation gives the expected logarithmic difference between P and Q, where the expectation is based on the probability distribution P.

(b) *Hellinger Distance:* The Hellinger distance between two probability distributions, say P and Q, can be defined as follows.

$$D_f(P||Q) = \frac{1}{\sqrt{2}} \sqrt{\sum_{i=1}^{n}(\sqrt{p_i} - \sqrt{q_i})^2}$$

It is a type of f-divergence measure and is defined in terms of the Hellinger integral, introduced by Ernst Hellinger in 1909 [48]. This distance measure has a direct relation to the Euclidean norm of the square root vectors difference, i.e.,

$$D_f(P||Q) = \frac{1}{\sqrt{2}} ||\sqrt{P} - \sqrt{Q}||_2$$

and is a special case of the *Mahalanobis distance*, when the given two classes have different standard deviations but similar means. In such a case, the *Mahalanobis distance* tends to zero, but the *Hellinger distance* grows depending upon the difference between the standard deviations. This was a major motivation for its introduction.

(c) *Total Variation Distance (TVD):* TVD measures the largest possible distance between P and Q as

$$D_f(P||Q) = \frac{1}{2} \sum_{i=1}^{n} |p_i - q_i|.$$

The total variation distance is bound in terms of the *K-L divergence*.

(d) *α-divergence:* The α-divergence measure is a generalization of *K-L divergence* between P and Q of order α and is defined as

$$D_f(P||Q) = \frac{1}{\alpha - 1} log_2 (\sum_{i=1}^{n} p_i^{\alpha} q_i^{1-\alpha}), \; where \; \alpha > 0.$$

When $\alpha = 1$, the α-divergence reduces to *K-L divergence* as

$$D_{\alpha=1}(P||Q) = \sum_{i=1}^{n} p_i \; log \frac{p_i}{q_i}.$$

We evaluate all four measures in the detection of DDoS flooding attacks, and for *α-divergence* we heuristically obtain the appropriate value for α to achieve the best possible classification accuracy.

2.8.2.4   Information Metrics

Entropy measures have been effectively used in distinguishing anomalous events from legitimate ones. In information theory, one can expect smaller entropy values, especially when low randomness is observed in the information variable, whereas for an information variable with a larger amount of uncertainty or randomness, such entropy value is expected to be high [92]. To estimate the randomness of a system accurately, researchers design measures based on statistical properties of variables. Shannon entropy [218], Renyi's quadratic entropy [204], Hartley entropy [218], Shannon's Generalized Entropy, generalized information distance, and *K-L* divergence are some well-known information theoretic measures that have been useful in network anomaly detection.

(a) *Hartley Entropy:* For a given discrete probability distribution, $P = p_1, p_2, p_3, \cdots, p_n$, such that $\sum_{i=1}^{n} p_i = 1$, $P_i \geq 0$, we can define *Hartley Entropy* as $H_0 = log_2 n$, where, the values of the p_is are the same and as a result, the maximum entropy value is achieved.

(b) *Shannon entropy:* If $\alpha \rightarrow 1$, then H_α converges to *Shannon entropy*, which is defined as follows.
$H_1(x) = -\sum_{i=1}^{n} p_i \; log_2 \; p_i.$

(c) *Renyi's Quadratic Entropy:* If $\alpha = 2$, it is referred to as *Renyi's Quadratic Entropy*, which is defined as follows:
$H_2(x) = -log_2 \sum_{i=1}^{n} p_i^2.$

(d) *Renyi's Entropy of order* α: If $\alpha \geq 0$, $\alpha \neq 1$ and $P_i \geq 0$, it converges to *Renyi's Entropy of order* α which is given below. $H_\alpha(x) = \frac{1}{1-\alpha} log_2(\sum_{i=1}^{n} p_i^\alpha)$.

(e) *Generalized Information Distance:* We can define *information distance* as an estimate of the divergence between a given pair of probability distributions. If P and Q are two discrete probability distributions, where $P = p_1, p_2, p_3 \ldots p_n$, $Q = q_1, q_2, q_3, \ldots, q_n$, and $\sum_{i=1}^{n} p_i = \sum_{i=1}^{n} q_i = 1$, $i = 1, 2, 3, \cdots, n$, then the generalized information distance between P and Q of order α is as follows. $D_\alpha(P\|Q) = \frac{1}{\alpha-1} log_2(\sum_{i=1}^{n} p_i^\alpha q_i^{1-\alpha})$

(f) *K-L Divergence:* In the above expression for generalized information distance between a pair of discrete probability distributions, i.e., P and Q, the value of α can be an arbitrary positive integer. When $\alpha \to 1$, the above expression converges to the *Kullback–Leibler* divergence measure [35], which is given below. $D_1(P\|Q) = -\sum_{i=1}^{n} p_i \, log_2 \frac{p_i}{q_i}$.
This measure is effective in differentiating attack traffic from legitimate traffic.

2.8.3 Discussion

Based on the above discussions, we observe the following.

- Mathematically, a similarity measure quantifies the strength of closeness between two instances using either all or a subset of attributes. In contrast, a dissimilarity or distance measure between a pair of instances quantifies how far apart they are.

- Typically, for two identical instances, the similarity is 1, whereas the dissimilarity is 0.

- Some proximity measures, such as Pearson correlation coefficients, Spearman rank correlation, or Hamming distance, are useful only after applying adequate preprocessing to avoid bias or outlier influence. However, such preprocessing often causes degradation of performance.

- Some proximity measures cannot retain the significance of individual attributes in high-dimensional space and hence result in unrealistic performance.

- For DDoS detection, the measure should be easy to implement, fast, sensitive, and accurate.

- To capture attribute-specific regulation (such as increase or high, decrease or low, and neutral) information, correlation-based measures are relevant.

- To compute significant differences in terms of selective attributes or features based on probability distributions, information metrics are useful.

2.9   Some Empirical Studies

DDoS attackers are continually improving their skills and sophistication to launch attacks by infecting unsuspecting hosts. There are normally two types of DDoS attack traffic that can compromise a host or a network: (a) high-rate DDoS attack traffic, which is similar to a flash crowd and (b) low-rate DDoS attack traffic, which is similar to legitimate traffic. Since both have characteristics of legitimate traffic, the use of appropriate measures or metrics is highly essential to distinguish between them accurately within a short interval of time.

Although several useful proximity measures or information metrics have been introduced by researchers as discussed above, each has its own advantages as well as disadvantages in the context of network intrusion detection. The performance of a machine learning based DDoS detection approach in terms of time and accuracy, is largely influenced by selection of a proximity measure or metrics. In this section, we present some empirical studies using benchmark and real-life DDoS attack datasets using three different groups of proximity measures and analyze their effectiveness in network anomaly detection. The proximity measures are chosen for the empirical study based on three factors: (i) speed, (ii) accuracy, and (iii) simplicity. We believe that such experimental analysis will help students and researchers in assessing the usefulness of such measures.

2.9.1   Using Information Metrics

Information metrics are known to be sensitive, scalable, and simple to implement when distinguishing anomalous traffic from legitimate traffic. In this experimental study, we make the following assumptions.

- *Assumption 1*: All TCP, UDP and ICMP flooding attack traffic generated and used at the victim end for this study, follow the rate dynamics specified by Mirkovic et al. [169].

- *Assumption 2*: Normal traffic follows the Gaussian distribution, whereas attack traffic is generated following the Poisson distribution.

- *Assumption 3*: Traffic is sampled every t_g minutes globally and the traffic for each global time interval is further sampled at t_l-second time intervals locally. In this study, t_g and t_l are considered *5 minutes* and *10 seconds*, respectively.

- *Assumption 4*: The in-and-out flow traffic is controlled at a router.

Table 2.1: Information metrics and variables used.

Name of Metric	Representations	Variables Used
Hartley entropy	$H_0 = log_2 n$	n
Shannon entropy	$H_1(x) = -\sum_{i=1}^{n} p_i \, log_2 \, p_i$	p_i, n
Renyi's quadratic entropy	$H_2(x) = -log_2 \sum_{i=1}^{n} p_i^2$	p_i, n
Generalized entropy	$H_\alpha(x) = \frac{1}{1-\alpha} log_2(\sum_{i=1}^{n} p_i^2)$	p_i, n, α
K-L divergence	$D_1(P\|Q) = -\sum_{i=1}^{n} p_i \, log_2 \, \frac{p_i}{q_i}$	p_i, n, P, Q
Generalized Information Distance	$D_\alpha(P\|Q) = \frac{1}{\alpha-1} log_2(\sum_{i=1}^{n} p_i^\alpha q_i^{1-\alpha})$	p_i, n, P, Q, α

It is also assumed [92] that the entropy value increases with the increase in randomness in the information variables, whereas with a decrease in uncertainty in the information variables, the entropy value becomes smaller. An information metric is useful in measuring such randomness in a system. In this empirical study, we use six different metrics to quantify the randomness in our network system (i.e., the testbed as shown in Figure 2.9). The names of the measures, their representations, and variables used are shown in Table 2.1.

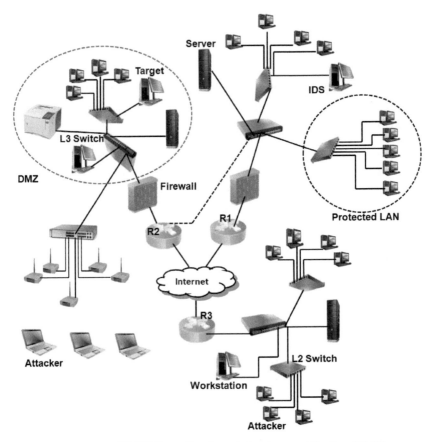

Figure 2.9: TUIDS testbed architecture with the DMZ.

2.9.1.1   Testbed Used

The TUIDS testbed was developed in the Network Security Laboratory of Tezpur University. It includes multiple networks and the hosts are divided into several VLANs. The testbed architecture with a demilitarized zone is shown in Figure 2.9. Each VLAN is attached to an L3 switch or an L2 switch inside the testbed. One can attack from both wired or wireless networks (possibly with reflectors), but the victim is inside the network. The attackers used the TUCANNON+ tool to launch attack traffic of all types, such as constant rate, increasing rate, pulsing rate, and subgroup attacks including all three protocols, i.e., TCP, UDP and ICMP. Further, the attack can be both low-rate as well as high-rate and direct as well as indirect. In this attack dataset, more than 6000 packets per second is considered a high-rate attack, whereas a low-rate attack is about 1000 packets per second, covering almost 55–60% of a full attack.

2.9.1.2 Datasets Used

In this empirical study the three different datasets viz., the MIT Lincoln Laboratory dataset [172], [164], [159], the CAIDA DDoS 2007 dataset [42] and the TUIDS DDoS dataset [88], are used to assess the effectiveness of the six information metrics and measures in detecting both low-rate and high-rate DDoS attacks. The MIT Lincoln Laboratory tcpdump dataset is used as a reference normal data, and is free of any attack traffic. In contrast, the TUIDS DDoS dataset includes both low-rate as well as high-rate DDoS attack traffic. It was prepared by launching TCP, UDP, and ICMP flooding attacks using the tool TUCANNON+ in a testbed architecture with a demilitarized zone as shown in Figure 2.9.

These CAIDA DDoS 2007 traffic traces contain both low-rate and high-rate attack traffic. It includes anonymized attack traffic of 5 minutes duration (300 seconds) captured during a DDoS attack on August 4, 2007. It contains only attack traffic to the victim and the responses from the victim. During preparation of the dataset, the non-attack traffic was removed as much as possible. Moore et al. [175] characterize a DDoS attack in the dataset as high-rate when there are more than 10,000 packets per second in the network. Similarly, a low-rate DDoS attack is one when there are 1000 packets per second covering 60% of the full attack. A brief statistical summary of this dataset [175], [26] is given in Table 2.2. Since a low-rate attack does not consume all the computing resources of the victim machine or the bandwidth of the network connecting the victim machine, to create a real low-rate attack scenario, low-rate attack traffic and legitimate traffic were mixed.

2.9.1.3 Results of Empirical Study

In this empirical study, as stated earlier, $t_g = 5$ $minutes$ and $t_l = 10$ $seconds$ were chosen as the sizes of global and local time windows, respectively, for analyzing legitimate and attack traffic. For faster identification of DDoS attacks, the study involved only three attributes, namely SIP (i.e., Source IP), DIP (i.e., Destination IP), and $protocol$

Table 2.2: Traffic features and details of CAIDA DDoS dataset.

Traffic Features	Values
Maximum capture length for interface	0:65000
First timestamp	1186260576.487629000
Last timestamp	1186260876.482457000
Unknown encapsulation	0
IPv4 bytes	37068253
IPv4 packets	166448
Ipv4 traffic	8079
Unique IPv4 addresses	136
Unique IPv4 source addresses	132
Unique IPv4 destination addresses	136
Unique IPv4 TCP source ports	4270
Unique IPv4 TCP destination ports	3348
Unique IPv4 UDP source ports	1
Unique IPv4 UDP destination ports	1
Unique IPv4 ICMP type/codes	2

for estimation of randomness in the system [26]. *SIP* may be spoofed, but may still be used to detect the source host that generates the attack. Similarly, *DIP* helps determine the target of the attack, and *protocol* is useful in determining the type of flooding attack in progress. In addition to these three, the *timestamp* attribute was used for sampling traffic using the sizes of the global and local windows. To assess the effectiveness of generalized information distance in detecting both low-rate and high-rate attacks, the order α was varied from 0 to 14, whereas for generalized entropy, the order α was varied from 0 to 15.

In this study, to compute probabilities from the dataset, we use classical probability distributions. Unique source IP addresses within a 10-second local time window are identified and individual probability values between 0 and 1 are computed for them. Then, entropy is computed for each probability value and all entropy values within a time window are summed up for total entropy. When computing probability, symbolic data are not converted to numeric values.

Figure 2.11 shows the effectiveness of a generalized entropy measure of order α in distinguishing attack traffic from normal traffic. Here, "spacing" indicates the difference or gap between the two traffic types.

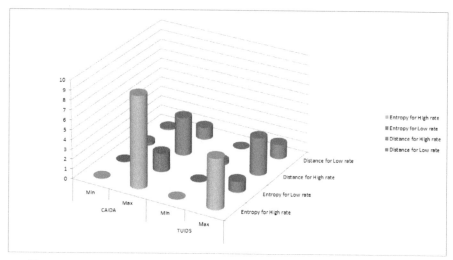

Figure 2.10: Spacing results for low-rate and high-rate attacks.

The more spacing that is shown by a metric or measure between the traffic types, the more effective the measure is. Figure 2.11 shows that spacing between normal and low-rate attack traffic is smaller than the spacing between normal and high-rate attack traffic. It is usual because low-rate attack traffic is almost similar to normal traffic.

Exhaustive experimentation was carried out with both the generalized entropy measure and information distance with the CAIDA dataset by varying the order α to assess its effectiveness in distinguishing both low-rate and high-rate attacks from legitimate traffic. Figure 2.10 shows the spacing results for both low-rate and high-rate attacks in comparison to normal traffic. We see in the table that spacing between normal and high-rate attack traffic is significantly higher than the spacing between normal and low-rate attack traffic for both the metric and the measure. In a similar fashion, the effectiveness of generalized entropy with the TUIDS dataset was evaluated and the results are shown in Figures 2.12 and 2.13 for distinguishing high-rate and low-rate attacks, respectively. To judge the suitability of information distance in DDoS detection, a similar experiment was carried out and the results are shown in Figures 2.14, 2.15, 2.16, and 2.17 for the CAIDA and TUIDS datasets, respectively. Overall, the generalized entropy measure is better suited for distinguishing attack traffic from normal traffic with an increase in the order value of α.

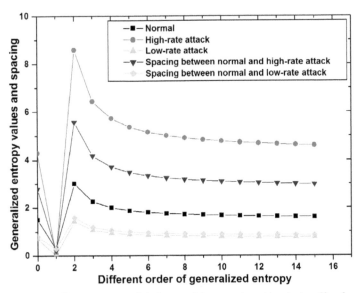

Figure 2.11: Differentiating high- and low-rate attack traffic from normal in CAIDA dataset using *Generalized Entropy*.

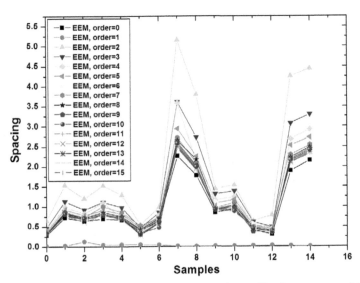

Figure 2.12: Distinguishing high-rate attack traffic from normal in TU-IDS dataset using *Generalized Entropy*.

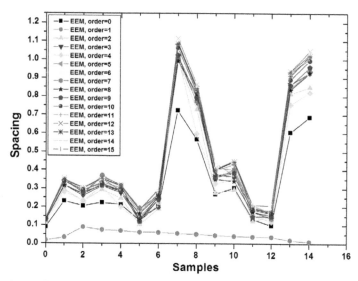

Figure 2.13: Distinguishing low-rate attack traffic from normal in TU-IDS dataset using *Generalized Entropy*.

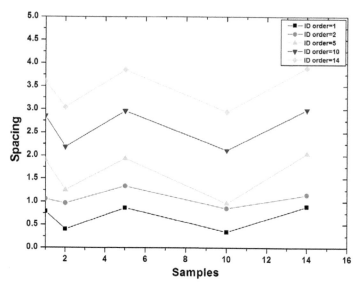

Figure 2.14: Distinguishing high-rate attack traffic from normal in CAIDA dataset using *Information Distance*.

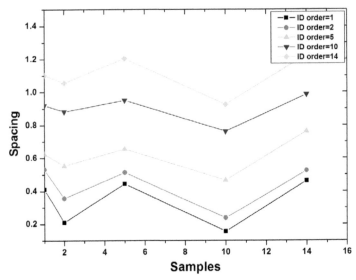

Figure 2.15: Distinguishing low-rate attack traffic from normal in CAIDA dataset using *Information Distance*.

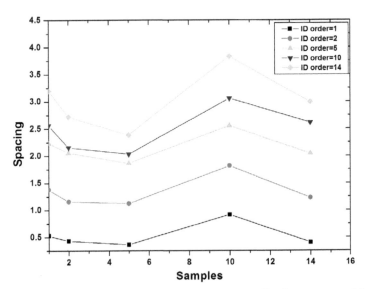

Figure 2.16: Distinguishing high-rate attack traffic from normal in TU-IDS dataset using *Information Distance*.

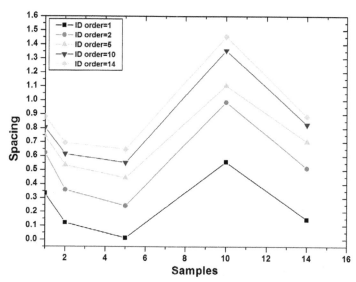

Figure 2.17: Distinguishing low-rate attack traffic from normal in TU-IDS dataset using *Information Distance*.

2.9.1.4   Discussion

We observe the following based on the results of the empirical study.

- The entropy measure performs better in detecting both low-rate and high-rate DDoS attacks when the order of the generalized entropy is increased.

- An information metric is preferred considering the computational complexity of the process because it is dependent on a small number of parameters for detection.

- With the increase in the value of the order, the performance of information distance improves over *K-L* divergence.

- Another important advantage of both generalized entropy and information divergence is that the value of α can be easily adjusted (increased or decreased) for better performance.

2.9.2   Using Correlation Measures

In this section, six well-known similarity measures are used. These are Pearson correlation [28], [143], Spearmen rank correlation [61],

Kendall correlation [133], shifting-and-scaling correlation [8], and the Normalized Mean Residue Similarity (NMRS) [158] measure, for an experimental study. These measures have already been used in various other domains and have been found effective.

Correlation between a pair of objects is a measure of how well they are related. The most common measure of correlation in statistics is the Pearson Correlation [28], [143]. It shows how linear the relationship is between two sets of data. The mathematical representation of Pearson correlation measure is given in Section 2.8.2.2. This standardized covariance value ranges from -1, indicating a perfect negative linear relationship, to $+1$, indicating a perfect positive relationship. A zero value suggests no linear association.

Spearman rank correlation [61] is used to test the association between a pair of ranked variables, or one ranked variable and one measurement variable. This correlation test is not dependent on any assumption about the distribution of the data. The formula used to calculate the Spearman rank correlation is given in Section 2.8.2.2.

The Kendall rank correlation [133] test is used to measure the strength of dependence between two samples, say P and Q, where each sample size is n. We know that the total number of pairings with P and Q is $n(n-1)/2$. The formula used to calculate the value of the Kendall rank correlation is given in Section 2.8.2.2.

SSSim is a robust correlation measure [8] that can handle shifting, scaling, absolute, and shifting-and-scaling correlations between a pair of objects. SSSim is robust in the presence of noisy data as this measure uses local means computed from values in a small interval. The mathematical expression for SSSim is given in Section 2.8.2.2.

NMRS [158] is a correlation measure that can detect shifted correlations effectively. The mathematical expression for the NMRS similarity measure is given in Section 2.8.2.2.

2.9.2.1   An Example

The correlation and similarity measures mentioned above can be used to evaluate relationships among objects. These measures play a key role in the learning process. One major difference among these measures is the type of correlation the measure can handle. Some types of correlations that may exist between a pair of objects are absolute correlation, shifting correlation, scaling correlation, and shifting-and-scaling correlation. Let us consider objects O_1, O_2, O_3, O_4, and O_5 as

Table 2.3: Example objects.

O_1	0.814	0.905	0.127	0.913	0.632	0.097	0.278	0.546	0.957	0.964
O_2	0.500	0.970	0.300	0.485	0.800	0.141	0.421	0.915	0.792	0.959
O_3	5.814	5.905	5.127	5.913	5.632	5.097	5.278	5.546	5.957	5.964
O_4	4.073	4.529	0.634	4.566	3.161	0.487	1.392	2.734	4.787	4.824
O_5	9.073	9.529	5.634	9.566	8.161	5.487	6.392	7.734	9.787	9.824

given in Table 2.3, with their corresponding visual representation in Figure 2.18. Let us compute distance and similarity values using the aforementioned measures to judge their effectiveness. Distance or similarity values among these objects using these measures are given in Table 2.4.

A distance measure like Euclidean distance is used to determine how close the values of two or more objects are. Closely situated objects in terms of values tend to bring the produced value toward zero. Correlation that is only concerned with closeness of values is called absolute correlation. Object O_2 is closest to O_1 compared to other objects and hence the pair produces the lowest Euclidean distance score. Another type of correlation that may exist between a pair of objects

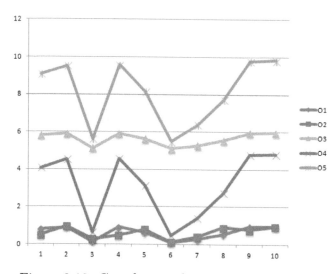

Figure 2.18: Correlation plot of example objects.

Table 2.4: Computed distance and correlations on example objects.

Object Pairs	Euclidean Distance	NMRS	Pearson	SSSim	Spearman	Kendall
O_1, O_2	0.7283	0.6773	0.7245	0.5522	0.6606	0.5111
O_1, O_3	15.8114	1.0000	1.000	1.0000	1.000	1.0000
O_1, O_4	8.9160	0.6000	1.000	1.0000	1.000	1.0000
O_1, O_5	24.0632	0.6000	1.000	1.0000	1.000	1.0000

is *shifting* correlation. In such correlation, an object can be obtained from the other object by adding a constant value to each of the features or observations. O_3 is obtained from O_1 by adding a constant 5 to all observations. Measures like *NMRS* can detect such correlation and produces the highest similarity score, i.e., 1. In scaling correlation, an object can be obtained from another object by multiplying each feature value by a constant. O_4 is obtained from O_1 by multiplying each feature value by a constant 5. In shifting-and-scaling correlation, an object can be obtained by performing a sequence of shifting and scaling operations on the features of the other object. It is worth mentioning that shifting correlation and scaling correlations are special cases of shifting-and-scaling correlation. O_1 and O_4 exhibits shifting correlation with a multiplicative constant 5, whereas O_1 and O_5 exhibit shifting-and-scaling correlation with a multiplicative constant 5 and a shifting constant 5. Pearson correlation, Spearman, Kendall, and SSSim measure can detect shifting-and-scaling correlation.

2.9.3   Using f-Divergence Measures

A common observation in DDoS flooding attacks is the sudden hike in packet arrival rate within a short interval of time or an abrupt rise in number of connection flows in the attacker's target network. One can expect that during a DDoS flooding attack, a major share of the active connections in the ith time window still appears in the $(i+1)^{th}$ time window. In this study, an ith connection flow, i.e., say CF_i is represented by $< SIP_i, DIP_i >$, where SIP_i and DIP_i represent the source IP and destination IP for i^{th} unidirectional flow, respectively. During a DDoS attack, usually the number of common connections becomes significantly high, whereas it drops when the scenario becomes normal. So, one needs to apply a simple, fast, yet accurate method that can help detect the attacks at least in near real time, if not in real time. *F*-divergence is one such potential measure based on probability theory, one that is efficient for this purpose. Typically, it computes the information distance between two probability distributions to find deviations.

To compute information distance between two given distributions, one can use all the attributes or can select the most relevant subset of attributes from each distribution. Use of a relevant and optimal subset of attributes can improve the performance of information distance significantly.

As an illustration, let us take two discrete probability distributions P and Q over a given space Ω so that P can be found absolutely continuous w.r.t. Q. For a convex function f, the divergence, i.e., say D_f of Q from P, can be computed as

$$D_f(P \parallel Q) = \int_\Omega f(\frac{dP}{dQ}). \qquad (2.7)$$

In this study, four different measures under f-divergence are considered for empirical study. These are *K-L*-divergence, Hellinger's distance, TVD and α-divergence. Although these measures are different or distinct, they are special cases of each other depending on the particular choice of f. The mathematical expressions for these measures are already given in Section 2.8.2.3. For faster detection of DDoS attacks, an optimal subset of relevant features is used. As f-divergence enables one to compute the divergence of two probability distributions, we consider sampled data values from two consecutive 5-second intervals, i.e., say for t and $t + 5$ seconds at a time. For processing convenience, the study considers a recursive binary tree data structure using a single key for each interval and for each type of flooding attack. It calculates the key for each attack type differently.

For ICMP flooding attacks, we compute the number of unique connection flows between a pair of consecutive 5-second intervals. A connection flow represents the aggregate number of packets sent from say, the ith SIP to the ith DIP in an interval. The study considers *connection size* as a relevant feature to compute f-divergence of a flow for each arrival of a packet in a flow. The extracted feature information is stored in a node in a binary tree with different components, viz., $< Uniq\_conn\_ID, SIP, Conn\_size_t, Conn\_size_{t+1}, Flag >$. The unique connection ID, i.e., $Uniq\_conn\_ID$, is computed from SIP and DIP addresses to represent a flow for each node, and this node is inserted in the tree with this unique ID as the key. The variables $Conn\_size\_t$ and $Conn\_size_{t+1}$ are used to store the size of a common connection flow in each consecutive interval. For each time interval t, the $Conn\_size_t$ of a flow is added to the size of every new packet if an already existing $Uniq\_conn\_ID$ is generated from its SIP and DIP address combination. Otherwise, a new node with a new $Uniq\_conn\_ID$ is created with its flag initially set to 0. In the next interval, i.e., at $(t+1)$, the $Uniq\_conn\_ID$ node flag is set to 1, if the same UID is generated when reading the packets. Once both interval samples are completely read and the tree is built, the nodes with flag value of 1 are accessed by pre-order traversal and their $Conn\_size_t$ and $Conn\_size_{t+1}$ are extracted to compute probability distributions. A node with flag value 1 represents common connections in two consecutive intervals and represents the two discrete probability distributions P and Q. This can be explained as follows: For a probability distribution P (or Q), let the distribution be an array of normalized connection sizes over n connections with probability p_i (or q_i) for the ith connection flow with connection size s_i is p_i or, q_i is equal to $\frac{s_i}{\sum s_i}$. Finally, we compute the f-divergence using these connection size probability distributions per connection flow and check whether the divergence value is above a preset normal threshold value, and if so, a flooding attack is confirmed, and these nodes with a high sum of $Conn\_size\_t$, $Conn\_size_{t+1}$ are marked as malicious connection flows.

To detect TCP SYN flooding attacks, the study considers the ratio of the number of TCP SYN and ACK packets to compute divergence. It takes a single sample at a time and attempts to compute all unique connection flows. For each flow, it computes the $Uniq\_conn\_ID$ value from the source and destination IP addresses and then creates a node with $Uniq\_conn\_ID, SIP, TCPSYNCount, ACKCount$ components, to be updated in the tree based on $Uniq\_conn\_ID$ as the key. From each sample, each node is updated with the TCP SYN and the ACK packet count for each connection flow. The study considers the sequence of TCP SYN packet counts as a probability distribution as P and ACK $packet$ $count$ as Q. f-divergence is calculated for both the distributions for each interval by considering all flows. If it detects that the overall TCP SYN and ACK ratio divergence exceeds preset normal threshold values, a TCP SYN flooding attack is confirmed. Finally, connection flows with abnormal divergence are marked as anomalous.

To detect UDP flooding, our study focuses on the feature called *destination port change* containing random destination port addresses. For each pair of consecutive intervals, we compute all unique connection flows and store them in the tree. We also compute the $Uniq\_conn\_ID$, which is simply a unique $<SIP, DIP>$pair to be used as a key. It flags a node with value "1" if the $Uniq\_conn\_ID$ is the same and fit represents a common connection for a consecutive pair of intervals. It represents the features as $dest\_port\_change\_count_t$ and $dest\_port\_change\_count_{t+1}$ in the tree node. These values, given in sequence, also represent the probability distributions P and Q. For each sample and for a time interval, say t, it updates the $dest\_port\_change\_count_t$ for each destination port number change for a connection flow by SIP address. Once the tree is constructed, one can access the nodes with flag 1 by pre-order traversal to compute the probability distributions P and Q and finally to compute the divergence between them.

For each measure, the approach can compute f-divergence in $O(nlog(n-1)) + O(n)$ time approximately, where n is the number of packets within a time interval t. The additional $O(n)$ time is required for pre-order traversal of the tree. In summary, it takes $O(nlogn)$ time.

2.9.3.1 Results

The performance of f-divergence measures was evaluated in terms of detection accuracy and execution time. We used three benchmark and one real-life datasets (generated using our own testbed as discussed earlier) to assess the effectiveness of these measures. The benchmark and real-life datasets used in this empirical study are the MIT Lincoln Laboratory dataset [172], [164], [159], the CAIDA DDoS 2007 dataset [42], and the UCLA[8] and TUIDS DDoS dataset [88]. We use both normal and attack traces from these datasets in isolation as well as in combination. The composition and traffic statistics for these datasets have already been discussed in Subsection 2.9.1.2. The CAIDA DDoS 2007 dataset mostly includes attack traces and corresponding responses from the victim. From this dataset we removed the normal traces as much as possible. The generation of the TUIDS DDoS dataset using our own testbed has already been discussed in detail in Subsection 2.9.1.1.

For each protocol-specific attack trace, we heuristically identify suitable ranges of threshold values for each member of the f-divergence

---

[8]http://www.lasr.cs.ucla.edu/ddos/traces/

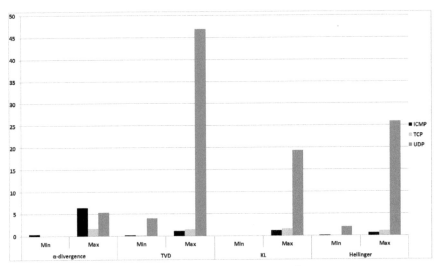

Figure 2.19: Threshold ranges for various f-divergence measures.

measure, for which a maximum divergence between a normal and attack trace can be achieved. For the α-divergence measure, we consider
$\alpha = 2$ because it obtains the highest divergence values to distinguish
attack traces from the normal for all three protocols. So, to compare
well with other measures, such as Hellinger distance, K-L divergence,
and TVD in terms of detection accuracy and computational performance, $\alpha = 2$ was used for the α-divergence measure throughout the
experimental study. To compute the threshold for detection of various
flooding attack types, we carefully examine the three types of benchmark normal traffic from CAIDA, MIT Lincoln Laboratory and UCLA
datasets for each of the divergence measures. Figure 2.19 shows the
threshold range for each measure and for each protocol-specific set of
attack traces.

A. Performance Evaluation in Terms of Detection Accuracy

To evaluate the performance of these four f-divergence measures, we
prepared three different datasets, namely, *Trace I, Trace II*, and *Trace
III* by injecting DDoS flooding attack traces at various proportions
into the normal traces of CAIDA, MIT Lincoln Laboratory, and UCLA
datasets in non-uniform proportions. We use a period of 300 seconds as
the total observation time for each of these new datasets. When injecting attack traffic, the motive behind injecting non-uniform proportions

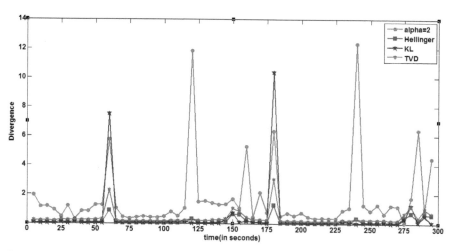

Figure 2.20: f-divergence for ICMP flood detection using *connection size* in Trace 1.

of attack traces is to avoid forming any specific patterns as well as to ensure the presence of various attack types based on rate dynamics, as discussed in Subsection 2.2.2.5.

Figure 2.20 shows the effectiveness of all the four f-divergence measures for the *Trace 1* dataset in detecting an ICMP ping flooding attack using *connection size* as the distinguishing feature. One can see from the figure that α-divergence can distinguish the attack spikes (i.e., peaks) more clearly than the other measures in the majority of cases. It is to be noted that the range of thresholds for α-divergence for detection of ICMP ping flooding is the highest (i.e., 0.40 to 6.38), which is also seen in Figure 2.19. Other measures such as K-L-divergence are able to differentiate these attack peaks, but not as clearly as α-divergence can. Similarly, for the TUIDS dataset, α-divergence shows the best performance in detecting ICMP ping flooding attacks in comparison to others, as seen in Figure 2.21. K-L-divergence establishes itself as a closed competitor of α-divergence in this case. For *Trace II* and *Trace III* datasets, which include TCP SYN flooding and UDP flooding attacks, it is evident from Figures 2.22 and 2.23 that α-divergence is the winner. In case of TCP SYN flooding detection, the threshold range for α-divergence is the highest and the distinguishing feature is the TCP SYN, ACK ratio. However, in case of a UDP flooding attack, with a smaller range of threshold values, α-divergence shows the best possible result using the *destination_port_change* as the distinguishing feature.

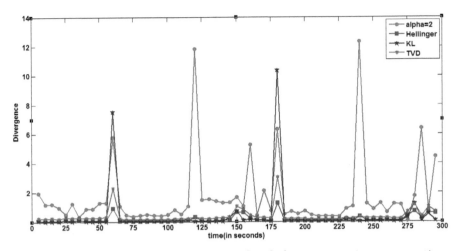

Figure 2.21: f-divergence for ICMP flood detection using *connection size* in TUIDS dataset.

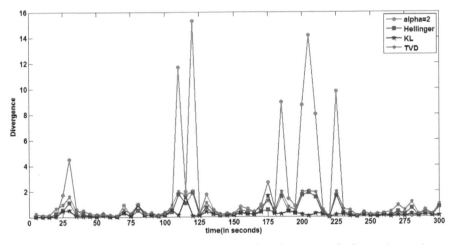

Figure 2.22: f-divergence for TCP SYN flooding attack detection using *TCP SYN ACK ratio* in Trace II.

B. Performance Evaluation in Terms of Computation Time

It is an essential requirement to detect DDoS attacks in real time. Although most victim-end detection systems show good detection accuracy, they often fail to perform detection in real time. It may be

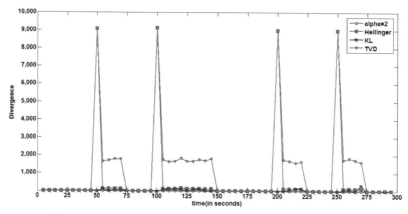

Figure 2.23: f-divergence for UDP flood detection using *destination port change* in Trace III.

due to (i) the use of a costly measure while differentiating illegitimate traffic from normal traffic, (ii) additional requirements imposed by a preprocessing task, and (iii) increased computational overhead. So, for every DDoS defender, it is necessary to carry out an exhaustive study of cost-effectiveness of various possible measures before deploying in a live defense system. In this empirical study, we also carry out an execution time performance analysis on these four f-divergence measures using those three traces. The results are shown in Table 2.5. One can see that none of the participating measures is a clear winner in terms of execution time performance.

Table 2.5: Execution time performance of f-divergence measures.

	Trace I		Trace II		Trace III	
	10 sec	300 sed	10sec	300sec	10 sec	300 sec
α-Divergence	1.84	499.4	0.002	0.064	0.021	1.211
Hellinger Distance	1.83	506.8	0.003	0.065	0.020	1.200
KL Divergence	1.85	500.3	0.003	0.063	0.022	1.211
TVD	1.84	501.1	0.002	0.066	0.022	1.211

2.9.4 Discussion

Based on the empirical study described in this section, we make the following observations.

- The study demonstrates that the performance of α-divergence is better than other similar measures.

- The study focuses on reducing the cost of divergence computation as much as possible when detecting attacks. In detecting ICMP ping and UDP flood attacks, when computing divergence for each pair of consecutive 5-second time intervals, it involves two probability distributions, i.e., P and Q, and accordingly, it constructs two recursive binary trees, i.e., a *primary tree* and a *secondary tree*. It starts with the primary tree for the initial interval, which is also used in the next consecutive interval to record feature values for common connections (i.e., node flagged as 1). Subsequently, it may grow if uncommon connections are detected (i.e., node flagged as 0). At time $(t+1)$, it constructs a secondary tree, which becomes the primary tree at time $(t+2)$ and again a new secondary tree is constructed. Once the divergence computation is over, the primary tree constructed at time $(t+1)$ is removed, and this process iterates until all samples are read. So, for these two attacks, the cost of divergence computation is low, as shown in Table 2.5.

- The case is further simplified when detecting TCP SYN flood attacks. It involves a single recursive binary tree construction at every 5-second interval when computing divergence. Once the TCP SYN ratio divergence computation is over, the tree is deleted.

- Although the search time may be a cause of concern as compared to fixed-sized data structures, we see in Table 2.5 that the computation time is significantly less for this data structure.

2.10 Chapter Summary

Based on all the discussion in this chapter, we can summarize a set of observations as follows.

(a) DDoS attacks are coordinated attacks launched using a large number of compromised machines. Such attacks can paralyze a victim network instantly, if an adequate defense is not deployed.

(b) Several design issues of the original Internet are responsible for increasing growth of Internet attacks. Some of these are (i) the existence of complex edges but simple cores, (ii) link bandwidth mismatch between core and edge networks, (iii) simple routing principles, (iv) lack of centralized network management, and (v) the habit of sharing reserved resources across data centers.

(c) DDoS attacks are categorized in various ways by various individuals. Typically, a DDoS attack can be (i) direct or indirect, (ii) direct or reflector based, (iii) protocol specific such as TCP DDoS flooding, UDP flooding, or ICMP flooding, and (iv) attacks classified based on rate dynamics such as pulsing, constant rate, increasing rate, or sub-group attacks.

(d) The desired characteristics of a DDoS defense system are real-time performance, scalability, maintaining QoS, and accurate source identification.

(e) A DDoS attacker chooses a definite target when attacking a victim network. The target can be (i) infrastructure, (ii) link, (iii) router, (iv) OS, or (v) the defense mechanism itself.

(f) Typically, a DDoS attacker follows a four-step strategy, viz., recruitment, exploitation, infection, and attack.

(g) Machine learning researchers help address the DDoS detection problem by adopting supervised learning or unsupervised learning methods. A supervised learning method has high detection accuracy when adequate and accurate knowledge is provided, but it cannot detect unknown attacks. In contrast, an unsupervised method can detect unknown attacks, although it suffers from high false alarms. Unsupervised methods are usually non-real-time, because they require more processing.

(h) Several similarity and dissimilarity measures have been introduced to work with machine learning algorithms. Each measure has its own advantages and limitations, and it is difficult to select a measure which is best for all types of applications and scenarios.

(i) Most measures are not scalable and their performance is affected by the increase in dimensionality of the relevant data or in the number of training data instances.

(j) To support effective DDoS attack detection, three desired qualities of a measure are: (i) sensitiveness, (ii) cost-effectiveness, and (iii) scalability.

(k) Among f-divergence measures, α-divergence performs better than others in most cases.

(l) Among information metrics, improved performance can be achieved when using generalized entropy by increasing the order of α.

(m) Some measures show better performance only after pre-processing the original test dataset. However, if we add the cost of preprocessing, the overall performance of such a measure is often inadequate for real-time or near-real-time detection of DDoS attacks.

Chapter 3

Botnets: Trends and Challenges

Along with rapid developments in Internet technologies, the professionalism and sophistication of those who commit Internet crimes have also been increasing exponentially. A major cause of such advancement in attack technology is the availability of open source attack resources. A DDoS attacker or a group of attackers hires or compromises a large pool of computers, referred to as *bots*, to launch attacks. To control the bots from a remote corner of the Internet, the attackers usually connect them to a remote Internet Relay Chat (IRC) server, to form what is called a *botnet*. Using such botnets, attackers flood the networks with spoofed IP addresses and generate spam emails, viruses, and worms. In general, botnets include thousands of bots. However, recently attackers have succeeded in reducing the size of a botnet to a few thousand with the ability to generate attack packets of variable intensity to make them less detectable. A medium-scale botnet of size, say 20,000, can be highly effective in damaging the Website of a corporate system with their combined bandwidth (20,000 uplinks with bandwidths of 56 Kbps for a total of 1092 Mbps), which may be higher than the bandwidth of many organizations' Internet connectivity. In the recent past, several effective botnets have been introduced. Some of these are Agobot, Spybot, RBot, and SDBot. Most of these bots provide for source IP address spoofing and generation of source ports, destination ports, TCP sequence numbers, and other fields that go into packet headers at random. Greater randomization generates more anomalies, making mitigation more difficult due to problems in computing packet signatures for filtering.

We stated in *Chapter 2* that botnets are currently being used by attackers to cause serious damage using both volumetric as well as application layer DDoS attacks. In the recent past, botnet technology has become quite sophisticated. We provide a discussion of botnet basics and their usage in DDoS attack generation in the next section. The evolution of botnet technology and its features in the context of DDoS attack generation are discussed in two categories, viz., (i) stationary botnets and (i) mobile botnets.

3.1 DDoS Attacks Using Stationary Botnets

In the recent years, most sophisticated and large-scale DDoS attacks have been launched using botnet technology. The main reason behind the popularity of botnet technology in DDoS attack launching is its increasing growth, flexibility, and power, which have enabled the generation of various types of DDoS attacks. The four important reasons that attackers prefer this technology are (i) inclusion of a large number of compromised nodes (i.e., zombies) to launch a high-intensity flooding attack within a short period of time, (ii) the ability to exploit protocols to bypass security mechanisms, (iii) difficulty in identifying the origin of the attack, and (iv) difficulty in distilling malicious traffic (especially low-rate DDoS attacks) from normal traffic in real time due to lack of any distinguishing features. Figure 3.1 shows an example of a DDoS attack using a botnet. Though botnets are now considered very effective in launching most sophisticated DDoS attacks, they originated from a text-based chat system, referred to as Internet Relay Chat (IRC) that organizes communication in channels. The main purpose of the IRC system was very affirmative and it provided services for message sharing, along with administrative support, simple games, and other services to chat users. In due course, bad actors came to understand and exploit its ability to execute malicious activities such as launching DDoS attacks to disrupt the services of a network.

3.1.1 Botnet Characteristics

Typically, botnets are characterized by the type of Command-and-Control (C&C) system used for communication. Communications be-

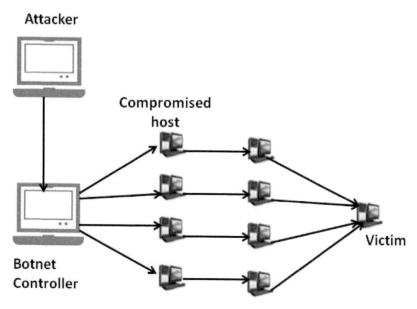

Figure 3.1: Botnet attack.

tween the botmaster and the bots take place according to the specification of the C&C system. Among the various C&C systems introduced so far, *centralized* and *distributed* mechanisms are commonly used for communication. Both types have their own advantages as well as limitations. To address these limitations, attacker masterminds have introduced another botnet technology of late, referred to as *peer-to-peer botnet*, which is considered more effective and difficult to defend against. To counter such botnet-based DDoS attacks, a network defender has to know the malware code and the possible enhancements that may have been incorporated in such code. Further, the topologies, protocols, and the botnet architectures used by the attackers need to be carefully studied during development of a DDoS defense. With the recent successful convergence of traditional telecommunication services and the Internet, the possibility of botnet-based DDoS attacks over essential network services, including 3G, 4G, and 5G wireless networks, has increased substantially.

3.1.2 Botnet Models

An attack mastermind typically uses any or a combination of three basic models when launching a botnet-based DDoS attack. These are

(i) the IRC botnet model, (ii) the agent handler model and (iii) the Web-based model. We discuss each of these models next.

3.1.2.1   Agent Handler Model

Generally, four players participate in this model for successful launching of a DDoS attack. These are (i) the master or the attacker, (ii) the handlers, (iii) the agents and (iv) the victim. The master or the attacker initially attempts to bring some hosts in a network under its control by compromising them. The handlers include some malicious software residing on remote machines that are used by the attacker. The purpose of choosing a set of victimized computers (handlers) to launch DDoS attacks is mainly to overcome the possibility of tracing the attack back to the attacker (client). The agents, i.e., the third set of players are practically responsible for performing the attack. They typically consist of software on compromised machines through which the attack is performed. One can imagine this set as a subset of handlers that reside on the same systems. Generally, in a DDoS flooding attack, the mastermind uses a large number of agents to make the attack effective within a short interval and the victimized (hacked) machines are used in the flooding attack without knowledge of their owners. To launch such a flooding attack, the attacker may exploit the weaknesses of protocols such as TCP, UDP, or ICMP. Another advantage of using such a large number of handlers is to conceal the malicious use of a handler computer. Finally, the victim, i.e., the fourth player, may be a single target machine or a group of target machines.

3.1.2.2   IRC-Based Model

The Internet Relay Chat (IRC), a text-based chat system that organizes communication in channels, unwittingly facilitated the birth of botnets. IRC-based DDoS attacks are now the most popular because of the ability to generate a huge volume of attack traffic instantly. Typically, this system, installed with a bot, can spread very fast and exploit multiple vulnerabilities automatically. After successful installation, a full backdoor generally exists on the system, including an IRC component to establish communication between the computer and a remote IRC server; this backdoor is controlled by the attacker. The bots or zombies used are responsive (can respond to commands), and are easy to control, create, or influence. An attack mastermind launches a DDoS attack through IRC by simply logging into a malicious IRC server, authenticates, and then instructs (by issuing commands) many zombies at once or individual bots within private windows. It is trivial to start and stop DDoS attacks via hundreds or thousands of zombies using this method. To remain invisible from the defenders, IRC botnet operators keep the size of bot herds small by rolling out updates and many minor variants of the code to create smaller botnets in dozens, if not hundreds, on various servers. The effect on a victim network is largely influenced by the architecture, topology, and protocol used in the botnet. Two crucial factors that judge its ability to avoid a single point of failure, such as the capacity to survive when authorities shut down a hostile IRC server, or to bypass the defense mechanism are the technology and size of the botnet used within such a model. IRC-based attacks may involve many different software code variants and protocols. Like agent-handler-based DDoS attacks, an IRC-based DDoS attack can also involve protocols like TCP, ICMP, or UDP.

3.1.2.3   Web-Based Model

Web-based models are effective alternatives for botnet command and control. Bots have multifaceted roles to play. They not only help gather statistics on a Website, but can also be configured and controlled via sophisticated PHP scripts and use encrypted communication. Compared to IRC, Web-based control has several advantages, such as (i) user-friendly interface that enables one to set up, configure and rent out easily, (ii) improved commands and reporting utilities, (iii) low bandwidth consumption due to distributed load, which enables the use of larger botnets, (iv) the simplicity in traffic concealment and difficulty in filtering due to the use of port 80, and (v) lower possibility of botnet hijacking.

In addition to the above, Web-based C&C has the ability to control botnets of any size. As a consequence, it becomes extremely difficult for a defender to locate the sources of DDoS attacks as well as to filter out such traffic over TCP port 80. Further, malicious actors continuously attempt to improve botnet technology to make DDoS attacks even more effective. Recently, malicious actors have introduced additional layers to the architecture to make the attack more complex. For example, in a distributed reflector DDoS attack, the attack mastermind exploits uncompromised devices that unwittingly play role in the attack. Another similar example is the exploitation of DNS servers as reflectors. In this example, the DNS server sends several times more traffic to the victim than was actually sent. So, network defenders must understand and predict trends in the evolution of botnet technology in advance to defend their networks. Defenders also need to analyze the attack trends in depth including extrapolation to the future to build appropriate strategies for defense. For example, with the recent use of peer-to-peer C&C systems, the next-generation of botnets will most likely be a hybridization of P2P.

3.1.3   Botnet Formation Life Cycle

Typically, the botnet formation life cycle can be presented using five distinct phases. The phases are (i) initial infection, (ii) secondary infection, (iii) connection, (iv) malicious activity, and (v) maintenance. Figure 3.2 shows the life cycle graphically. In Phase 1, the initial infection takes place through the botnet mastermind who sends malware to infect target hosts, with bots as payloads. In Phase 2, the attacker attempts, through the infected machine, to log into an IRC server or another communication medium to establish the botnet. The owner of the botnet is paid by spammers for access rights in Phase 3. In Phase 4, the spammer instructs the botnet to send malicious code or spam to a large number of machines in the victim network. Finally, the maintenance and update tasks are executed during Phase 5.

3.1.4   Stationary Botnet Architecture

Based on the availability of machines to compromise and according to a set of pre-specified objectives, a mastermind may plan to set up a botnet with various architectures. With the growing development of botnet technologies, most recent attackers prefer complex communication structures with multiple or hybrid network topologies, rather than the early centralized structure for communication among bots and servers. Figure 3.3 shows three distinct botnet architectures commonly used by attackers.

3.1.4.1   Botnet Topology

Four types of botnet topologies are used by most attackers. (i) In the *star* topology, a single centralized C&C resource component communicates with all bot agents. This central component is responsible for

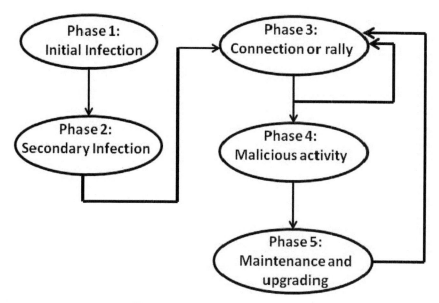

Figure 3.2: Botnet life cycle.

issuing new instructions directly to each bot agent. (ii) The *multi-server* topology, a logical extension of the star topology, provides C&C instructions to bot agents by using multiple servers. To manage the botnet, communications take place among the multiple command systems. If any of the individual servers fails to participate or is detached permanently from the network, the remaining servers handle the situation and control the botnet. (iii) In contrast, a *hierarchical* topology attempts to compromise and then propagate the bot agents among themselves. Such bot agents have the ability to proxy new C&C instructions to previously propagated progeny agents. However, updated command instructions generally suffer latency issues, which sometimes makes it difficult for an operator to use the botnet for real-time activities. (iv) In the *random* topology, no centralized C&C infrastructure exists. Signed (as authoritative) commands are injected into the botnet via any bot agent to instruct the agent to automatically propagate commands to all other agents.

3.1.4.2   Protocols Used

Three communication protocols are commonly used by attackers in a botnet. (i) The IRC protocol is used to transmit messages to other bots in the botnet. This protocol facilitates both one-to-one and one-to-many conversations. However, a limitation of this protocol is that one can easily block IRC traffic using appropriate security devices. (ii) The HTTP protocol is another widely used protocol, with the advantage that it is able to bypass the security system during communication. It is usually difficult to identify malicious HTTP traffic from legitimate traffic due to its similarity to legitimate traffic. (iii) Finally, the P2P protocol has recently become more popular among the attackers because of its distributed support.

3.1.4.3   Botnet C&C Systems

To counter a DDoS attack, it is very important for a defender to identify the C&C system used by an attacker. In general, a mastermind adopts any of three different C&C server approaches, viz., central, P2P, and hybrid, as shown in Figure 3.3. Some botnet researchers also add a fourth type of approach, known as the random C&C server approach. We analyze them in the context of DDoS attack generation.

(a) *Central C&C server*: This C&C server is mostly preferred because of its simplicity and low latency. It also provides an anonymous, real-time and efficient platform for the botmaster. A botmaster can exploit this server for direct communication with the bots. However, a C&C server suffers from several limitations. Two such common limitations are (i) single point of failure, i.e., failure of the server may lead to failure of the botnet, since no bot can receive any messages and (ii) the messages received by the servers from a host can be triggered and sent by defenders also. An IRC botnet is typically configured based on a client-server model to send text messages to the IRC server from a client or even from a server to another server. It is able to function in a distributed environment and its four major functions are (i) access list management, (ii) file movement, (iii) sharing of clients, and (iv) sharing of channel information. An attacker typically follows four basic steps to execute an IRC-based botnet attack. (i) Creation, where the attacker finds highly configurable bots in the Internet and adds malicious code or modifies existing code. (ii) Configuration, where a victim machine is connected to a selected host automatically, as long as the bot remains on that machine. To enable restricted access or to protect the channel for personal or for business purposes, the attacker

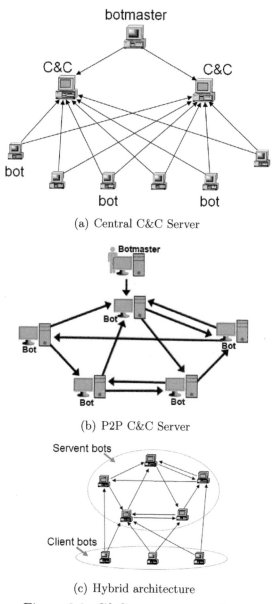

(a) Central C&C Server

(b) P2P C&C Server

(c) Hybrid architecture

Figure 3.3: C&C server approaches.

may also configure the system. (iii) Infection, where bots start propagation directly or indirectly. In case of direct propagation, the attacker uses virus programs to exploit vulnerabilities of the services or operating systems. In contrast, the attacker uses other programs as proxies to spread bots in indirect propagation. Sometimes, the attacker also uses distributed malware through DCC (Direct Client-to-Client) file exchange on IRC or P2P networks. Once an adequate number of vulnerable machines are compromised, they are employed to spread the infection process, saving time for the attacker to add other insecure victims. Two common examples of vulnerable systems are Windows 2000 and XP SP1, where the attacker often can find unpatched or insecure (e.g., without firewall) hosts. (iv) Control, where the attacker sends instructions to a group of bots via an IRC channel to carry out malicious tasks.

(b) *P2P C&C server*: This architecture has recently gained tremendous popularity, because (i) it is reliable and robust in comparison to the centralized architecture, (ii) it cannot be shut down easily, (iii) its design is simple, and (iv) it has a high survivability rate. Recently, most people have started to depend on this approach to share their resources, programs, documents, movies, and games. This approach maintains a seed list with each host, and when a bot receives a message, it forwards it only to the private list of seeds. Another advantage of the P2P architecture is that the botmaster needs to connect to only one of the bots (peers) to send instructions over the network and each host periodically connects to its neighbor host to retrieve instructions from the botmaster. However, an important limitation is that it gives no guarantee of message delivery. The three most commonly found P2P architectures are discussed below.

   (i) *Unstructured C&C server*: An unstructured C&C server is free of the restriction to send messages from one host to another. If the system is not maintaining a seed list, the bot collects information to identify another bot by scanning the network. In this architecture, the botmaster initially sends an encrypted message to any one of the hosts over the network. It is a simple, yet secure structure, where the discovery of a host does not affect other hosts. The two major advantages of this architecture are (i) low design complexity and (ii) high survivability. However, it has limitations such as (i) low message latency and (ii) no guarantee of message delivery.

   (ii) *Structured C&C server*: A structured C&C server is relatively more efficient than its unstructured counterpart. The effective use of a distributed hash table (DHT) [152] makes its routing effective. It creates a mapping between the content and its corresponding locations. Few commonly used examples of DHTs are CAN [202], Pastry [207], Kademlia [161], Tapestry [287], and Pchord [103].

(iii) *Superpeer P2P overlay [23]*: In a superpeer P2P network, all peers are not considered equal. A small subset of peers are temporary servers and carry out network functions, such as search and control. Bots belonging to this category usually have a valid IP address and are not under firewalls or DHCP. Some commonly found example applications of this type are Skype, Fasttrack, and Gnutella. The high visibility and more vulnerability to attacks make this design less preferable to most botnets.

(c) *Hybrid*: A hybrid C&C system is designed by deriving the benefits of both centralized and P2P models. It includes both servant bots and client bots. A servant bot includes both static and routable IP addresses that behave both as client as well as server. In contrast, client bots include dynamic and non-routable IP addresses. This category of C&C system can also be placed behind firewalls without having connectivity to the Internet.

(d) *Random C&C system*: This simple and secure C&C system is designed based on the principle that a single bot should know at most one other bot. The sender bot or controller of this system initially scans the Internet at random to identify another bot. Once found, it sends an encrypted message. An attractive feature of this design is that detection of just a single bot is not enough to compromise the full botnet. However, it suffers from three major shortcomings, viz., (i) high message latency, (ii) frequent detectability of the random probing behavior, and (iii) no guarantee of message delivery.

3.1.5 Some Stationary Botnets

Most sophisticated DDoS attacks in recent times have been launched using botnet technology. During the past few years, several significant developments in botnet technology have been introduced. We present a few commonly used bots for launching various types of attacks.

1. *Agobot*: This multi-threaded bot, authored by a German programmer called Axel Ago Gembe, was developed using C++, an assembly language. It is considered the pioneer IRC bot used for attack generation. Agobot is known for its four important features, viz., (i) it is able to initiate port scanning to identify other hosts and infect them, (ii) it can launch DDoS attacks by executing programs and commands, (iii) it uses a password-protected IRC client control interface, and (iv) it can update and remove installed bots from a remote location.

2. *Forbot*: This botnet is derived from Agobot and it operates in a centralized mode during command communication.

3. *SDBot*: SDBot is able to perform several backdoor and information stealing activities. This bot exploits any vulnerabilities found and network shares during propagation.

4. *RBot*: This bot enables the creation of a large family of backdoors| remote administration utility programs. After successful installation of these backdoors, it allows a remote user to access and control it over the Internet. A remote user with malice can control the infected hosts, usually without the knowledge or consent of the original user(s). The user can also use the backdoors remotely to perform a set of activities on the infected machine such as stealing data, executing commands, or accessing other machines on a local network.

5. *Phatbot*: Phatbot is another descendent of Agobot. It uses the P2P botnet architecture and communicates using IRC channels. Phatbot allows a remote attacker to compromise the victim machine and add it to a P2P network. It sends a large volume of spam emails or floods Websites with data using the network to knock them offline.

6. *Conficker*: This powerful and effective computer worm can infect millions of users instantly. It exploits vulnerabilities and flaws in Windows software and attempts to mount dictionary attacks to steal administrator passwords to propagate during the formation of a botnet. It is extremely difficult to defend against Conficker's approach as a combination of several advanced malware techniques.

7. *Spybot*: Spybot is a modified version of SDBot. It allows one to connect and communicate with a designated IRC server and to receive commands through private channels from the botmaster.

8. *MegaD*: MegaD is a mass spamming botnet, which was identified in 2007. MegaD allows one to interact with four types of C&C servers, viz., master servers (MS), SMTP Servers (SS), drop servers (DS), and template servers (TS).

9. *Srizbi*: Srizbi is a collection of computers (zombies) infected through the Srizbi Trojan Horse. A *botnet herder* controls this botnet by sending commands to these computers. The effectiveness of the Srizbi botnet in terms of operations depends on a number of servers included in the operation through which individual bots are controlled. Srizbi includes a collection of redundant copies of servers to protect the botnet from being crippled in case of system failure.

10. *Torpig*: Torpig allows one to steal sensitive information such as credit card data and bank account information from its victims. It is a dangerous Trojan horse to infest the Internet. It applies phishing attacks to extract additional, sensitive information from the victim machines.

11. *Grum*: Grum is a spam email sender botnet. It includes two types of control servers in its design. One type of control server push configuration updates to the infected computers and the other type instructs the botnet concerning the content of spam emails to send.

12. *Cutwail*: Cutwail is a simple yet effective spam email sender botnet that uses a Trojan component called *pushdo* to install the bot on the victim machine. The bots are able to connect directly to the C&C server, and to receive instructions about emails to be sent. After successful delivery, the bots generate statistics on email delivery and error messages (if any) and report to the spammer.

13. *Rustock*: This bot is a rootkit-enabled backdoor Trojan that assists in the distribution of spam emails. Rustock can transmit more than 25,000 spam messages per hour from an infected ma-

chine. Rustock is able to generate 13.82 billion daily junk mails by including 470,000 to 690,000 computers.

14. *EggDrop*: EggDrop is the first botnet that used IRC as a C&C server.

15. *GTbot*: GTbot launches flooding attacks with huge volumes of text messages using a legitimate IRC channel as a C&C server. It initially accesses an IRC channel with a large volume of traffic and then joins the target channels, and attempts to flood them with endless repetitive data. This bot causes normal users to become disconnected or their IRC clients to freeze, because it cannot process the rapidly scrolling flood of garbage data fast enough. GTbot can flood up to 150 kbps of data through the IRC server and often incurs huge costs to the owner, who usually gets free or cheap service, with high penalties for extra bandwidth consumption.

16. *Sinit*: This is another backdoor Trojan that allows users with malicious intentions to access a machine and connect to a distributed botnet. Sinit uses P2P technology during communication.

17. *Bagle*: Bagle, which was first introduced in 2004, can be used in proxy-to-relay email spam. Bagle is more effective than Rustock. The number of computers included in Bagle is estimated to be between 180,000 and 280,000, which can pump out 8.31 billion spam emails in a day.

18. *SpamThru*: SpamThru shares information with other peers, such as source IP and destination addresses, port addresses, and software versions of the control server and template servers using a custom P2P protocol. In this bot setup, all peers are aware of each other and the botnet is usually maintained by a central server. The control server is shut down, and the spammer can update the other peers with the location of a new control server, as long as the spammer controls at least one peer.

19. Kraken: Kraken, another spam Trojan, is used to spread spam from an infected machine. It communicates with C&C using encrypted messages and can communicate with TCP and UDP protocols.

20. *Bobax*: Bobax is known to be a wide spanning botnet with a large footprint. It uses plaintext HTTP for communication with the C&C server. This worm exploits the DCOM and LSASS vulnerabilities on Windows systems.

21. *Asprox*: This botnet emerged in 2007. It allows one to launch SQL injection attacks on Websites and to send phishing scams.

22. *Rxbot*: Rxbot, a Windows-based worm, is designed using an IRC C&C server. It can be used for malicious activities such as spam mail sending, identity stealing, fraud click, and to generate DDoS attacks.

23. *Nugache*: Nugache is designed by customizing the Trojan worm. It allows P2P communication without any C&C server, which makes it not easily detectable. Nugache provides a new level of resiliency for the botnet.

24. *Waledac*: This is a sophisticated worm that can be downloaded and then used to execute binaries. It can act as a network proxy, send spam, mine infected computers for confidential data such as email addresses and passwords, and launch DoS attacks. It enables propagation using social engineering and certain client-side vulnerabilities.

25. *Donbot*: This is a specially designed botnet to transmit pharmaceutical and stock-based email spam. Donbot allows one to use approximately 125,000 individual computers to send up to 800 million spam messages in a day.

26. *Festi*: Festi can be used as an email spammer as well as for launching DoS attacks. It is designed based on the client server C&C mechanism, where a set of servers is used to manage the botnet.

27. *TDL-4*: TDL-4 is an effective and new-generation botnet. It allows one to infect up to several million machines. In 2011, TDL-4 infected more than 4.5 million machines within the first three months. It infects the master boot record of the target machine, making it extremely difficult to identify.

Table 3.1: Comparison of stationary botnets.

Botnet	Year	No of Nodes	Architecture	Attack Type	Protocol Used	Platform	Reference
GTbot	1986		Centralized	DDoS	IRC	Windows	[156]
EggDrop	1993		Centralized		IRC	Windows, Linux	[3]
Agobot	2002		Centralized	DDoS	IRC, HTTP	Windows	[247]
SDBot			Centralized	DoS	IRC	Windows	[166]
RBot	2003		Centralized	DoS	IRC	Windows, Linux	[203]
Sinit	2003		P2P		IRC/ HTTP	Windows, Linux	[284]
Bagle	2004	230,000	Centralized, P2P	Spam sending	IRC	Windows	[274]
Phatbot	2004		P2P		HTTP/ IRC	Windows	[274]
SpamThru	2006	12,000	P2P	Sending spam	IRC	Windows	[132]
Nugache	2006	160,000	P2P		IRC	Windows	[232]
Rxbot	2006		Centralized		IRC	Windows	[19]
Spybot			Centralized	DoS	IRC		[150]
Rustock	2006	150,000	Centralized	Sending spam, DDoS	HTTP	Windows	[125]
MegaD	2007	500,000	P2P	DDoS		Windows	[102]
Srizbi	2007	400,000	Centralize	DoS, DDoS	HTTP	Windows, Linux	[132]
Storm	2007	160,000	P2P	DDoS	IRC	Windows	[232]
Conficker	2008	10.5 million	P2P	Buffer over-flow	HTTP	Windows	[165]
Torpig	2008	180,000	Centralized	Phishing, man-in-the-middle	IRC	Windows	[231]
Grum	2008		Centralized	Sending spam	IRC/ HTTP	Windows	[125]
Asprox	2008	15,000	Centralized	SQL injection	HTTP	Windows	[30]
Bobax	2008	185,000	Centralized		HTTP/ UDP	Windows	[274]
Kraken	2008	400,000	Centralized		HTTP	Windows	[98]
Waledac	2009	90,000	P2P	Sending spam	IRC	Windows, Linux	[248]
Cutwail	2009		P2P	DDoS	IRC	Windows	[65]
Donbot	2009	125,000	Centralized	DDoS	TCP	Windows	[230]
Festi	2010	25,000	Centralized	DoS, email spam	HTTP	Windows	[114]
TDL-4	2011	4.5 million	P2P	DDoS, DoS		Windows	[91]

3.1.6 DDoS Attacks Using Mobile Botnets

A mobile botnet is a collection of compromised smartphones, which are remotely controlled by a botmaster via C&C channels. In recent times, many intruders have been attracted to exploit these mobile devices as a means for launching DDoS attacks because of their ability to communicate with Internet services through various techniques such as Evolution Data Optimized or Enhanced Voice Data Only (EVDO), Enhanced Data Rates for GSM Evolution (EDGE), High-Speed Downlink Packet Access (HSDPA), Universal Mobile Telecommunication System (UMTS), and General Packet Radio Service (GPRS). Generally, a DDoS attacker uses a mobile platform during the initial stage of the launching because it has limited battery power, limited network traffic, and no fixed IP address [221]. An example mobile botnet architecture is shown in Figure 3.4.

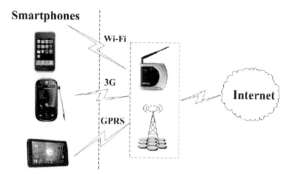

Figure 3.4: Mobile botnet architecture.

3.1.6.1 Mobile Botnet Characteristics

From the constraints as presented above, it can be understood that mobile environments are generally less secure. But the characteristics of mobile botnets make it very difficult to detect them. It is also difficult to detect malware that attack mobile devices. Some inherent challenges posed by mobile botnets are discussed below.

1. *Developed with long-term intentions*: A DDoS attacker develops a mobile botnet with long-term intentions and the botmaster tries to maintain the botnet safe and uncovered by applying various strategies.

2. *Distributed security management*: Generally, a mobile botnet lacks central security management. It can track and monitor security threats and update security policies directly on mobile devices.

3. *Social engineering*: In recent times, most mobile botnet developers use social engineering approaches to propagate in the network.

4. *Flexibility*: An attack mastermind regularly updates bots and botnets, and changes the codes periodically. The attacker also changes botnet control strategies frequently and develops improved methods to recover and restore the detected bots, within a short time.

5. *Works in silent mode*: A mobile botnet developer always avoids unnecessary or suspicious use of CPU, memory, or other computer resources, which may help identify its presence.

6. *Resource limitations*: Mobile device resources such as CPU, memory, and battery life are limited. Therefore, existing botnet detection solutions are often inadequate for mobile botnets.

7. *Use standard protocols*: Most attackers establish their communication infrastructure using standard protocols. In recent botnets, the standard HTTP protocol is used to impersonate normal Web traffic and to bypass current network security systems.

8. *Device-specific characteristics*: Some characteristics are specific to mobile devices such as mobility, strict personalization and various types of connectivity, technology convergence, and a variety of capabilities.

9. *Diversity in infection*: Typically, a mobile botnet developer uses different communication media (e.g., MMS, SMS, and Bluetooth) along with the Internet to spread with diversity. An important advantage of this diversity is that it makes it difficult to detect infection processes using current security systems.

3.1.6.2   C&C Mechanisms in Mobile Botnet

The botmaster in a mobile botnet is mainly responsible for controlling channels for compromised nodes. So, if one can block the channel for the botmaster, the botnet will not be able to function. In a mobile botnet, typically three types of C&C mechanisms are used.

1. *GSM-based (SMS-based) C&C*: A botmaster uses a phone to control the botnet in this C&C mechanism.

2. *Internet-based (IP-based) C&C*: This C&C is similar to the P2P-based mechanism used in traditional network botnets.

3. *Local wireless C&C*: The botmaster in this mechanism injects a command and allows it to travel through the net.

The C&C channel plays a major role in a mobile botnet. It is responsible for circulating commands from the botmaster to the mobile bot. So, a mobile botnet-based attacker needs to be careful with this channel in designing the botnet. In a mobile attack process, the attacker may use four different channels during communication.

1. *SMS C&C channel*: SMS communication is a convenient way of sending or receiving textual information between two communicating parties. This C&C has four important features.

   (a) The server of the service provider stores messages when the recipient's mobile device is switched off.

   (b) Communication propagates through SMS or MMS functions.

   (c) It can support multiple sending and receiving channel options.

   (d) It can hide malicious content.

   To prevent detection of commands sent as SMS messages by a remote user, each mobile bot intercepts all incoming SMS messages before they reach the inbox. SMS messages containing the specific passcode are kept aside whereas the other SMS messages are allowed to pass through the inbox.

2. Bluetooth C&C channel: This mobile phone-based botnet uses Bluetooth to propagate control messages. It is almost similar to an Internet-based P2P botnet.

3. HTTP C&C channel: In addition to Bluetooth and SMS channels for retrieval of information from the server, HTTP is commonly used to transmit information for the C&C channel. This channel

Table 3.2: Comparison of mobile botnets.

Botnet	Year	Platform	Architecture	Attack Type	Protocol Used	Ref.
Zeus	2007	Windows Android	Centralized	Mobile banking	HTTP	[74]
Tiger	2010	Android	P2P	Private data theft	HTTP	[74]
Droid Dream	2011	Android	P2P	Download malicious applications	HTTP	[74]
Andbot	2011	Android	Centralized	Theft of private data	HTTP	[268]
Geinimi	2011	Android	P2P	Illegal transactions	IRC/HTTP	[194]
MDK	2012	Android	P2P	Theft of private data	HTTP/IRC	[79]

is used to communicate information between the mobile bot and control server.

4. Hybrid C&C channel: This channel overcomes almost all the limitations of a single point of failure. It includes three major components: (i) C&C channels, (ii) a propagation vector, and (iii) a mobile botnet topology. Typically, a hybrid design makes use of multiple C&C channels to satisfy various objectives. It attempts to ensure that there is no single point of failure in the topology, the cost of command dissemination is low, network activities are limited, and battery consumption per bot is low.

With rapid developments in cellular networks and Internet access capabilities of smartphones and tablets using Wi-Fi, GPRS, 3G, and 4G, the use of mobile botnets has become the trend. Many security experts contend that large-scale attacks can and will be launched from mobile networks. Till now, most DDoS attacks have been generated from a network of malicious computers using an IRC-based architecture or an agent-handler architecture. But in recent times, networks of mobile devices or mobile botnets have also started to become significantly involved in launching DDoS attacks. For example, Android.DDoS.1.origin is an Android Trojan that can be used to mount DDoS attacks from a mobile botnet. This Trojan is able to create an application icon that looks almost like a normal application to a legitimate user. It can connect to a remote server and transmit the phone number of the compromised device to illegitimate parties and then wait for further SMS commands. The Trojan can launch a DDoS attack against a specified server by sending SMS messages.

Table 3.3: Comparison between mobile botnet and stationary botnet.

Features	Mobile Botnet	Stationary Botnet
Use of IP address	Private	Public
Battery power	Limited	Unlimited
Bandwidth	Limited	High bandwidth
Collection of	Mobile devices	Stationary devices
Central security management	No	Usually yes
C & C protocol	IRC, HTTP, P2P	SMS, MMS, Bluetooth

3.1.7 Some Mobile Botnets

The C&C center of a mobile botnet governs a network of compromised mobile devices such as smartphones and tablets. A general comparison between mobile botnets and their stationary predecessors is given in Table 3.3. We can clearly see that there is a clear distinction between these two types of botnets in terms of power backup, available bandwidth, use of IP addresses, and the existence of centralized management. Some example mobile botnets are mentioned below.

1. *Andbot*: Andbot adopts a centralized C&C topology and uses an effective C&C system called URL Flux [268]. It is attractive because of three important features: low cost, stealth, and resilience.

2. *Waledac*: This Web-based mobile botnet uses HTTP for communication through channels. It is very effective as a spam mailer and in this botnet, each infected mobile device communicates with others to exchange lists of active proxy servers. Waledac communicates among infected devices using MMS messages on the mobile network.

3. *Ikee.B*: This simple botnet operates on jailbroken iPhones with almost the same capabilities as computer-based botnets. It has several attractive features such as the ability to scan the IP range of iPhone networks, look for vulnerable iPhones on a global scale, and self-propagation.

4. *Geinimi*: This is another effective Trojan malware that can steal personal data on a user's phone and transmit it to remote servers

using an Android botnet. After injection and installation on a user's phone, the malware can receive commands from a remote server allowing the owner of the server to control the phone.

5. *MDK*: MDK is considered as the largest mobile botnet in China. This botnet can very quickly infect a large number of devices. It is a new variant of *Android.Backscript*, which uses the Advanced Encryption Standard (AES) algorithm to encrypt data.

6. *Zeus*: This botnet mainly uses social engineering approaches to infect a large variety of mobile operating systems such as Windows Mobile, Android, Symbian, and BlackBerry. Zeus or Zitmo infects a mobile phone by sending an SMS message that contains a fake URL to dupe users to download a security certificate which is, in fact, the Zitmo bot. Zeus can also intercept messages received from banks to customers and authenticate illegal transactions by stealing mobile Transaction Authentication Numbers (TAC).

7. *DroidDream*: DroidDream is a cleverly designed, silent botnet that does not make any unusual or suspicious use of CPU, memory, or other resources, which may uncover its activities. This botnet is typically activated at night (11 pm to 8 am) when mobile users are usually asleep. It attempts to access the root privileges on infected mobiles and tries to steal confidential information by installing a second application.

8. *Tiger*: Tiger is able to capture not only private SMS data but also can record voice call conversations and even background sounds. It is a fully SMS-controlled bot that can detect and uncover C&C messages.

3.2   Chapter Summary and Recommendations

In this chapter we have noted that the requirements for designing an effective DDoS attack launching tool using a stationary botnet are different from those for a mobile botnet. A mobile botnet-based attack launching tool places additional demands on the planners and schemers due to limited bandwidth, limited battery backup, lack of central security management, lack of firewall protection as compared to a stationary botnet-based tool. The attacker and the defender need to be aware

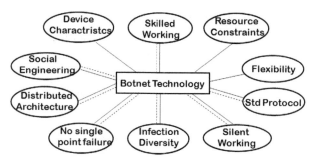

Figure 3.5: Major factors of botnet design.

of these issues while developing tools that attack or defend against a DDoS attack.

During design of a botnet architecture, a DDoS attacker generally considers the factors shown in Figure 3.5. The most relevant issues for stationary botnet design are connected with dotted lines, whereas the issues for mobile botnet design are connected with solid lines.

An important observation is that P2P botnet communication is preferable over centralized networks. A P2P communication is generally too complex to be disrupted by the defender. Further, the failure of a single bot does not have much impact on the entire network. In this design, as commands pass through intermediate peers in a P2P network, it is more difficult for analysts to identify bot controllers and to determine the size of a network. Furthermore, just increasing the size of a botnet may not always be effective if the goal is to inflict maximal damage. Increased size increases the visibility of the botnet. A botnet with a relatively small size, say between 15000 and 20000 bots can be quite effective in damaging a victim's Website or server if their combined bandwidth can be utilized properly with appropriately skillful coding. In general, the low-rate attacks (50–70% of full attack) with random variation in the pulse, amplitude, and interval are more likely to bypass the defense system.

With rapid developments in botnet technology and increasing use of smart phones, mobile botnets have emerged as an effective platform for attackers to launch cellular network attacks such as SMS spam, DDoS attack, and click fraud. In contrast to stationary botnets, a mobile botnet's design is influenced by factors such as device-specific resource constraints (e.g., battery life) and flexibility. The coder for mobile botnets must pay attention to these factors. Further, smart phones are usually more vulnerable to an attack because getting access to a mobile phone through an SMS command and control system or via Bluetooth [285] is easy. Furthermore, the P2P topology for mobile botnets allows botmasters and bots to publish and search for commands in a P2P fashion, making detection and disruption much harder. Attack planners and designers also prefer the use of HTTP in mobile botnet communication, because it helps hide the contents of the communication.

Chapter 4

DDoS Detection

Today, the world is being computerized and Internetized at an astonishing speed. To support this phenomenal growth, service providers are trying their best to provide the utmost quality of service. In this competitive environment, an aspect that stands out is security, which is indeed an extremely serious topic of concern. As we have discussed in the previous chapters, an intrusion or attack may be fast or slow. We refer to a DDoS attack as *fast* when it generates a large number of packets or extremely high-volume traffic within a very short time, say a fraction of a minute, to disrupt service. An attack is referred to as a *slow* attack, if it takes minutes or hours to complete the process.

To counter the rapid emergence of external and internal threats to networks and resources, researchers have looked at a variety of approaches such as intrusion detection system (IDS), intrusion prevention system (IPS), intrusion response system (IRS), and intrusion tolerance system (ITS). Among these, IDS and IPS are important components of a layered security infrastructure. To execute an attack on a network or a system, as discussed in *Chapter 2*, an attacker generally follows four main steps [25]: (a) the attacker scans the whole network to find and recruit vulnerable host(s); (b) the vulnerable hosts are then compromised for exploitation by the attacker using malware or backdoor programs; (c) the attacker infects the compromised hosts to create a base for effective launching of an attack, and (d) finally, the attack is launched using the compromised hosts.

4.1 Modules of a DDoS Defense Solution

A generic DDoS defense solution is comprised of three modules, viz., *monitoring*, *detection*, and *reaction*. In this section, we discuss the functions of these three modules of DDoS defense.

4.1.1 Monitoring

This module allows one to monitor services being used on a network and to match against activities that we should see. To perform such monitoring activities, it collects necessary information on the state of the network at various points within the network. This module also helps identify unauthorized services within a network. For identification of such unauthorized services, one should look not only at external traffic but also at internal traffic. Otherwise, one will miss internal hosts involved in unauthorized activities.

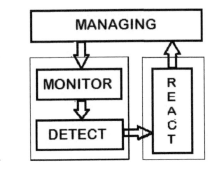

Figure 4.1: Modules of a DDoS defense system.

4.1.2 Detection

This module aims to identify any misuse or anomalous behavior in a network and generate reports to the administration. The module may also try to stop an intrusion attempt, but this is neither required nor expected. Intrusion detection is primarily focused on identifying possible intrusive patterns, incidents, or activities, and reporting them in a timely and meaningful manner. Typically, a detection module analyzes relevant network traffic information to identify possible security breaches, which include both misuses and anomalies, either by using a supervised approach (using prior knowledge of intrusions) or by using an unsupervised approach (without using prior knowledge of intrusions).

4.1.3 Reaction

A reaction module of a DDoS defense system typically reacts with two basic components, viz., a *passive* and an *active* component. The passive component, composed of a set of procedures, is involved in the inspection of the system's configuration files to detect inadvisable settings, inspection of the password files to detect inadvisable passwords, and inspection of other system areas to detect policy violations. In contrast, the active component, which is composed of another set of procedures, reacts to known methods of attack and generates system responses. It can respond to suspicious events in several ways, which include displaying an alert, logging the event, or even paging an administrator.

4.2 Types of DDoS Defense Solutions

In this section we discuss a categorization of DDoS defense based on the approach used, the nature of control applied, the infrastructure used, the deployment strategy used, and the type of technique applied.

4.2.1 Based on Approach Used

An approach to DDoS defense is developed with one or more of the four major objectives viz., (a) to detect DDoS attacks at an early stage, (b) to prevent DDoS attacks from occurring at all if possible, (c) to react with appropriate action(s) on detection of DDoS attacks, and (d) to improve the tolerance of the victim network. We discuss DDoS detection in detail in this chapter. DDoS prevention, reaction, and tolerance are discussed in detail in the subsequent chapters (i.e., in *Chapters 5 & 6*, respectively).

An intrusion detection system (IDS) is an application that monitors a network or system for malicious activities or policy violations. Some systems may additionally try to stop an intrusion attempt, but this is typically not expected from an IDS. If it detects any threat, anomalous patterns, or policy violations, it alerts the system or network administrator. So, the objective of an IDS is to detect and inform active defenders about intrusions. An IDS uses techniques that may detect

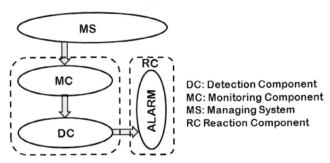

Figure 4.2: Intrusion detection system: a generic view.

suspicious activities either at the network or at the host levels. Figure 4.2 shows a generic view of an IDS. The four basic components of an IDS are managing, monitoring, detection, and alarm generation.

- The *managing component* oversees traffic flow in the network. It provides traffic information to the monitoring component for analysis.

- The *monitoring component* monitors traffic and analyzes the behavior of the network.

- The *detection component* detects any suspicious behavior with respect to the normal working nature of the network. If any abnormal behavior is detected, it communicates with the alarm-generation component.

- If any abnormality in the traffic is detected, the alarm-generation component raises an alarm to inform the administrator, so that the intrusion can be handled appropriately.

4.2.2   Based on Nature of Control

In this section, we discuss the classification of defense systems based on the control structure used to counter DDoS attacks. One can use three basic ways to control detection and prevention of DDoS attacks, viz., centralized, hierarchical, and distributed.

4.2.2.1   Centralized DDoS Defense

In a centralized defense system, each detection engine generates alerts locally and sends them to a central server. The server attempts to

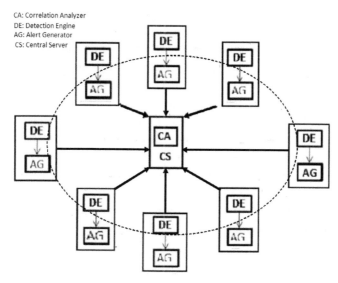

Figure 4.3: Structure of centralized DDoS defense.

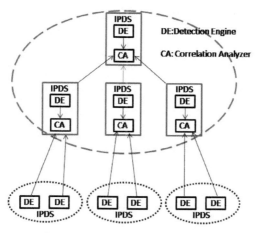

Figure 4.4: Structure of hierarchical DDoS defense.

correlate the alerts and analyze them. Using this approach, an accurate detection decision can be made based on all available alert information. However, a major limitation of this approach is that the central server is crucially vulnerable; any failure of this server leads to the collapse of the whole process of correlation. In addition, the central server should be prepared to handle a high volume of data received from the local detection elements within a short interval of time.

4.2.2.2 Hierarchical DDoS Defense

In this structure, the whole system is divided into several small subsystems based on features such as geography, administrative control, and software platforms. The detection and prevention systems at the lowest level work as detection elements while such a system at a higher level is able to serve as an intrusion detector and a correlation handler. A system at a higher level can correlate alerts from both its own level and from lower levels. The correlated alerts are then forwarded to a higher level for further analysis. This approach is more scalable than the centralized approach, but still suffers from the vulnerability of the central unit. In addition, the higher-level nodes have a higher-level abstraction of the input, which may limit their detection coverage.

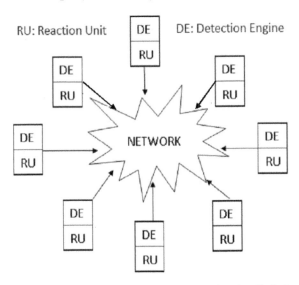

Figure 4.5: Structure of a distributed DDoS defense.

4.2.2.3 Distributed DDoS Defense

A distributed DDoS defense system avoids the use of a centralized unit to process information. It is comprised of fully autonomous systems with distributed management control. All participating detection and prevention systems have their own components communicating with each other. An important advantage of a fully distributed DDoS defense system [146] is that although the network entities do not have complete information about the network topology, it is possible to have a scalable design since there is no central entity responsible for doing all the correlation work. Further, local alarm correlation is simpler in this structure. However, a fully distributed DDoS defense system is also not free from limitations [289]: (a) All alert information may not be available during decision making, so accuracy may suffer. (b) Inadequate alert information (usually has a single feature like IP address) may be a bottleneck in appropriate decision making, especially in detecting large-scale distributed attacks.

Looking at the different approaches used to control DDoS defense, we observe the following.

- Each control structure has its own advantages and limitations.

- Appropriateness of a control structure depends on the network under consideration, its structure, size, and how the network is constructed.

- In centralized defense, the central server plays a major role in the decision-making process. The server covers the entire network with no redundancy.

- In hierarchical or distributed DDoS defense, each level can detect attacks and can react accordingly in its own neighborhood. Each level or each unit usually handles a low volume of data.

4.2.3 Based on Defense Infrastructure

In this section, we discuss defense systems based on the infrastructure used. There are two types, viz., host-based and network-based.

4.2.3.1 Host-Based DDoS Defense

In a host-based DDoS defense system, data is analyzed by individual computers, which serve as hosts. Typically, it uses an agent-based network architecture, where a software agent resides on each of the hosts in the system. The detection and prevention engine processes data that accumulate automatically, such as event and kernel logs. Such a DDoS defense system also monitors activities such as which program accesses what resources. Accordingly, it also flags anomalous usage. A host-based DDoS defense system also monitors the state of the system and makes sure that everything is in order, which is necessary for effective functioning of anomaly filters.

Table 4.1: Infrastructure-based defense: a comparison.

Infrastructure Used	Strengths	Limitations
Host based	-Can detect and verify insider attacks as the attackers reside on host. -Can decrypt encrypted packets in incoming traffic. - Doesn't require any additional hardware.	-Vulnerable to both direct attacks and attacks against host operating system. -Vulnerable to DoS attacks. -Performance overhead may increase.
Network based	-Can work in large networks. -Usually passive in nature and can be easily deployed without disruption to normal network operation. -Less susceptible to direct attack.	-When size of network is large, the system may fail to recognize attacks. -Cannot analyze packets which are encrypted. -Often found unreliable in terms of detection accuracy.

4.2.3.2 Network-Based DDoS Defense

A network-based DDoS defense system sniffs packets or extracts network flow information either from the router or from stored network traces and analyzes them for identification of misuses or anomalous behaviors. A network-based IDS (NIDS) can be supervised, unsupervised, or hybrid. A supervised NIDS uses prior knowledge in the form of signatures, profiles, or references when identifying misuses. In contrast, an unsupervised NIDS attempts to identify anomalous patterns without depending on any form of prior knowledge. Such a NIDS is able to detect unknown or novel attacks. If any suspicious or anomalous behavior is detected, it triggers an alarm and passes the message to the central computer system or an administrator, and generates an automatic response.

4.2.4 Based on Defense Location

A DDoS defense system can also be characterized based on its location of deployment. Based on three possible locations of deployment, such systems can be categorized as victim-end, intermediate, and source-end system. We discuss each of these categories and analyze their pros and cons.

4.2.4.1 Victim-End DDoS Defense

A victim-end DDoS defense system is generally deployed in the routers of the victim network. The detection software stores information about known intrusion signatures or profiles of normal behavior. This information is updated by the processing elements as new knowledge becomes available. The stored intrusion signatures and procedures for other critical events such as false alarms are updated. The processing element is responsible for frequent storage of configuration data, which are the results generated at intermediate stages. Typically, a victim-end detection approach is able to provide better detection accuracy than other approaches, because it gets more scopes to analyze the traffic at the cost of higher resource consumption. An important disadvantage is that these approaches detect the attack only after it reaches the victim and detecting an attack when legitimate clients have already been affected may be pyrrhic victory.

Most DDoS defense mechanisms are deployed at the victim end for effective detection and defense of a system. Victim-end detection systems detect attacks either in a reactive or proactive manner. Unlike the other two DDoS defense approaches, a victim-end defense approach cannot provide complete protection from DDoS attacks when the rate of attack traffic is very high. The DDoS attack may have already damaged the victim network. So, in many high- rate attacks, victim-end-based DDoS defense is not adequate. Besides, a victim-end defense system can drop all incoming traffic when the traffic rate is very high and as a consequence, legitimate traffic still cannot travel across the network through congested links in other parts of the network and make it to the victim. A victim-end detection architecture is shown in Figure **??**.

4.2.4.2 Source-End DDoS Defense

A source-end DDoS defense system operates in a fashion similar to the victim-end defense. It can be considered the best approach from a deployment perspective, if we want to stop intrusion at an early stage. It is able to prevent congestion not only on the victim side, but also in the whole intermediate network. Source-end defense can stop the attack traffic before reaching the target network and it also reduces the chance of collision by filtering attack traffic before it mingles with other attack traffic flow in the network. Further, with this DDoS defense, it is not

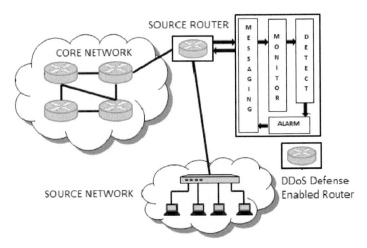

Figure 4.6: Source-end DDoS detection: a generic architecture.

only easy to perform traceback but it can also achieve high detection accuracy due to low network traffic flow aggregation at the source end. However, a major difficulty with this defense is that during an attack, the sources of attack are typically distributed widely and the behavior of a single source is almost like in normal traffic. In addition, from an implementation perspective, deployment of such a defense system at the source end is also extremely difficult. A source-end detection architecture is shown in Figure 4.6.

So, the main advantage of source-end DDoS attack detection is that it can protect a network near the point of attack generation, reducing the chance of severe damage to the victim network. However, it may cause collateral damage [115] to legitimate traffic. Mirkovic et al. [171] propose a source-end DDoS defense system called D-WARD to defend DDoS attacks at the source end. According to the authors, the source end is the only effective deployment location to achieve better response selectiveness in case of high-volume, high-spoofing flooding attacks, and as a result it should be a key building block for a distributed defense system.

4.2.4.3   Intermediate Network DDoS Defense

An intermediate network defense is designed to overcome the limitations of source-end and victim-end DDoS defense by balancing the problems of attack detection accuracy and bandwidth consumption.

A major difficulty with such a defense system is its deployability. You must employ the detection system in all routers on the Internet to achieve maximum detection accuracy, because the unavailability of this scheme on only a few routers may cause failure of the detection and traceback processes. Thus, full practical implementation of this scheme is practically impossible as it requires re-configuration of all the routers on the Internet.

Network-based defense mechanisms are deployed mainly on the routers of the network system. The main advantage of a network-based defense mechanism is that proper actions can be taken in the routers against malicious traffic before such malicious traffic is forwarded to the victim machine. Suspicious network traffic filtering in the edge or core routers of a victim machine is another advantage of a network-based defense. Some well-known network-based defense mechanisms are (i) router-based packet filtering [189], (ii) detecting and filtering malicious routers [173], and (iii) pushback [115]. The main drawback of the network-based defense mechanism is the overhead incurred due to large network size. Such detection mechanisms are not very effective and efficient for real-time defense against DDoS attacks. An intermediate end detection architecture is shown in Figure 4.7.

So, from the pros and cons analysis of these three DDoS defense approaches based on location, one can make the following observations.

- The resource requirements at the three locations are not the same.

- Each location has its advantages and disadvantages, which we list clearly in Table 4.2.

- Legitimate clients suffer most in the victim-end approach compared to the source-end and intermediate network approaches.

- Balancing the amount of resources needed to handle an attack and the volume of traffic for legitimate clients is tougher in source-end and intermediate locations.

4.2.5 Based on Techniques Used

During the past two decades, a large number of DDoS detection and prevention techniques have been developed. These techniques have been mostly developed using various statistical, data mining, and machine learning, soft computing and knowledge-based techniques. We

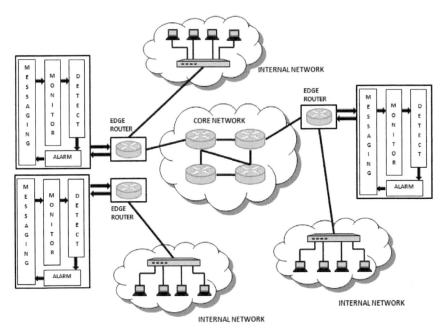

Figure 4.7: Intermediate DDoS detection: a generic architecture.

introduce and discuss some popular DDoS detection, prevention, reaction, and tolerance techniques next.

4.3   DDoS Detection Techniques

Detection of distributed denial-of-service attacks is broadly studied in two categories: *misuse detection* and *anomaly-based* detection. Misuse detection searches for definite patterns (i.e., *signatures, rules*, or *activities*) in the captured network traffic to identify previously known DDoS intrusion types. Such detection techniques usually exhibit high detection rates with low numbers of false alarms. However, a misuse detection technique fails to detect unknown DDoS intrusion types. Anomaly-based DDoS detection techniques aim to identify novel intrusion types in addition to detection of known types. Such techniques analyze network traffic behavior and attempt to detect unusual patterns at an early stage. We discuss each of these two major categories of detection techniques below.

Table 4.2: DDoS defense based on locations: a general comparison.

Defense Location	Advantages	Disadvantages
Victim-end	-Shows good performance using stored known intrusion patterns or signatures. -Takes advantage of the availability of resources during detection.	- If detection is not fast, legitimate clients may be affected. -Often unreliable in terms of detection accuracy in the presence of new attacks.
Intermediate	- Legitimate clients suffer less. - Can balance between bandwidth consumed by an attack and resources used for detection.	- Defense deployability is the major critical issue. - All routers in the network must employ the detection scheme. - Failure at a few routers can cause damage to the whole detection process.
Source-end	- Can avoid congestion and collateral damage to the whole network. - Legitimate clients suffer less.	- Deployment of such a defense solution is usually cost-effective. - Often fails to distinguish attack traffic from normal traffic.

Table 4.3: Misuse detection techniques: a comparison.

Signature-Based	Rule-Based	State Transition
-It matches the pattern of attack against stored patterns. -Database is quickly updated on discovery of a new attack.	-Rules are defined by analyzing attacks. -Uses the rules as conditions to detect an attack.	-Needs to identify the states of a system and transitions among them. -Single or multiple changes can cause transitions among states of the monitored system.

4.3.1 Misuse Detection

In misuse detection, the defenders initially define the abnormal system behavior and then they define other behavior as normal. In contrast, an anomaly detection approach uses the reverse approach, defining normal system behavior first and defining any other behavior as abnormal. In other words, anything we don't know as bad is normal in misuse detection. Using attack signatures in IDSs is an example of this approach. The performance of an IDS in terms of detection accuracy depends

entirely on how adequate the knowledge of known attacks is and how
well the detection engine can use it during detection. A defender with
well-crafted knowledge of known attacks can make an effective use of
this detection approach and can achieve high detection accuracy and
low false alarms.

4.3.1.1   Signature-Based DDoS Detection

A signature-based detection or misuse detection scheme stores sequences
of patterns and signatures of attacks or intrusions in a database. When
an attacker attacks or when an intrusion occurs, the IDS attempts to
identify its class by matching against a predefined set of attack signatures that are already stored in the database. On a successful match,
the system generates an alarm. In this approach, the semantic characteristics of an attack are analyzed and details are used to form attack signatures. The attack signatures are organized using appropriate
data structures to facilitate faster search using audit data logs generated by computer systems. It uses well defined known attacks to build
a database of attack signatures. During detection, a signature-based
IDS matches string log data or audit data against the stored signatures
in the database for identification of attack. If it encounters and recognizes a new attack, quick appropriate actions are taken to update the
signature database for up-to-date performance.

4.3.1.2   Rule-Based Detection

Rule-based detection systems are built using a number of if-then rules.
Experts develop rules by analyzing attacks or misuses and then transform them into conditional rules, which are later used by inference
modules of the IDS to compare against monitored data (usually logs)
to detect any misuse.

4.3.1.3   State-Transition Techniques

A state-transition technique represents the misuses or attacks as a sequence of activities. An activity or a group of activities may cause
transition from one state of a monitored sensor to another, and can
eventually reach the alert state of a monitored system.

4.3.2 Anomaly-Based DDoS Detection

Anomaly-based detection techniques first establish the normal behavior of a subject, which may be a user or a system. If an action is found to deviate significantly from the normal behavior or pattern, it is recognized as anomalous or intrusive. So, if the defender can properly establish a normal activity profile for a system, it can also flag all system states that vary from the normal profile significantly. So, in an anomaly-based detection approach, two distinct possibilities may arise: (a) false positives, which are anomalous activities that are flagged intrusive, but are not intrusive, (2) false negatives, which are anomalous activities that are flagged as non-intrusive but are intrusive. The main advantage of anomaly detection is that it can detect unknown attacks.

In the past two decades, the world has seen a good number of anomaly-based DDoS detection approaches and systems [157], [244], [144], [68], [151], [227], [27], [142]. In addition to these software-based DDoS defense solutions, a large number of hardware-based network security solutions have also evolved, as explained in [49]. To counter DDoS attacks that use both low-rate and high-rate traffic, researchers use a variety of approaches such as statistical, machine learning and data mining, soft computing, and knowledge-based. We introduce some prominent solutions under each category, discuss methods used, and analyze their effectiveness.

4.3.2.1 Statistical Techniques

The effectiveness of statistical methods have already been established in anomaly-based intrusion detection. A statistical approach initially defines normal user behavior based on what is acceptable within system usage policies. If a monitored behavior is found to deviate significantly from predefined normal behavior thresholds, it is considered anomalous activity and an attack. Most methods are designed to detect network anomalies using various statistical and information theoretic measures such as deviation, cumulative sum, correlations, entropy, mutual information (MI), and covariance. We discuss few prominent statistical methods below.

Chen et al. [54] introduce a victim-end change-point (DCP) detection system to detect abrupt traffic anomalies across multiple network domains using change aggregation trees (CATs). In this system, each network domain corresponds to a single autonomous system (AS) and

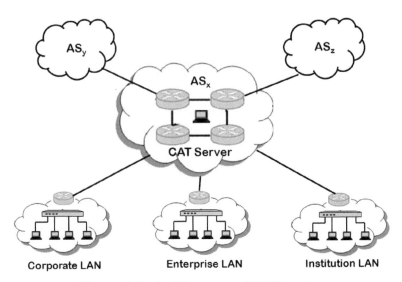

Figure 4.8: Architecture of DCP system.

the AS domain is supported by a CAT server to gather traffic change information sensed at the routers. To produce an effective global consensus across multiple domains, the CAT servers exchange flooding alert information and to resolve any conflicts at various service provider domains, if they arise, a secure infrastructure protocol (SIP) is introduced. The protocol helps establish trust among them. In Figure 4.8, the system architecture of the DCP system is shown. It shows multiple AS domains such as A_x, A_y, and A_z for deployment of the system. Each domain is equipped with a central CAT server. The DCP system acts to (i) detect traffic changes, (ii) aggregate changes detected, and (iii) collect alerts over collaborative CAT servers. It maintains the root of the CAT at the last-hop domain server. In the change aggregation tree, each node represents an attack-transit router (ATR), whereas the edges of the tree correspond to the links among the ATRs. The CAT servers of a DCP system may communicate with each other through VPN (virtual private network) channels or through an overlay network. The DCP system uses the non-parametric CUSUM (cumulative sum) statistic to solve the change detection problem. The cumulative deviation is significantly higher than random fluctuation during a DDoS flooding attack. DCP detects such abrupt changes in traffic flows at the router level through the CAT mechanism. The reliability of DCP was established over 16 domains. According to simulation results, 4 domains are enough to achieve 98% detection accuracy for TCP SYN

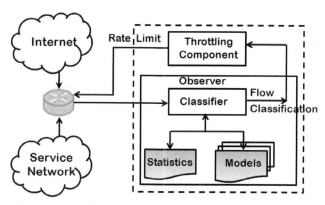

Figure 4.9: Architecture of the D-WARD system.

flooding attacks, whereas for UDP flooding attacks, it produces less than 1% false alarms.

D-WARD [168] is a source-end DDoS defense system developed using a statistical supervised approach, deployed at source-end networks to detect and stop attacks generated from these networks. The authors configure D-WARD with a pre-specified set of addresses, with an objective to police (its *police address set*) their outgoing traffic and to monitor two-way traffic between the police address set and the rest of the network. Figure 4.9 shows the architecture of D-WARD. The *classifier* and the *throttling component*, as shown in the figure, are the core components of this architecture. D-WARD gathers online traffic characteristics, compares them with pre-defined normal traffic models, and attempts to rate-limit those flows which are non-complying. It is able to adjust the rate-limit dynamically as and when flow behavior varies, and can hence recover fast from mis-classified legitimate flows. D-WARD ensures good service to legitimate traffic by profiling individual connections. However, scalability and real-time detection of novel attacks are two major issues with this source-end DDoS detection system.

The author of [50] introduces an effective DDoS detection method based on the two-sample t-test. The author first investigates the SYN arrival rate (SAR) sampling distributions of normal traffic and checks whether they conform to a normal distribution or not. The method attempts to distill DDoS attack traffic from legitimate traffic by (a) computing the deviation of incoming SAR from normal SAR and (b) finding the difference between the numbers of SYN and ACK pack-

ets. The method initially compares the differences between the overall
means of the incoming traffic arrival rate and the normal traffic arrival rate by the two-sample t-test. If it finds a significant difference,
it confirms that traffic may include attack traffic. However, in case
of a low-rate DDoS attack, its arrival rate test may not be helpful,
and hence the backlog queue may become full. In such a case, Chen's
method compares the two groups with different numbers of SYN and
ACK packets by the two-sample t-test. If it finds significant difference,
it confirms that the traffic includes attack traffic. Like most other detection schemes, two major issues with Chen's method are inability (i)
to detect both high-rate and low-rate DDoS attacks with high detection accuracy in real time and (ii) to handle large DDoS attacks in real
time.

Saifullah [208] develops a DDoS defense system with weight-fair
router throttling to protect Internet servers. The mechanism depends
on a distributed algorithm, which is responsible for performing weight-
fair throttling at the upstream routers. The author uses weight-fair
throttling because it controls (increases or decreases) the traffic destined to the server with leaky buckets at the routers, depending on the
number of users connected directly or indirectly. Initially, the routers
underestimate the ability of the server to survive, and hence update
the rate (increases or decreases) based on a server's feedback sent to
its child routers and eventually propagates downward to all routers, to
protect the server from any sudden initial attack. The author establishes the effectiveness of the method using NS-2 simulation. However,
the drawbacks of the previous methods are not all overcome.

In another effort, Akella et al. [9] introduce several key challenges
to support an ISP network in detecting attacks targeted on it or targeted on external sites using the ISP network. The authors introduce
an effective method to detect anomalous traffic at the router level using normal profiles. The profiles for normal traffic are generated using
stream sampling algorithms. The authors establish that one can generate these profiles reasonably and accurately. Further, it is cost effective
and can help identify anomalies with low false positives at the router.
Furthermore, it keeps a provision to improve confidence levels in the
decision-making process at the ISP router level by exchanging information among such routers. When classifying aggregated traffic as
anomalous or normal, a router collects opinions (i.e., suspicions) from
all other routers and makes a decision based on them. Initial results

show that a router profile is able to capture key characteristics of the traffic and can identify anomalous traffic with high accuracy.

Another effective method [191] to detect bandwidth attacks by observing the arrival rate of new source IP addresses was introduced by Peng et al. The method, referred to as SIM (source IP address monitoring) works in two phases: (a) *offline learning*, where a learning engine is used to keep an IP address database (IAD) up to date by adding new source IP addresses and by deleting expired IP addresses, and (b) *detection and learning*, where statistics are gathered on incoming traffic during the current time interval to estimate the number of distinct IP addresses arriving during the interval to decide whether a DDoS attack is occurring or not, with reference to a user-defined threshold. Two major attractive features of SIM are (i) it dynamically changes the attack signature, which makes it hard for the attacker to counter the detection scheme and (ii) it exploits an advanced non-parametric change detection technique called CUSUM [277] to achieve high detection accuracy. The effectiveness of SIM was established using trace-driven simulation. Two major limitations of SIM are (i) it cannot detect low-rate DDoS attacks and (ii) the detection performance is highly dependent on the threshold value, although determining appropriate threshold value is a difficult task.

In recent years, with the advancement of botnet technology in terms of both sophistication and scalability, the types of DDoS attacks have also grown significantly. A mastermind, in order to continue using botnet-based attack launching practices, attempts to take advantage of novel anti-forensic methods to disguise attack traces, such as code obfuscation, memory encryption [111], peer-to-peer implementation technology [100], [20], [57], resurrection using fresh code pushing [57], or mimicking flash crowd traffic [126], [212]. Flash crowd is legitimate traffic that is usually an unexpected, sudden burst of traffic accessing a server, and may be due to breaking news. An attack mastermind can adopt a concrete strategy to launch DDoS attacks by simulating or by mimicking the traffic patterns of flash crowds to fly under the radar. Such a DDoS attack is referred to as a *flash crowd attack*.

Most existing DDoS detection systems face difficulty in countering such DDoS attacks. Yu et al. [281], in their investigation of sizes and organizations of botnet-based attack launching practices, observe that current attack flows are more similar to each other compared to flash crowd flows in a community network. Based on this observation, the authors present a discrimination algorithm to distill DDoS attack traffic from flash crowds. Their method exploits a flow correlation coefficient as the similarity metric. The authors initially establish a DDoS attack detection model for a community network with a potential victim. Then a theoretical proof is put forward to show that one can distill attack flows from flash crowds with knowledge of botnet sizes and organizations. Finally, they corroborate their theoretical findings with experimental results using real-life flash crowd datasets and by using attack launching tools in several scenarios.

Multivariate Correlation Analysis (MCA) is an effective approach to measure abrupt variations in network traffic. This has been established by Jin et al. in their SYN flooding attack detection model [123]. The authors show that MCA can be used to identify anomalous traffic in a network in a simple yet effective way. It is possible to differentiate anomalous traffic from legitimate traffic using correlation analysis over multiple features in real time. For correlation-based analysis, the authors initially generate a normal profile based on a selected set of features of normal traffic. Next, to test whether incoming traffic is normal or anomalous, it uses the same correlation analysis to generate a test profile, which is matched against the normal profile. If it finds the test profile deviating from the normal profile significantly above a predefined threshold value, the method considers the test profile anomalous. An added advantage of this MCA-based method is that it is also able to detect subtle attacks, which it can differentiate from normal behavior. The authors establish the effectiveness of their method in terms of (i) detection accuracy and (ii) real-time performance in DDoS attack detection.

Cheng et al. [55] develop an effective DDoS attack detection method using multiple salient features such as abrupt traffic variation, non-uniformity in flow patterns, distribution patterns of source IP addresses, and concentration of target IP addresses. Their method, based on an IP flow feature value (FFV) algorithm, uses a linear prediction technique for detection of both attack and legitimate flows. The authors establish their method based on experimentation using real-life intrusion datasets.

Udhayan and Hamsapriya [249] use a statistical segregation method (SSM) to achieve high detection accuracy in DDoS attack detection. The method operates on network flow traffic over consecutive intervals, and for detection of attack, it maintains attack state conditions. It samples the flow in consecutive intervals, computes the mean as the parameter, and sorts the samples with reference to this parameter. Finally, to segregate attack flows from legitimate ones, it performs a correlation analysis. SSM has high detection accuracy and a low false alarm rate. In addition to that, they evaluate SSM against several other its closed counterparts. Li et al. [150] introduced another effective DDoS attack detection method using entropy. The method initially computes the patterns of distribution of the header attributes in the network packets and then computes cumulative entropy to monitor behavior of network traffic for an interval of time, instead of discriminating it as abnormal traffic after detecting it as abnormal. Next, it identifies anomalous patterns dynamically based on time instead of a threshold value set a priori. If it finds non-conforming patterns or behavior to continue for a significantly long duration of time, it marks the pattern as anomalous.

In another effort, Feinstein et al. [76] developed a statistical DDoS attack detection method based on entropy. The method attempts to identify anomalous traffic by computing entropy and sort distribution of packet attributes based on frequency. It computes entropy of the source addresses for a packet window of size, say 1000, to measure the randomness or uniformity of the addresses. If it finds the amount of randomness is significantly high, it recognizes the scenario as attack. The authors' observation is that in normal conditions, the entropy of the source addresses is less than in attack conditions.

Low-rate DDoS attack traffic is very similar to normal traffic. As a result, an accurate identification of such a low-rate attack is challenging. Xiang et al. [268] attempt to address this problem by introducing an efficient detection mechanism and a traceback technique using information theoretic measures. Their method uses a generalized entropy measure to find the difference between legitimate traffic and attack traffic, and then uses an information distance metric for detection of low-rate DDoS attacks. The authors establish by experimentation that the generalized entropy can detect an attack earlier than the traditional Shannon metric. Further, their information distance metric performs better than the Kullback–Leibler divergence approach. In addition, the authors introduce an IP traceback scheme based on the information distance metric, and establish it as capable of tracing the origin of all attacks in a short time. The authors use (i) the MIT Lincoln Laboratory Scenario (attack-free) inside tcpdump dataset[1] as the normal

---

[1]http://www.ll.mit.edu/ideval/data/

traffic and (ii) the low-rate DDoS attack scenario from CAIDA as the DDoS attack traffic to test the algorithms.

In another approach, Qi et al. [122] show that dynamic entropy is effective in identifying specific types of malicious traffic. They introduce a novel dynamic entropy-based detection model to detect DoS attacks. This model takes advantage of NetFlow conversation correlation at different perspectives in a group of correlated events like request and reply. To establish the effectiveness of dynamic entropy, the authors include an experimental study of dynamic and static entropy change rates in anomaly detection and compare performance. The authors opine that dynamic entropy can help sense the occurrence of anomalous traffic more accurately than static entropy.

Yu et al. [275] present another fast and lightweight detection scheme for identification of flooding attacks. The method collects SNMP MIB traffic records from SNMP agents to analyze the security status of a network and a system. Their method initially uses SNMP MIB statistical data, which are collected from SNMP agents, instead of gathering raw packet data from network links. Then they select SNMP MIB features by an effective feature selection mechanism and collect data using the optimal set of features by a mechanism of MIB update time prediction. In the second step, the authors use a machine learning approach based on Support Vector Machines (SVM) for attack classification. The authors claim that with appropriate tuning of MIB and SVM, one can achieve high detection accuracy in efficient time. The authors collect MIB datasets from real experiments involving a DDoS attack every 15 seconds on average to validate their method. Experimental results show that the method is able to detect network attacks with high accuracy and low false alarms in less than 15 seconds.

Most defense methods discussed above focus on the IP and TCP layers to protect resources from DDoS attacks. However, such methods are often inadequate in handling new types of application layer attacks. To address this issue, Xie et al. [271] introduce an effective scheme for early detection and filtering of application layer DDoS attacks. The authors use an extended hidden semi-Markov model to investigate and describe the browsing patterns of Web surfers. To overcome the additional overhead due to the model's large state space, the authors also report a forward algorithm, which allows an online implementation of their model. To estimate the user's normality, the authors use entropy of the HTTP request sequence fitting to the model as a criterion.

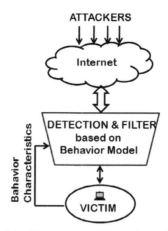

Figure 4.10: Xie et al.'s filtering strategy based on behavior model.

Figure 4.10 shows the use of the detector and the filter. As shown in
the figure, the filter, which resides between the Internet and the victim, receives an HTTP request and tries to identify it as anomalous or
legitimate. If it identifies the request as legitimate, it allows it to pass
through the filter toward the victim. To validate their model, the authors perform several experiments using real traffic data collected from
an institutional Website and by generating an App-DDoS attack traffic.
Experimental results show that with an appropriate threshold setting,
their model can yield 98% detection accuracy and 1.5% false positive accuracy. Further, their algorithm is able to reduce the memory requirement significantly and can help improve computational performance.

   In addition to these, several other novel and effective statistical
methods have been developed   [261], [140], [155], [237], [181], [5] to
counter DDoS attacks of both low-rate and high-rate types. However,
most of these methods have been developed to protect resources from
either high-rate attacks or from low-rate attacks, but not both at the
same time. Further, most methods are dependent on multiple user parameters, which are often crucial, greatly influencing the performance
of the system, when in fact, the correct estimation of such parameters
is a difficult task.

   Based on the above discussion on a number of prominent statistical
methods for DDoS detection, we summarize as follows.

- A statistical method typically monitors user behavior in a network and tries to observe occurrences of deviations (if any) with

reference to predefined normal behavior thresholds. If it can identify any such non-conforming pattern or activity, it concludes that a DDoS attack is occurring.

- The effectiveness of a statistical method is dependent on (i) the reliability of the process of gathering legitimate user behavior, (ii) modeling of legitimate user behavior, and (ii) determination of the deviation threshold.

- One can develop an effective statistical method for DDoS detection by appropriate use of a statistical and information theoretic measure such as deviation, cumulative sum, correlations, entropy, mutual information (MI), and covariance.

- To be effective operationally, a statistical method requires time to tune itself to a network environment. Once it is tuned and the appropriate predictive model(s) is built, the method can show detection performance of up to 100%. However, the tuned parameter values for such a model may vary from network scenario to scenario.

- With the evolution of botnet technology, variations in DDoS attacks have also been increasing. As a consequence, developing a generic predictive model for a large variety of DDoS attacks has become challenging.

4.3.2.2 Machine Learning and Data Mining Techniques

Machine learning (ML) and data mining play a significant role in the development of efficient detection mechanisms to protect resources from network intrusion due to their ability to help a system learn from the environment without being explicitly programmed [25]. This growing branch of AI enables a system to learn using mainly two distinct approaches (i) *supervised learning*, where the learning algorithm uses prior knowledge (i.e., *labeled* instances) to predict class labels of previously unknown instances and (ii) *unsupervised learning*, where the learning algorithm attempts to identify groups of similar instances or the underlying organization of the data without any prior knowledge. An unsupervised learning algorithm uses similarity or dissimilarity measures to group instances or identify the organization of data. In addition to these, many researchers like to define two other approaches when categorizing learning algorithms. These are *semi-supervised learning*, where the algorithm has access to partial knowledge (i.e., say, a set of labeled pure "normal" or "legitimate" instances) prior to predicting the class labels of previously unknown test instances, and *hybrid learning*, where the learner takes advantage of both supervised and unsupervised learning. A good number of machine learning and data mining algorithms [27] have been used to detect both low-rate and high-rate DDoS attacks. We discuss some prominent DDoS detection methods that use machine learning and data mining techniques.

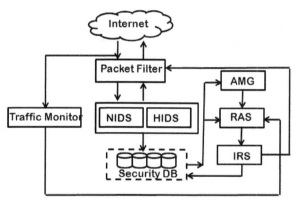

Figure 4.11: The NetShield system and its components.

Hwang et al. [110] introduce an efficient DDoS defense solution, referred to as *NetShield*, to protect network resources such as servers, routers, and client hosts from becoming victims of DDoS flooding attacks. NetShield attempts to identify DDoS flooding attacks using a data mining approach to protect any IP-based public network in the Internet. This detection software can not only defend against DDoS flooding attacks, but can also detect, prevent, and respond to other malicious network worms or virus attacks. It is able to generate a class-specific intrusion report and can assess residue risks.

The NetShield software is designed using a simulator at the USC Internet Wireless Security Laboratory. In addition to a packet filter, a traffic monitoring module, and a security database, the NetShield system comprises four basic modules, viz. (i) a detection module consisting of both host-based (HIDS) and network-based intrusion detection system (NIDS), (ii) an alarm matrix generator (AMG), (iii) a risk assessment system (RAS), and (iv) an intrusion response system (IRS). Figure 4.11 shows the structure of the NetShield software. It can be seen from the figure that all these four basic modules get support from the packet filter, traffic monitor, and the security database. The authors keep all attack and response information in a security database, which is maintained and dynamically updated centrally. The HIDS is designed to identify handler or zombie activities in a network. The NIDS actively detects flooding attacks by analyzing incoming traffic. The responsibility of the traffic monitor is to observe incoming network traffic to identify traffic characteristics and to distill irregular bursty traffic toward detection as a DDoS attack. The AMG module is responsible for generating alarms, once an attack type is confirmed. The performance of NetShield was evaluated in a testbed environment by carrying out a benchmark evaluation experiment. Although NetShield is able to reduce some risks of DDoS attacks, some can be blocked only partially. In addition to DDoS flooding attack detection, it can be extended to provide defense against other attack types.

Chen et al. [54] present another DDoS defense system using a data mining technique, referred to as the DDoS Container, which operates in inline mode to inspect, examine, and manipulate ongoing traffic. DDoS container is based on a NIDS that helps identify and manipulate DDoS traffic in real time. The system initially tracks connections established during a DDoS attack and normal applications, maintains state information for each session, carries out stateful inspection, and finally, attempts to correlate data between sessions. It performs stream reassembly and dissects the resulting collections by protocol. The framework of DDoS container is shown in Figure 4.12. The figure shows that the system maintains several types of information to support DDoS detection, including white and black lists of source IPs, a free session pool, defunct session information, active session information and a frequency table. Such information is accessed by various components of the DDoS container, such as the protocol decoder, session correlator, traffic arbitrator, traffic distinguisher and message sequencer. The three main transport mechanisms used by this system are TCP, UDP, and ICMP to communicate among clients, handlers, and agents during a DDoS attack. It treats such traffic uniformly so that one can process packets and/or message streams during a DDoS attack in an unbiased manner. In case of encrypted DDoS traffic, the authors improve detection accuracy using deep inspection and by analyzing behavior. Once successfully detected, the DDoS container generates alarms to take necessary actions to block packets and

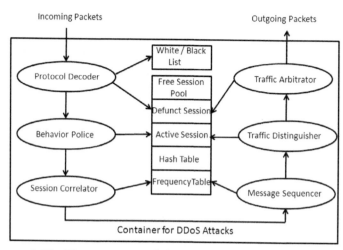

Figure 4.12: The conceptual framework of a DDoS container.

to terminate the session. The authors establish the effectiveness of the framework in several network settings.

The Naive Bayes (NB) classifier is an effective classifier for 2-class and n-class problems. Vijaysarathy et al. [254] use a Naive Bayes classifier to develop a defense solution to counter TCP and UDP attacks in real time. The system uses a window-based architecture to analyze incoming TCP and UDP traffic. It splits the incoming traffic according to a window of a given size and processes the traffic in a window with reference to a training model using the NB classifier to provide a real-time response. The authors establish the effectiveness of their method in terms of classification accuracy using 10-fold cross validation. However, the performance of this method is largely dependent on the threshold value used during detection, and appropriate estimation of the threshold value is difficult, since it may vary from network to network and from one attack type to another.

In another effort, Gaddam et al. [83] develop a detection method using cascading decision tree learning and clustering. It combines ID3 decision tree learning and k-means clustering for cascading, using two specific rules, i.e., (i) the nearest-neighbor rule and (ii) the nearest consensus rule. These two rules help obtain a concrete decision on attack traffic classification. The approach uses k-means clustering to group traffic samples into a fixed, say N, number of clusters and then each cluster of instances is used to train the ID3 algorithm. The authors justify the use of clustering because it ensures the association of each training instance with only one cluster. However, in case of traffic patterns with the occurrence of a nested cluster (i.e., cluster(s) within a cluster) or overlapped cluster patterns, the method requires special care while training the ID3 algorithm, and as a consequence, in refining decision boundaries. The method can detect attack traffic with satisfactory accuracy, however, like the previous scheme, it also requires an appropriate threshold setting during ID3 training. Further, it cannot detect both low-rate and high-rate DDoS attacks at the same time or in real time.

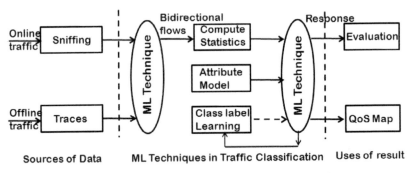

Figure 4.13: Machine learning in DDoS attack detection.

Most classification-based DDoS detection schemes typically use as features a set of header fields (e.g., port number, source IP, or protocol) to classify the DDoS attack traffic. However, a common limitation with these schemes is that often, applications do not use the port numbers required by convention. In addition, if the protocol information is in encrypted form, such methods consume a lot of computation to identify the protocols. So, keeping these in mind, Zander et al. [283] develop a DDoS attack detection scheme using ML techniques, which depend on flow statistics rather than a set of header attributes. The scheme applies ML techniques at two levels for automated traffic classification. Figure 4.13 shows the architecture of Zander et al.'s approach. We see in the figure that the scheme initially classifies the sniffed packets into bidirectional flows, and then uses a NetMate traffic analyzer to compute flow characteristics based on these sampled bidirectional flows received from the initial classifier. The computed flow statistics are fed to a second level of classifiers to predict the class labels of the previously unknown instances based on flow characteristics with reference to a flow attribute model. The method shows good classification performance with a low false alarm rate. Further, the method also shows an effective use of the learned class label information for the previously unknown instances in Quality of Service (QoS) mapping.

Zhong et al. [288] also present a DDoS defense solution using data mining techniques. The authors use fuzzy c-means (FCM) clustering [70] and the Apriori algorithm [94], [262] to build a network traffic threshold model and a packet protocol status model to support DDoS attack detection. The method receives current normal traffic and defines the normal model using k-means clustering. The Apriori algorithm is used by the authors to mine packet protocol status information, whereas FCM clustering is applied to build protocol status model. The authors establish their method to be effective in detecting SYN flooding attacks with 100% accuracy. However, a major limitation of this method is its inability to perform in real time.

In most cases, to train learning algorithms with appropriate labeled datasets for both legitimate and illegitimate classes of instances may not be possible. Often, labeled instances representing possible attack classes are not available, and to assign labels manually for such instances is a time-consuming process. As a consequence, semi-supervised learning becomes relevant. Erman et al. [73] introduce a defense solution that can operate both offline and in real time to classify network traffic using semi-supervised learning. The increasing development of applications and their evolving nature has made classification of network traffic a challenging task. The authors' observation is that flow-based classification is more effective than packet content-based classification due to the unpredictable nature of features. The authors introduce a semi-supervised DDoS classification scheme, which exploits distinctive flow characteristics of applications when they communicate on a network. Their scheme can handle both known and unknown applications. The scheme uses only a few labeled, but many unlabeled, flows to train. A distinguishing feature of their scheme is that it considers two pragmatic classification issues, viz., longevity of classifiers and the need for retraining of classifiers. The authors establish the effectiveness of their method by empirical evaluation on Internet traffic traces that span a 6-month period. The results show that the method can classify attack traffic with high detection accuracy for both flow and byte, i.e., greater than 90%.

Both supervised and unsupervised learning algorithms have advantages and disadvantages in detecting anomalies from network traffic in real time. As a result, some researchers have developed effective DDoS

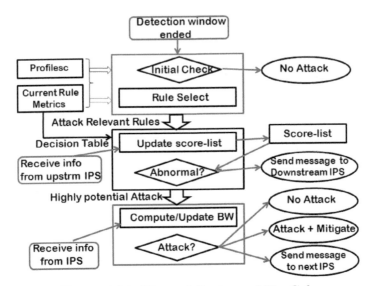

Figure 4.14: The architecture of FireCol.

detection solutions by exploiting the benefits of both supervised and unsupervised learning. One such example solution is Shon et al.'s [220] detection method, which uses a hybrid machine learning approach called *enhanced SVM*. The authors are of the opinion that among the variety of machine learning techniques, Support Vector Machines (SVM) are most effective in classifying anomalous patterns or behaviors. Unsupervised learning can be best used in anomaly identification to obtain low false alarm rates with an enhanced SVM method, using an appropriate combination of both one-class SVM and soft-margin SVM methods.

Francois et al. [82] present a very effective detection method for DDoS flooding attacks. The method, referred to as *FireCol*, is composed of several IPSs located at various ISPs, which provide virtual protection rings around the target hosts to counter DDoS attacks and allow collaboration by exchanging specific traffic information. The architecture of FireCol is shown in Figure 4.14. It provides protection by maintaining virtual rings or shields around registered customers. Each virtual ring of FireCol's defense is formed by a set of IPSs maintained at the same number of hops from the customers. The authors assign each IPS instance the task of aggregate traffic analysis within a configurable detection window. FireCol maintains a *metric manager* that is responsible for computing the frequencies and entropies of each rule, where each rule represents a specific traffic instance to monitor, and is essentially a traffic filter that works based on ports or IP addresses. The *selection manager* is responsible for estimating the deviation of the recent traffic profile compared to pre-recorded ones. On the basis of estimated deviation, it selects the relevant profile rules and transmits toward the *score manager*. The *score manager* plays a crucial role also. It assigns a score to each selected profile rule by using a decision table based on entropy, frequency information, and the scores obtained from upstream IPSs. It considers a *low score* with reference to a given threshold, as indicative of low attack potential and forwards the corresponding traffic instance to a downstream IPS for score computation. In contrast, a significantly high score is considered to indicate high attack potential and subsequently triggers ring-level communication for a validation of the decision to ensure or to dismiss the attack based on whether the actual packet rate passing through the ring exceeds the pre-defined client's capacity. So, a major advantage of this method is that it generates no false positives, as each potential attack is well verified. FireCol is scalable and is able to detect DDoS attacks at an early stage. Experimental results show its robustness and high accuracy in simulation environments, real Internet topologies, and with the DARPA'99 dataset.

In addition to these, several other significant efforts have been made by researchers to apply data mining and machine learning techniques to develop effective DDoS detection systems. For example, Ramamoorthi et al. [200] present an effective anomaly detection system, developed using an enhanced SVM (ESVM) with string kernels. The authors claim that their method is able to detect DDoS attacks on both network and transport layers with high accuracy. Further, the detection accuracy of ESVM with string kernels is higher than one-class SVMs, binary SVMs, and SVMs with string kernels. Farid et al. [75] present a decision tree-based adaptive intrusion detection method that distinguishes attack from normal behavior with 98% accuracy. In this method, a stochastic approach is used to split the dataset into sub-datasets until all the sub-datasets belong to the same class. Lee et al. [144] propose a method for proactive detection of DDoS attacks by exploiting an architecture consisting of a selection of handlers and agents that communicate, compromise, and attack. The method performs cluster analysis. The authors experiment with the DARPA 2000 Intrusion Detection Scenario Specific Dataset to evaluate the method. The clusters show that traffic corresponding to each phase of the attack scenario

gets partitioned well and the clusters can also detect precursors of a
DDoS attack as well as the attack itself. Sekar et al. [217] investigate the design space for in-network DDoS detection and propose a
triggered, multistage approach that addresses both scalability and accuracy. Their contribution is the design and implementation of LADS
(Large-scale Automated DDoS Setection System). The system makes
effective use of data (such as NetFlow and SNMP feeds from routers)
readily available to an ISP.

Dainotti et al. [62] present a cascade architecture for detection
of DDoS attacks using a traditional change-point detection approach
combined with wavelet analysis. The system makes an effective combination of adaptive thresholding and cumulative sums with continuous wavelet transforms for anomalous pattern identification for the
detection of DDoS attacks. The system was validated using publicly
available attack-free traffic traces superimposed with anomaly profiles
obtained using real DoS attack tools as well as time series of commonly
known behaviors. From the results obtained through offline evaluation,
the authors claim that the system can accurately detect a wide range
of DoS attacks.

Another systematic method using wavelet transformation for detection of DDoS attacks is introduced by Li and Lee [151]. The authors
feel that characterization of network traffic with behavior modeling
could be a good source of guidance for DDoS attack detection. The
authors explore the ability of wavelet analysis to capture and model
complex temporal correlation patterns across multiple time scales at
low cost. They make effective use of energy distribution to detect
DDoS attack traffic based on wavelet analysis. Legitimate traffic has
limited variation in energy distribution over time. On the other hand,
during a DDoS attack, such distributions will have significant variations within a short interval of time. Using experimental results, the
authors show that the spike caused by the occurrence of DDoS attacks
in energy distribution variance can be well captured by appropriate
wavelet analysis.

Xia, Lu, and Li [267] introduce a defense system for DDoS flooding
attacks using intelligent fuzzy logic. The system provides a real-time
solution for DDoS attacks in two stages. In *stage 1*, they detect the
change point(s) of Hurst parameters caused by DDoS flooding attacks
based on statistical analysis of network traffic using discrete wavelet
transform (DWT) and Schwartz Information Criteria (SIC). In *stage*

2, they use intelligent fuzzy logic in an effective manner to dynamically decide the intensity of DDoS attacks. The authors show the ability of their method based on NS2 simulation with various network traffic characteristics and attack intensities.

A low-rate DDoS attack has significant ability to conceal its traffic because of its similarity with normal traffic. Xiang et al. [268] propose two new information metrics —(i) the generalized entropy metric and (ii) the information distance metric —to detect low-rate DDoS attacks. They identify the attack by measuring the distance between legitimate traffic and attack traffic. The generalized entropy metric is more effective than the traditional Shannon metric [160]. In addition, the information distance metric outperforms the popular Kullback–Leibler divergence.

Another effective DDoS attack detection scheme with IP traceback based on entropy variations is reported in [279]. In this work, the authors show the usefulness of constant monitoring, observation, and storage of short-term information such as entropy variations at routers. When there is significant deviation in entropy variations, the scheme detects the occurrence of a DDoS attack and initiates a pushback tracing procedure to find the origin of the attacks. Experimental results establish the effectiveness of both the detection and the traceback scheme.

An effort by Zhang et al. [286] develops a low-rate DDoS (LDDoS) attack detection scheme using statistical analysis of the flow level of network traffic. The authors introduce a CPR (Congestion Participation Rate)-based approach for identification of low-rate DDoS (LDDoS) attack traffic. They assume that a flow with a high CPR value signals an LDDoS attack and hence consequently drop packets. To establish the scheme, the authors carry out NS2 simulation and testbed experiments using Internet traffic traces, and claim that the method can detect LDDoS flows with high detection accuracy. Gelenbe and Loukas [87] introduce a mathematical model to evaluate the benefits of DDoS defenses that drop attack traffic. The authors establish their model using simulation results and testbed experiments. Further, the authors present an autonomic defense mechanism based on the CPN (Cognitive Packet Network) protocol. They establish that the mechanism is capable of tracing back flows coming into a node automatically. In another effort, Yuan and Kevin [282] develop a scheme to monitor network-wide macroscopic effects for detection of DDoS flooding attacks. The authors claim that their method can detect DDoS attacks with various rate dynamics, i.e., constant rate, increasing rate, pulsing rate, and subgroup attacks.

Based on the discussion in this section, we summarize as follows.

- A machine learning or data mining technique can be supervised, unsupervised or hybrid. A carefully designed supervised method is able to show high DDoS attack detection accuracy, if precise, certain and sufficient knowledge is provided for training. However, such methods are incapable of detecting unseen attacks. On the other hand, an unsupervised machine learning or data mining technique can detect unseen attack, in addition to known attacks. Hybrid methods take advantage of both supervised and unsupervised learning techniques.

- For consistently high performance of supervised learning methods, it is essential to provide complete, precise, up-to-date, and relevant training data, which is often not possible for all network situations.

- Dimensionality reduction and feature selection have important roles to play in the development of cost-effective and real-time DDoS defense.

- Ensemble or combination learners are able to classify anomalous traffic with high detection accuracy, but usually cannot provide real-time performance.

- A supervised machine learning or data mining technique implemented in both hardware and software, one that uses an optimal subset of features with up-to-date knowledge, could be ideal for DDoS detection in all network situations.

- An appropriate use of information theoretic measures can help develop an effective IP traceback mechanism for identification of the source or origin of DDoS attacks.

- Sensitivity to user parameter(s) while classifying the network anomalies, is a major issue with most machine learning or data mining techniques.

4.3.2.3 Soft Computing Techniques

Unlike traditional computing approaches, which are brittle in noisy or unexpected situations, soft computing solutions are known for their tolerance of imprecision, uncertainty, partial truth, and approximation. The basic principle that guides soft computing is to achieve a low-cost, and robust solution by exploiting the tolerance for imprecision, uncertainty, and partial truth. The five major approaches in soft computing are fuzzy logic, neural computing, evolutionary computation, machine learning, and probabilistic reasoning. The ability of soft computing methods has already been established in solving complex pattern matching and machine intelligence problems in many real-life application domains. Such methods are useful in solving problems, especially in situations when the information about the problem itself is insufficient and the possible solutions are also imprecise and uncertain. The ability of soft computing has been confirmed by network security researchers in differentiating anomalous traffic from legitimate traffic with high detection accuracy and low false alarm rates.

As we discussed in the previous subsections, most DDoS detection systems suffer from high computational cost, when they try to achieve high detection accuracy. To address this issue, some researchers prefer to use classifiers that are adaptive and incremental to minimize the cost of processing. The presence of uncertain or imprecise information is also a major issue when analyzing and evaluating the performance of DDoS attack detection methods. To overcome both hurdles, adaptive, incremental, soft computing approaches have been used. One can use a fuzzy set theoretic approach for handling uncertainty in network traffic and for better interpretation of rules. Similarly, appropriate use of neural networks can help improve the learning ability and the generalization of the network. So, by accumulating the benefits of both these soft computing techniques, Kumar and Kumar [141] develop a DDoS detection system, referred to as *NFBoost*, using an ensemble of adaptive and hybrid neuro-fuzzy inference systems (ANFIS). Since a single classifier may be biased and can make mistakes in training traffic samples, the authors overcome such bias by creating an ensemble of classifiers and by combining their output using an appropriate combination function. Figure 4.15 shows the framework of the adaptive and hybrid neuro-fuzzy inference system. The authors use the gradient learning approach and the fuzzy c-means (FCM) algorithm for learning and initialization of the fuzzy subsystem. The number of nodes used in the input layer is the product of the number of inputs and the membership functions for each input. The method can deal with both discrete and continuous attributes in a dataset, which is useful for dealing with real-time intrusion. Using simulation results, the authors show that NFBoost, with a weight update distribution strategy can detect DDoS attacks with 99.2% accuracy and with low false alarm rates. The authors also claim that the cost per instance is much lower than the other competing methods. Further, NFBoost performs better than other ensemble methods with a gain of up to 8.4%.

In another effort, Jalili et al.   [120] develop an effective DDoS detection system using a statistical pre-processor and applying an unsupervised neural net. Their method, also referred to as SPUNNID, initially extracts a set of eight statistical features from real-life network traffic by using a pre-processor to form a training vector for the neural net. The features extracted are (i) percentage of ICMP packets, (ii) percentage of UDP packets, (iii) percentage of TCP packets, (iv) percentage of SYN in TCP packets, (v) percentage of SYN+ACK in TCP packets, (vi) percentage of ACK in TCP packets, (vii) average packet header size and (viii) average packet data size. To extract these features and to analyze the traffic based on these features for identification of DDoS attacks, the method divides the packet traffic into smaller time intervals, say each τ seconds long. Once the features are successfully extracted for each time interval, it forms a training vector to support analysis of network traffic using the neural net to recognize each time interval as normal or as DDoS attack. During evaluation of their method, the authors carried out an experimental study on the effects of several crucial parameters such as size or length of τ, parameters related to neural net, viz. (i) the number of appropriate clusters, (ii) the number of epochs and (iii) the vigilance parameter and its value. Experimental results show that SPUNNID is able to recognize attack traffic 94.9% and in the best case, it requires 0.7 second to detect DDoS attack.

Siaterlis and Vasilis [222] explore and show the ability of multi-layer perceptron (MLP) as a classifier in detecting DDoS flooding attacks using several statistical detection metrics obtained through passive measurements. The authors use five statistical metrics such as UDP ratio (i.e., (incoming bits/sec)/(outgoing bits/sec)), ICMP ratio (i.e., (outgoing bits/sec)/(incoming bits/sec)), flow length, flow duration, and flow-generation rate. These features are fed to the MLP for effective

detection of DDoS flooding attacks in near real time. The method uses
a supervised learning approach that uses these metrics to train the
multi-layer feed-forward network to classify the state of the monitored
edge network as DDoS source, DDoS victim, or legitimate. The authors
use the MLP as an algorithm to fuse together all detection metrics and
the method overcomes the site-specific threshold dependency. Simulation results show that the method is able to detect flooding attacks
with high detection accuracy.

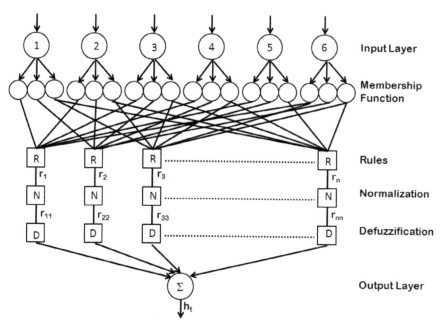

Figure 4.15: The hybrid neuro-fuzzy inference system.

In another ANN-based approach, Gavrilis and Dermatas [86] use
radial-basis function neural networks (RBF-NN) for faster detection of
DDoS attacks. Their method is based on a relevant subset of statistical features extracted from short-time window analysis using captured
packet traffic. The system comprises three modules, viz. *data collector,
feature estimator* and *DDoS detector*, which are sequentially connected.
The data collector is responsible for gathering packet traffic in terms of
a selected set of attributes, such as source port, SEQ number of clients,
window size, SYN, ACK, FIN, PSH, URG, and RST flags. It gathers
statistics for each time frame in terms of frequency of occurrence for
six different flags, i.e., SYN, ACK, FIN, PSH, URG, and RST. The

observation was that these flags could be a good source of information
for detection of DDoS attacks. The feature estimator is dedicated to
estimation of the frequency of the flags and the number of distinct values for the source ports, SEQ number and window size for each time
frame. Finally, the third module, i.e., the DDoS detector, uses the
RBF-NN by activating with a nine-feature vector for each time frame.
The occurrence of a DDoS attack is sensed by the most active output neuron. The method is able to analyze network traffic based on
statistical features estimated in short time windows and shows 100%
detection accuracy and 0% false alarms in real time.

Another fast detection method for DDoS defense using fuzzy esti-
mators was proposed by Shiaeles et al. [219]. The method works in two
phases. In the initial phase, it performs the task of DDoS attack detection. Then it identifies malicious IP addresses. A major advantage of
this method is that it not only detects DDoS attacks, but also identifies
malicious source IPs before the victim service suffers from exhaustion
of resources due to the attack. Empirical evaluation shows that the
method achieves an 80% success rate in attack detection. In another
similar effort, fuzzy logic was used by Xia et al. [267] to detect DDoS
attacks in real time. Like the previous one, this method also works
in two phases. In phase I, the method performs a statistical analysis
on the captured and preprocessed network traffic data using discrete
wavelet analysis. Then it calculates the intensity of DDoS attack using fuzzy logic. The method performs satisfactorily for DDoS attack
detection accuracy, giving real-time performance.

In addition to the above, many other methods have been introduced
in the recent past. Su [236] presents a method for DDoS attack detection using a weighted KNN classifier. The method computes a weight
value for each feature and identifies a relevant subset of features for
effective classification. The author claims that their method is able to
classify attack traffic with 97.42% accuracy for known attacks and 78%
accuracy for unknown attacks. Chonka et al. [58] present a chaos-
theory-based DDoS attack detection algorithm. The authors use real
network packets and flow traffic and investigate the self-similar patterns
for the normal traffic. These patterns are then used as benchmarks for
detection of DDoS attacks. For detection purposes, the authors train
a neural network using the self-similar legitimate traffic for classification of illegitimate or DDoS attack traffic. For detection, the authors
use the Lyapunov equation to differentiate the attack traffic from the

normal. For evaluation, they simulated the prediction algorithm using benchmark DDoS datasets, including the DARPA LLS DDoS 1.0 dataset from MIT. The results show that the detection accuracy is from 88% to 94% with a 0.05% to 0.45% false positive rate. Nguyen and Choi [179] develop another proactive DDoS attack classification method using a k-nearest neighbor classifier using a subset of features. Initially, the authors select an optimal subset of features relevant for DDoS attacks by breaking the attack traffic into phases. Next, they apply the KNN-based method to classify the network status during each phase of a DDoS attack. The results show that the method performs with high detection accuracy.

Wu et al. [265] explore the ability of decision trees and gray relational analysis in the detection of DDoS attacks. The authors use 15 attributes to monitor the incoming and outgoing packet traffic to estimate packet or byte rate. The authors also estimate the TCP, SYN, and ACK flag rates to understand traffic flow patterns. A decision tree is used to classify the abnormal traffic flow with reference to the pre-specified known traffic flow patterns, using a novel similarity matching technique. Their method is followed by an effective traceback mechanism to track the origin of the attack based on the similarity matching. The method performs satisfactorily in detecting DDoS attacks and in locating the origin of the attack source with high accuracy.

Gong et al. [89] develop an intrusion detection mechanism using Genetic Algorithms (GA). The authors initially generate a set of effective classification rules by applying GA on network audit data. They use a support-confidence framework to estimate the fitness of the rules. These rules are then used to identify anomalous traffic in real time. Two major advantages of this method are that (i) it is easy to implement and (ii) it can detect intrusions with high accuracy due to its simple rule representation and the effective fitness function. The authors establish their method with experimental results using benchmark DARPA datasets of intrusions.

Though the aforementioned classifiers developed using soft computing techniques are able to classify DDoS attacks satisfactorily, each uses subjective thresholding and produces false alarms. To overcome individual biases of these classifiers, an ensemble of several soft computing and hard computing techniques is introduced by Mukkamala et al. [177]. The authors use an ensemble of three classifiers, i.e., Support Vector Machines (SVM), Artificial Neural Networks (ANN),

and Multivariate Adaptive Regression Splines (MARS) to achieve high
detection accuracy by combining these learning paradigms without any
hybridization. To design the ensemble, the authors initially construct
different connection-oriented models carefully to achieve the best possible performance. Once the ensemble is constructed, test data is fed
to the individual models and the respective outputs are recorded. To
obtain the best output that maximizes classification accuracy, majority
voting is used to detect the attack class. It is shown that the proposed
ensemble can outperform the individual classifiers, i.e., SVM, ANN,
and MARS for all types of DoS and other attacks in many datasets.

In another similar approach, Abraham and Jain [7] develop multiple soft computing models for network intrusion detection. The authors explore the effectiveness of multiple classifiers, viz., fuzzy-rule
classifiers, decision trees, support vector machines, linear genetic pro-
gramming, and an ensemble method for fast intrusion detection. They
experiment in three phases: (i) data reduction, (ii) training, and (iii)
testing. In the first phase, i.e., in data reduction, the authors select
a relevant and optimal subset of features. In the training phase, they
construct different soft computing models using the training data to
obtain maximum generalization accuracy on unknown test patterns.
Finally, in the third phase, test data are passed through the saved
trained models for intrusion detection. They evaluate their method
using the KDD dataset and claim that the fuzzy classifier can detect
almost all attack classes with 100% accuracy in the KDD dataset.

Another neuro-fuzzy classifier was introduced by Toosi et al. [245]
to classify abnormal or non-conforming traffic patterns. The authors
use a fuzzy inference module, referred to as the *fuzzy decision engine*,
to detect malicious network traffic. The engine is used to generate a set
of fuzzy rules without the intervention of human analysts. To optimize
the ruleset, the authors use a genetic algorithm. The method is shown
to perform satisfactorily with the KDD-CUP99 intrusion dataset for
all attack class types.

Chimphlee [56] introduces a rough-fuzzy enabled soft computing
approach to handle the anomaly detection problem. The author uses a
fuzzy-rough c-means (FRCM) clustering algorithm to differentiate attack traffic from normal traffic. It assigns a membership value within
the range 0 to 1 to each test instance when partitioning the traffic.
It partitions the test instances into three groups, viz., lower approximation, boundary, and negative regions. The author evaluates the

method using the KDD-CUP99 intrusion dataset and shows that it can perform detection with 82.46% accuracy with a 91.45% detection rate and a 24.8% false alarm rate, whereas the traditional k-means algorithm performs with 76.0% accuracy only with a 91.81% detection rate and a 16.9% false alarm rate.

From the above discussion on various soft computing methods introduced for malicious traffic identification, we observe the following.

- Use of rough sets, fuzzy sets, and neural networks, in isolation or in combination, can enhance the performance of a DDoS detection system, especially in situations when information about the legitimate and attack traffic is insufficient, imprecise, and uncertain.

- Like the approaches discussed in the previous subsections, soft computing techniques also depend on multiple user parameters. The performance of most soft computing methods is highly sensitive to minor changes in the values of these parameters. At the same time, the accurate estimation of these parameters is difficult.

- Most soft computing methods achieve high detection accuracy and low false alarm rate, at the cost of high execution time, which is not desirable, especially in case of DDoS attack detection.

- The performance of supervised and semi-supervised soft computing methods is significantly better than that of unsupervised soft computing methods. However, some unsupervised soft computing methods are able to detect unseen attacks from even uncertain, imprecise, and insufficient traffic information in some situations.

- A soft computing method, capable of handling both known and unknown attacks in all situations with insufficient, imprecise, and uncertain information with high detection accuracy in real time, is still needed.

4.3.2.4 Knowledge-Based Techniques

In DDoS attack detection, a knowledge-based approach may be able to identify known classes of DDoS attacks. In this approach, it is understood that the defender uses prior knowledge acquired from the history of previous DDoS attacks when developing a defense solution. Based

on prior knowledge, the defender creates a set of rules or signatures
for each of the known attack types, and during detection, the newly
occurring network events are matched against these predefined rules
or signatures. If there is a match, it raises alarms, otherwise, considers it normal. Two major advantages of a knowledge-based technique
are (i) faster detection and (ii) high detection accuracy with low false
positives. Several effective knowledge-based techniques have been introduced to counter DDoS attacks. These techniques mostly belong to
one of the four distinct categories, viz., rule-based filtering, signature
analysis, self- organizing maps, and state-transition analysis. For each
of these categories, we discuss some prominent techniques introduced
for DDoS defense.

Rule-based filtering is an effective way to mitigate known DDoS
attacks. Unlike statistical methods, a rule-based filter usually requires
much less time for setup and to initiate detection [99]. Once a set of
unambiguous, non-redundant and maximally covering rules is created,
the system can initiate detection immediately. An effective rule-based
filter can show detection performance up to 100% for known DDoS
attack types. The false positive rate shown by a carefully built rule-
based filter is also very low. The time requirement for maintaining the
rule-base is also significantly lower than statistical approaches. However, for unknown vulnerabilities, especially for zero-day DDoS attacks,
such rule-based filters are ineffective since the corresponding rules are
not available. Further, for large variations in DDoS attacks, the rule
repository becomes very large, and hence the time needed to match may
become high. Considering recent DDoS attacking scenarios, most attacks have large variations and they propagate swiftly. So the defender
must develop a light defense solution to counter such varied attack
types in minimum time. Kim et al. [135] present a rule-based defense
method to support fast detection of multiple DDoS attack types. The
framework of their method is shown in Figure 4.16. The method initially collects traffic data for fixed time intervals. Then it analyzes the
traffic using the rule engine, as shown in the figure. The method has
a group of rules to identify anomalous traffic, and it attempts to make
an effective use of this rule set to detect DDoS attack types in real
time. It makes a swift decision using this rule set during the occurrence of a DDoS attack type. In addition, the method has a provision
to thoroughly investigate the alarm-generation process to reduce the
rate of false alarms and to assign weight to the rules. During analysis,

the method considers nine typical factors, viz., TCP octet, TCP flows, TCP packets, UDP octet, UDP flows, UDP packets, TCP source port variation, TCP destination port variation, and source IP address variation. It considers a process as normal, if the result of the analysis does not exceed critical values. Otherwise, it is judged abnormal and subsequently the corresponding source IPs are blocked. The method also has provision for post-alarm diagnosis and for recomputing the critical values to reduce false alarms. The authors establish satisfactory performance of the method using real network traffic.

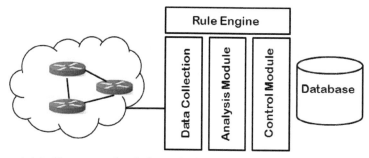

Figure 4.16: Framework of the rule-based DDoS detection mechanism.

Another approach to DDoS attack detection using inductive learning [59], [198] and a Bayesian classifier [95] is reported in [182]. The authors endow an alarm agent with a tapestry of reactive rules for detection of DDoS attacks. The authors monitor TCP flag rates and absence or presence of flooding attacks to create state-action rules. They exploit the regularities in DDoS attacks to help in identification and to enable the alarm agent. To obtain the rules, the authors use machine learning algorithms, using the results of TCP flag rates. They use a spectrum of approaches to support detection of various attacks on Websites. For evaluation, the authors used a simulated network environment using Linux machines, as shown in Figure 4.17. It consists of (i) a Web server using Apache, (ii) Web clients, (iii) DDoS attackers, (iv) network monitoring devices including a packet collecting agent, and (v) an alarm-generation agent. In this environment, they measure TCP flag rates. To generate normal and attack traffic models, the method uses two settings, one using a normal Web server and the other with a Web server with DDoS attacks. To evaluate the effectiveness of the compiled ruleset generated for the alarm agent using three well-known classifiers, C4.5, CN2, and Bayesian classifier, the authors express the performance obtained in terms of the ratio {total

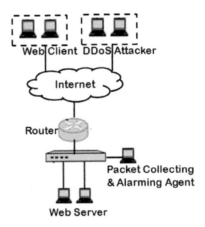

Figure 4.17: Simulated network environment with web clients, attackers, server, and the proposed agent.

no of alarms–(number of false alarms + number of missed alarms)}
: *{total number of alarms}*. According to the authors, the rules constructed are qualitative and the detection performance is satisfactory in comparison to similar techniques.

Thomas et al.'s victim-end *NetBouncer* [242] is another effective knowledge-based defense solution to protect network resources from DDoS attacks. The authors claim that *NetBouncer* is a practical solution with high performance. The basic idea is to distinguish legitimate and illegitimate uses of the resources and to make the resources available only for legitimate use. As incoming traffic flows, NetBouncer uses a long list of established legitimate clients for reference. If incoming packets are not from any legitimate client, it administers a variety of legitimacy tests. If it finds that the client passes these tests, *NetBouncer* adds it to the legitimate list and subsequent packets from the client are accepted until a certain legitimacy window expires. A traffic management subsystem controls the transmission of legitimate packets by applying various bandwidth management and rate control schemes to ensure that legitimate clients cannot be a cause of bandwidth misuse and that target servers are not overwhelmed at any cost even though the traffic appears to be legitimate.

Another effective knowledge-based DDoS defense solution was proposed by Wang et al. [258]. The authors introduce a formal and systematic approach for modeling DDoS attacks using an augmented attack tree (AAT)-based DDoS detection algorithm. Using the model, the authors capture delicate changes that occur in network traffic due to the occurrence of DDoS attacks and the corresponding transitions in network states considering transmission of network traffic on the primary victim server. The authors use the AAT-based DDoS model (ADDoSAT) to assess potential threats from anomalous packets on the primary victim server and to detect such attacks. The AAT-based bottom-up detection algorithm identifies possible DDoS attacks. Unlike traditional attack tree modeling approaches, Wang el al.'s approach is advanced feature-based and it provides additional information, especially about the state-transition process. Consequently, the model can overcome the limitations of CAT modeling. Based on experimental results, the authors claim that their method is able to detect DDoS attacks with high detection accuracy and at an early stage.

Considering the previous discussion of various knowledge-based computing methods, we observe the following.

- In a knowledge-based approach, the defender uses prior knowledge acquired from the history of previous DDoS attacks when developing a defense solution.

- A knowledge-based DDoS detection technique can use rule-based filtering, signature analysis, self-organizing maps, or state-transition analysis.

- A carefully designed rule-based DDoS detector can usually initiate its detection operation right away and show very high detection accuracy and low false positive rates.

- Most rule-based DDoS detectors suffer due to the need for instant processing of a large number of rules to handle large variations in DDoS attacks. Ideally, we need a light defense solution, yet almost complete.

- A generic knowledge-based DDoS defense solution based on state-transition or any other analysis that can handle all types of DDoS attacks in multiple network environment still does not exist.

4.4 Chapter Summary

In the above sections, a large number of statistical, soft computing, machine learning, and data mining and knowledge-based DDoS detection techniques have been discussed. Based on the analysis of their salient features and performance issues, we summarize their effectiveness as follows.

- In a statistical method for DDoS detection, typically user behavior is monitored, and if there is significant deviation from predefined normal behavior thresholds, the non-conforming or anomalous activity is considered an attack. So, the success of such methods is highly dependent on (i) how data about the legitimate user behavior is gathered, (ii) how legitimate user behavior is modeled, and (ii) how the deviation threshold is decided.

- Statistical methods typically use various statistical and information theoretic measures such as deviation, cumulative sum, correlations, entropy, mutual information (MI), and covariance.

- If a precise, certain, and sufficient source of knowledge is available for training, a supervised machine learning technique can help detect DDoS attacks with high detection accuracy.

- An unsupervised data mining technique with a carefully chosen proximity measure can help detect unseen attacks in addition to known attacks.

- By appropriate hybridization of supervised and unsupervised machine learning and data mining techniques or by using an appropriate combination of learners, one can achieve high detection accuracy for both known as well as unknown attacks.

- A carefully designed rough-fuzzy or ANN-based DDoS detection system can handle both known and unknown attacks with high detection accuracy, even if the situation does not provide sufficient, precise, and certain information. However, like other approaches, a soft computing technique depends on multiple user parameters and these parameters are crucial for performance.

- A rule-based DDoS detection system is typically faster than other detection approaches. With an unambiguous, non-redundant, and maximally covering ruleset, it can show detection performance of up to 100% for known DDoS attack types.

- A light-weight DDoS defense solution using both supervised and unsupervised learners implemented on both hardware and software, using an optimal subset of features with up-to-date knowledge could be ideal for DDoS detection in multiple network situations.

Chapter 5

DDoS Prevention

An intrusion prevention system (IPS) is considered an "upgraded" version of an intrusion detection system [69]. Both monitor network traffic and/or system activities for malicious activity; however, unlike an IDS, an intrusion prevention system is able to actively block intrusions that are detected. Typically, an IPS does so by generating alarms, dropping malicious packets, resetting the connection, and/or blocking traffic from the offending IP addresses. A generic view of an intrusion prevention system is shown in Figure 5.1. The managing system, monitoring component, and detection component are almost similar to those in an IDS, but instead of the *reaction component* in this system, prevention procedures are applied. The prevention engine applies a set of procedures based on the pattern of behavior of the suspicious traffic by working closely with the *managing system*. The responsibility of the managing system is to manage the traffic flow and to apply the procedures provided by the prevention engine.

5.1 DDoS Prevention Techniques

Intrusion prevention is performed by a software or hardware device that can intercept detected threats in real time and prevent them from moving closer toward victims. It is an useful approach against DDoS, flooding, and brute force attacks. Today, the general lack of adequate security infrastructure across the Internet is a major cause of the tremendous pressure faced by Internet Service Providers to prevent and mitigate DDoS attacks on their infrastructure and services, on their own.

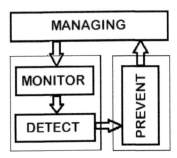

Figure 5.1: Intrusion prevention system: a generic view.

Prevention of DDoS attacks in real time is a live network security problem. One can consider an IPS as an extension of an IDS. Although IPSs and IDSs both examine network traffic searching for attacks, there are critical differences. IPSs and IDSs both aim to detect malicious or unwanted traffic and both can potentially do so well, but they differ in their response generation. For effective prevention, one must be able to detect source(s) early and then initiate appropriate action(s) to identify the attack sources. Since DDoS is a coordinated attack, it is not straightforward to identify the attack sources in real time. Further, spoofing of source IP addresses in the attack packets complicates attempts at reliable DDoS prevention.

A good number of DDoS prevention methods have been developed recently. Most prevention methods act upon detection of DDoS attacks in one or more of the following ways: (a) by reconfiguring the security mechanisms such as firewalls or routers to block future attacks, (b) by removing malicious content from the attack traffic by filtering out possible attack packets, or (c) by appropriate browser setting and by reconfiguring other security and privacy controls to avoid occurrence of future attacks. However, for effective DDoS prevention, identification of true attack source(s) is an essential task. Although identification of the true source of attack is a daunting task due to open and decentralized structure of the Internet, several novel approaches have evolved in the recent past. IP traceback is one such powerful candidate among the mechanisms used to identify the true source of attacks in a network.

5.1.1   IP Traceback

As we have discussed earlier, in a DDoS attack, attackers mostly use zombies or reflectors to send attack packets to the victim machine using spoofed IP addresses. One can attempt to detect the attack source manually as well as automatically. It may be performed either at the victim end or from intermediate routers and traced back to the original source end. Typically, a hop-by-hop traceback mechanism is used from router to router. Therefore, for successful identification of the attack source, co-operation among networks is highly essential. However, manual traceback is a tedious and time-consuming process. To expedite the process, researchers have introduced automated traceback schemes. An effective traceback mechanism should have the following properties.

- The traceback mechanism should be cost-effective.

- The involvement of ISPs should be low.

- It should not incur any additional memory cost in routers or switches.

- It should produce low network overhead.

- The false positive rate of detection should be low.

- The deployment of the traceback system should not be a problem.

- The traceback mechanism should be able to identify the original source of attack with the help of a single packet.

To understand the working of a traceback scheme, let us introduce an automated example using the traceback scheme developed in [279] using a variation of Shannon's entropy. For illustration, we use the example network shown in Figure 5.2. In this example network, we have six LANs (viz, $LAN_1, LAN_2, \cdots, LAN_6$) and five routers (viz, $R_1, R_2, \cdots, R_5$). Multiple attackers from LAN_1, LAN_3, and LAN_6 target a single victim. So in a DDoS attack, the flows destined to a victim include both legitimate flows as well as a combination of attack and legitimate flows. In Figure 5.2, a flow such as f_3 is a legitimate flow, whereas f_1 and f_2 are combinations of attack and legitimate flows. Typically, during a DDoS attack, the volume of flow increases significantly within a short interval of time. So, one can observe a significant change in the traffic pattern at routers R_2 and R_4 and also at the victim. In contrast, at routers R_1, R_3, and R_5, such changes or variations will not be visible due to the absence of attack flows. Once such variations are sensed by the victim, typically the defender attempts

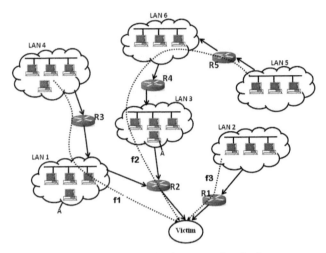

Figure 5.2: An example network for traceback demonstration.

to push back to the LAN(s), that are suspected to be involved in the attack. One can carry out such an exercise by using information metrics (such as entropy) to quantify the variations in the traffic at the routers and the victim. In other words, one can measure the changes in randomness of flows at the routers or at the victim for a given interval of time. Based on the discovery of significant flow variations at the victim machine in terms of entropy, the defending agent may be able to guess that high-rate attack sources are somewhere behind R_2, but not behind R_1, since no significant entropy variation is sensed here. Accordingly, the network defender will send a traceback request to R_2 to locate the possible source of DDoS attacks. Like the victim, based on entropy variations sensed, router R_2 may identify that DDoS attacks are from two sources, one behind LAN_1 and the other behind LAN_3. Subsequently, the traceback request can be forwarded to the edge routers of LAN_4 and LAN_6, i.e., R_3 and R_4. Similarly, at both these routers, entropy variations will be estimated and if significant change is detected in any one or at both routers, action will be taken accordingly. In the sample network, R_3 can infer that attack sources are from LAN_1. However, R_4 will infer that attackers are from LAN_3 and also are behind R_4. Accordingly, the traceback request needs to be forwarded further to upstream routers, say R_5, to locate the attack from LAN_6.

It is worth mentioning that such an entropy-based traceback scheme is useful and effective only when the following assumptions are valid.

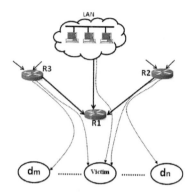

Figure 5.3: Tracing attack flows at the router.

Assumption 1: During a DDoS attack, a dramatic change of network traffic occurs in a very short period of time, say in *seconds*. In case of non-DDoS attacks, such changes or variations also may occur, but it happens over a longer duration, may be *minutes*.

Assumption 2: During a high-rate DDoS attack, attack packets are generated by a large number of bots or zombies, usually *thousands* [279], and hence the number of attack packets are significantly higher compared to the normal or legitimate flows.

Assumption 3: In both attack and non-attack cases, the number of flows at a given router is stable.

Assumption 4: In a given interval of time, only one DDoS flooding attack takes place.

To overcome such restrictions, recently several novel traceback schemes using variants of Shannon's entropy [218] have been developed [278], [280], [269], [240]. These schemes use information theoretic or information distance measures with an objective of identifying the attack source with low network overhead and with low false positive rates. The measures commonly used for sensing the attack at a router are Shannon's generalized entropy, collision entropy or Renyi's quadratic entropy [204], extended entropy [218] and Kullback–Leibler divergence or information distance [36]. The authors of specific papers mostly attempt to establish their chosen measure in terms of effectiveness in sensing the variation between the attack traffic and the legitimate traffic. Several additional traceback schemes have also been developed using either link testing or by using various packet-marking and logging schemes. So we broadly classify these schemes into four categories: (i) link testing, (ii) packet marking, (iii) packet logging, and (iv) ICMP Traceback Messages.

5.1.1.1   Link Testing

In link testing, the victim conducts a test on each of its incoming links as a probable input link for a DDoS attack traffic. If the test result is positive, it contacts the upstream router(s) closest to the victim. The contacted router then initiates an interactive traceback process recursively with its upstream routers until the true source of attack is identified. This scheme has at least three main advantages: (i) it can discover attackers of flooding attacks reliably, (ii) it is cost effective due to relatively low network overhead, and (iii) the scheme can be replicated in a distributed manner easily. It has several limitations as well. One major limitation is the generation of additional traffic, which usually consumes significant network resources. One can apply link testing to detect attack sources in two distinct ways: (i) input debugging and (ii) controlled flooding. These two link testing methods are introduced next.

In the *input debugging* scheme, the first task is to recognize an attack at the victim. Once an attack is recognized, the next task is to generate an attack signature based on the common features of attack packets. The victim then sends a message to an upstream router for installation of an input debugging filter on the egress port. It is expected that such a filter will reveal the associated input ports and the upstream routers responsible for generation of the attack traffic. The process is repeated recursively until the source of the attack is detected. This scheme is often successful in identifying the true sources of DDoS attacks because of its distributed nature. Its limitations include facts such as (i) the cost of management of resources used to support prevention is significantly high, (ii) the network and router overhead is large, (iii) it consumes a significantly large amount of time to communicate with upstream routers, and (iv) it requires skilled network professionals for effective traceback operation.

The *controlled flooding* traceback scheme, introduced by Burch and Cheswick [39], works automatically without the involvement of network operators. The scheme floods the incoming links on the router with high rate (bursty) network traffic and then observes the response from attackers. It chooses the incoming links nearest the victim, and uses a pre-generated map of Internet topology, including a few selected hosts. There is a high dropping probability for packets (including the attacker's packets) travelling across the loaded links. The victim can infer the attack links by computing the changes in packet arrival rates. This process is then recursively applied on the upstream routers until the source of attack is reached. It is a very effective traceback technique. However, like the previous schemes, it also suffers from three major limitations: (i) It has high management overhead, (ii) It requires coordination among routers or switches or even ISPs, and (iii) It requires skilled network administrators.

5.1.1.2 Packet Marking

Packet marking is a significant recent addition to the techniques used for identification of the origin of DDoS attacks. In a packet-marking scheme, routers mark forwarding packets either deterministically or probabilistically, with their own addresses. So, when an attack occurs, the victim uses the marked information associated with the packet to trace back to the attack source. Packet-marking-based traceback schemes have been developed in two ways: (a) deterministic packet marking, commonly known as DPM schemes, and (b) probabilistic packet marking, also known as PPM schemes.

The *probabilistic packet-marking (PPM)* scheme, introduced by Savage et al. [210], does not require prior knowledge of the whole network to build an attack tree, i.e., a map of the routers along the path of the attack. One can use this marking during an attack or even after an attack has occurred. In this scheme, the IP header has only a single field to store the marking information. Each router on the path from the source to the destination writes down its unique identifier in the entry in the packet header with some probability. By writing into the field, routers overwrite any previous entry that was present there. The victim can reconstruct the path from the source to itself on receiving a large number of packets.

A major advantage of this scheme is that there is no need for any additional network traffic like ICMP traceback, router storage for logging, or packet size increase. In this scheme, each router performs an information injection event using a 16-bit identification field in the IP header for every forwarding packet. Out of 16 bits, it uses 5 bits for maintaining hop count information and the remaining bits for the message that the router wants to send to the destination of the packet. If the message is too long, fragmentation is performed to make it smaller in size with some bits indicating the fragment offset and data fragment. During a DDoS attack, a victim can reconstruct the message with the help of a hash function interleaved in the original message it received from the router. However, a major limitation of the PPM scheme is high processing overhead in the victim during the reconstruction of the path.

In *deterministic packet marking (DPM)*, each outgoing packet is marked by the router with its own unique identifier. This mechanism is similar to the IP record-route option and it uses the marking information during reconstruction of the attack path at the victim. Savage et al. [210] calculate the optimal value for the marking probability to be $1/d$, where d is the length of the path.

Goodrich et al.'s [90] randomize-and-link approach is an improvement over the probabilistic packet-marking scheme from security and practicality points of view. The core concept is that each router fragments its message M into several words and these words are included randomly in b reusable bits together with a large checksum. Though the approach is efficient, it wastes b precious bits. The checksum codes significantly reduce the ability of an adversary to inject false messages that collide with legitimate ones. The main strength of this approach is that it can easily recognize 8-fragment messages or higher from hundreds of routers, even when attackers inject packets to slow down the approach. Moreover, this approach does not require any prior knowledge of the whole network.

Xiang et al. [270] propose an optimized version of DPM called flexible DPM (FDPM) that provides a defense system with the ability to find real sources of attacking packets. Compared to link testing, packet logging, ICMP traceback, PPM, and DPM, FDPM provides more flexible features to trace IP packets and gives better performance. In some situations, the method uses a service field in the IP header; to store mark information. It uses two fields in the IP header, one is the fragment ID and other is the reversed flag. The sender of a packet assigns an identifying value to the ID field that helps assemble all fragments of a datagram. Compared to DPM, FDPM is simpler and more flexible during path reconstruction. FDPM is effective in terms of low false positive rates as well as the number of packets needed to reconstruct one source, the high number of sources that can be traced in one traceback process, and the high forwarding rate of traceback-enabled routers. Major pros of FDPM include easy implementation, low processing cost, low bandwidth overhead, suitability for attacks other than (D)DoS, scalability, and the lack of inherent security flaws.

Alwis et al. [11] propose a network topology-based packet-marking (TBPM) scheme, which is distinct from other similar schemes. It embeds network topology information in a data packet to be marked. The main problem with traditional packet-marking methods is that they mark the identity of the edge router through which a packet enters a network. However, during flooding attacks, the edge router may be unreachable from the node under attack. The node can defuse the attack close to its source with the help of information about the route that the packet has traversed through the network. This is practically possible even when the edge router is unreachable, and therefore, this approach can restore functionality of the internal network in the presence of DoS attacks at the edge routers. Space efficiency in the form of a constant marking field and processing efficiency in the form of minimum router support are two major advantages of this scheme. However, it also suffers from limitations such as (i) a high false positive rate, (ii) a high number of required packets, (iii) low capability for packet tracing, and (iv) an inflexible marking rate that cannot adapt to the load of the participating router.

5.1.1.3 Packet Logging

In the packet logging approach, routers store packet information so that such information can be used to trace an attack long after the attack has completed. One can use data mining techniques on the logged packet data to determine the path that the packets may have traversed. Many variations of packet logging methods have been proposed. Snoeren et al. propose [223] a hash-based IP traceback mechanism that records the packet digest in an efficient data structure. This method needs a significant amount of memory to store the logged information. To overcome this problem, Broder and Mitzeamacher [34] propose the use of bloom filters to minimize storage overhead significantly. The main advantages of this method are (i) it stores packet log information historically for future investigation, (ii) it is easy to trace back, and (iii) it can be easily deployed in a distributed manner. However, it requires high storage space to store historic data, and also has high network overhead and high management overhead.

5.1.1.4   ICMP Traceback Messages

In this mechanism, the router generates ICMP traceback messages that include the content of forwarded packets along with information about adjacent routers and sends them to the destination. When flooding attacks occur, the victim uses these ICMP messages to construct attack graphs back to the attacker. The traceback messages help the victim find the original source of the attack. This mechanism relies on an input debugging capability that is not enabled in many router architectures. As a result, it may be difficult to establish a connection between a participating router and a non-participating router. ICMP traceback is effective in terms of network overhead as it incurs low management cost. Moreover, the approach can be distributed easily and is able to effectively detect attack paths during flooding attacks. However, this approach generates high additional network traffic and creates many false ICMP messages. ICMP messages can be distinguished easily and hence may be filtered or rate limited differently from normal traffic. The main disadvantages of this method are (i) computational overhead is high if the network is large, (ii) detection of multiple attack paths is difficult, (iii) IP traceback is difficult due to the stateless nature of Internet routing, and (iv) manual IP traceback is tedious and difficult.

5.1.1.5   Discussion

Although a large number of IP traceback schemes have been proposed under categories such as link testing, packet marking, packet logging, and ICMP traceback messages, several issues remain to be resolved satisfactorily.

- *Network Overhead:* Most link testing schemes suffer from (i) high resource consumption, (ii) have high management overhead, and (iii) require skilled network operators. A link testing scheme that may be able to locate the true source of DDoS attacks by alleviating these limitations is necessary.

- *Processing Overhead:* Packet-marking schemes are useful and effective in preventing DDoS attacks in real time. However, most such schemes suffer from one common disadvantage, viz., high processing overhead at the victim during reconstruction of the path. So, a PPM (probabilistic packet marking) or DPM (deterministic packet marking) scheme that is able to prevent DDoS attacks in real time with low processing overhead at the victim is wanted.

5.1.2 Filtering Techniques

Filters provide a useful and powerful mechanism to protect network resources from DDoS attacks. Several filtering techniques have been introduced by network security researchers. In this section, we discuss three commonly used, but effective approaches to filter DDoS attack traffic, especially with spoofed source IP addresses.

5.1.2.1 Ingress and Egress Filtering

Ingress and egress filters are very useful in DDoS attack prevention. Ingress filtering rules are useful to filter the traffic coming into a local network, whereas egress filtering rules are set to filter the traffic leaving a local network [239]. When setting ingress and egress filtering rules, one requires a reference point to avoid confusion and conflict. As an illustration of these two filtering mechanisms, consider the example situation shown in Figure 5.4, in the context of the original filtering proposal of Ferguson and Senie [77].

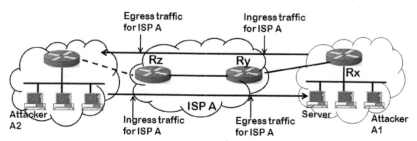

Figure 5.4: An example network to demonstrate ingress and egress filtering.

We see in the figure that ISP A provides access to the Internet to the network of an institution or organization, referred to as a *leaf* network. In the leaf network, router Rx is the edge router, connecting to an edge router of ISP A, i.e., router Ry. ISP A has another edge router, i.e., router Rz, through which connectivity is provided to other networks. According to the proposal, ingress and egress filters allow access to packets that come into a network or leave a network if their source addresses match a pre-defined range of source IP addresses.

Let us consider a scenario. Assume that attacker $A1$ is inside the institution's network and is sending packets with spoofed IP addresses to the *Server*. Also assume that router Ry of ISP A is equipped with an input filter, and is connected to the institution's network. Assume also that we have set a rule that the input filter will only allow packets with source IP addresses with the prefix 202.141.129.0/24. If the attacker $A1$'s packets with spoofed source IP addresses do not have such a prefix, the filter will simply drop these packets at router Ry. Such a filtering facility provided by router Ry is referred to as ingress filtering. Similarly, in another scenario, assume the attacker $A2$ is outside of both ISP A and the institution's network, and is sending packets with spoofed source IP addresses to the *Server* inside the institution's network. Also, assume that these source IP addresses are set to watch for the ones with prefixes other than 202.141.129.0/24. Like the previous case, router Rz, which is equipped with an input filter, will simply drop these packets due to non-match with the pre-defined range of IP addresses. Such a filtering operation performed at router Rz is referred to as ingress filtering. On the other hand, if the filtering operation is performed at router Ry, it would be called egress filtering.

By now, it is clear that to apply such filtering operations, one has to know the expected range of source IP addresses at a port. If such a range can be predicted correctly, both ingress and egress filtering work successfully. However, in many enterprise networks with complex topologies, such prediction may not be correct and as a consequence, legitimate traffic may be dropped, which is undesirable! To ameliorate the situation, researchers address this issue using various approaches to build adequate knowledge of correct IP ranges to watch for.

In general, the network of an institution or an organization is created with a simple topology. Acquiring knowledge about the expected source IP ranges of the network in such a case is not a difficult task. Thus, ingress and egress filtering is usually effective. When such networks are deployed, filtering operations are relatively easy to install because sufficient additional computing resources can be spared. Another significant advantage of filtering is that it can be applied not only to source IP addresses, but also to port numbers, protocol types, destination IP addresses, and other attributes of concern. However, such filtering may not always be effective in the case of DDoS attacks. Since, recent trends in launching DDoS attacks is to use large peer-to-peer botnet technology, an attacker may compromise a large number (of the order of *thousands*) of hosts to generate the attack traffic. An attacker does not have to spoof source IP addresses, and hence can bypass the ingress/egress filtering easily.

5.1.2.2   Router-Based Packet Filtering (RPF)

Router-based packet filtering is an extension of ingress filtering, introduced by Park and Lee [189]. The main principle behind this approach to filtering is that in the core of the Internet, for each link usually only a limited set of source addresses is valid for generation of legitimate traffic on the link. So, if any deviation is detected in an IP packet on a link, one can suspect that the source address is spoofed, and accordingly filter the packet. The working principle of the technique is as follows. Initially, the Internet must be divided into a collection of routing domains referred to as Autonomous Segments (AS). Each AS may represent multiple networks, and is administered by a single entity, which may be an organization, an institution, or a corporation. A border router is responsible for routing traffic between ASs using a gateway protocol called Border Gateway Protocol (BGP) and depending on the topology used, each *AS* (which is identified by a 16-bit unique ID) can operate with more than one such border routers. Thus, following their terminology, the whole Internet can be viewed as an interconnection of border routers. In summary, this technique attempts to filter traffic with spoofed source IP addresses using the information available about the world-wide BGP topology.

Let us consider an example situation with eleven *AS*s or nodes, as shown in Figure 5.5. The attacker *R3* is in *AS3* and attempts to flood a target *R6* in *AS6*. Assume that the attacker spoofs the source address

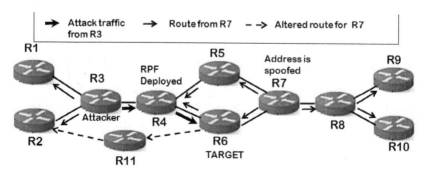

Figure 5.5: A demonstration of router-based packet filtering.

as if it is coming from $R7$ in $AS7$ and also let the filtering technique be deployed at $R4$ in $AS4$. The traffic generated from $R3$ can be prevented by filtering if $R4$ is aware of the network topology. Considering the traffic path shown in the figure with the normal directed edge from $R7$, which is the spoofed address of attack traffic, it will not be possible for traffic generated from $R7$ to reach at $R4$ where the filter engine is deployed on the link from $R3$ to $R4$. Therefore, we can confidently say that attack traffic with the spoofed source address of $R7$ will be filtered by the RPF at $R4$.

Although, an RPF has several advantages from the perspective of DDoS prevention, it has some limitations as well. Recent DDoS attack masterminds are very clever and are likely to use both carefully chosen spoofed source IP addresses and genuine source IP addresses when launching attacks. As a result, one may not find this filtering technique effective against DDoS attacks. Therefore, both router-based filtering approaches (viz., ingress / egress filters and RPF) may fail to prevent attack traffic, especially, when dynamic Internet routing is used. To address this issue, the following protocol has been introduced.

5.1.2.3   Source Address Validity Enforcement (SAVE) Protocol

Li et al. [148] introduced the SAVE protocol to enable update of the expected source IP address information dynamically on each link. Like previous techniques, it blocks IP packets with source IP addresses which are not included in the expected list of source IP addresses for a given link. SAVE frequently updates information about all destinations by propagating valid source IP addresses, so that each router can build an up-to-date incoming table relevant for each link of the router and accordingly can block any unexpected source IP addresses. Like ingress filtering and RPF, SAVE also assumes that for each link of the router, the expected source address space is known a priori and is stable. A major advantage of the SAVE protocol in comparison to ingress filtering and RPF is that it can overcome the problem associated with asymmetries of Internet routing by updating the incoming table for each link regularly. However, in case of DDoS attacks, like the previous two filtering techniques, SAVE is also not safe, since recent DDoS attacks may not be dependent on spoofing.

5.1.3 Rate Control

Rate control is another effective approach to prevent DDoS attacks based on pre-specified prevention criteria. It attempts to control or limit the arrival rate of packets matching the DDoS attack criteria. Such schemes are carefully designed so that legitimate flows are minimally harmed. Further, unlike pushback schemes, typically such a scheme does not incur any extra overhead during prevention, and as a consequence, does not create a situation of denial of service by itself. Furthermore, rate control is also considered less severe than other packet filtering schemes. Used with a DDoS defense method that leads to too many false positives, such rate control schemes can be more effective than the usual packet filtering schemes. An appropriate rate limiting scheme shapes packets, which is good because other Internet sources are forced to respect constraints imposed on their forwarding rate.

5.2 Chapter Summary

Based on the discussion of various DDoS preventive measures introduced in the recent past, we make the following observations.

- Although filtering techniques prevent DoS/DDoS attacks by handling the IP spoofing problem, they have become outdated and ineffective due to (i) non-dependency of most recent DDoS attacks on IP spoofing, (ii) difficulty in deployment, and (iii) inability to handle IP spoofing within the same network.

- Ingress and egress filters can prevent DDoS attacks with high accuracy, especially when the source IP addresses are spoofed. However, in case of high-rate DDoS attacks without IP spoofing or carefully chosen spoofed IP addresses, such filters may not perform effectively.

- RPF has several advantages, but still has one serious limitation. It may not perform well against DDoS attacks generated by large botnets without source IP spoofing, especially when dynamic Internet routing is used.

- Rate control has no significant extra overhead during prevention and is generally more effective when the DDoS defense method leads to too many false positives.

Chapter 6

DDoS Reaction and Tolerance

An intrusion response system (IRS) monitors the health of a system continuously based on IDS alerts to effectively handle malicious or unauthorized activities. It applies appropriate countermeasures to prevent problems from worsening and to return the system to a healthy mode. A notification system generates alerts when an attack is detected. An alert can contain information such as attack description, time of attack, source IP, and user accounts used to attack. Typically, an IRS automatically executes a preconfigured set of response actions based on the occurrence of a specific type of attack. This approach is more automated than the IDS approach, where an administrator is required to take such response actions manually. Unlike an IDS, here no human intervention is required. So, there is no delay between intrusion detection and response. Figure 6.1 shows a generic structure of an IRS. The four basic components of a generic IRS are a detection component, a reaction component, a monitoring component, and a managing system. Unlike IDSs and IPSs, the reaction component of an IRS includes a response system, which uses a predefined approach to respond to any intrusion automatically.

6.1 Intrusion Response System (IRS)

Once anomalous or intrusive behavior is detected by an intrusion detection system (IDS), it is desirable that appropriate action(s) be taken to minimize the damage and to guarantee protection of computing and

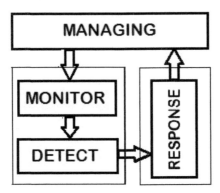

Figure 6.1: Intrusion response system: a generic view.

network resources. Actions or corrective measures taken to thwart attacks and to ensure safety of the resources are commonly known as *intrusion responses (IRs)* [229], [127]. In an IDS, such response activities are considered integral to it when monitoring, tracing, and analyzing system activities. However, an intrusion response system (IRS) has its own existence and it has an important role to play in DDoS defense. An IRS is dedicated to constantly observing the health of a networked system based on alerts received from IDSs, and to take appropriate actions for effective handling of malicious activities to bring the networked system back into a healthy state. In the past two decades, although IDS research has been able to attract considerable attention of the computer science research community, very little attention has been given to IRS research. The following may be reasons for poor progress on the IRS front.

- Developing an adaptive and dynamic IRS that can thwart most DDoS attacks most of the time is very difficult.

- Deployment of such a system in automatic mode to provide real-time services is very challenging as well.

6.1.1   Intrusion Response (IR) and Its Types

Intrusion response can be of various types based on the approach used to generate it. An IR can be generated manually, semi-automatically, or automatically based on alerts received from an IDS. But, in all these types of IR generations, a human analyst or system administrator has a direct or indirect role to play. Especially, in case of a manual and semi-automatic IRS, involvement of such human analysts with adequate knowledge and experience is a must to select an appropriate course of actions. An IR can also be *proactive* or *reactive*. A reactive IRS generates the response only after the attack is confirmed. In contrast, a proactive IR is generated only after a probabilistic analysis of the network behavior indicates the possibility of occurrence of a DDoS attack in the near future. Similarly, an intrusion response may be generated in active or passive mode. In an active IRS, the system does not just notify the administration with attack details, but also takes necessary actions to minimize the damage by the DDoS attack and to prevent repeated such attacks in the near future. In contrast, a passive IR just notifies the system administrator about the occurrence of an attack. Considering the three basic types of responses, viz., passive, proactive, and reactive, to show relationships among them using different attack time frames, a response model was developed by [12]. We explain it next.

6.1.1.1 A Model to Demonstrate Relationships among Responses

In this model, the authors [12] establish the relationships among the three basic types of responses, viz., passive, proactive, and reactive, using three distinct *time frames*. Once an attack is detected by an IDS, the types of responses that can be generated at various stages and their inter-relationships, are shown using three time frames (represented by three *dotted horizontal lines*) viz., $T_{n-\gamma}$, T_n and $T_{n+\gamma}$, as shown in Figure 6.2. These time frames also represent two stages viz., (a) before an intrusion alarm (i.e., *normal* or *pre-attack* stage) or during the interval $T_{n-\gamma}$ to T_n, and (b) after an intrusion alarm (i.e., *post-attack* stage) or during the interval from T_n to $T_{n+\gamma}$. In addition to these stages, another stage is introduced in this model, i.e., stage III or the post-reaction response stage, which is also referred to as the *investigation* stage.

Stage I: Pre-attack Stage

During the pre-attack stage, i.e., during the interval from $T_{n-\gamma}$ to T_n, prior to detection of any attack by the IDS, proactive response generation is active. This stage plays two significant roles to defend and protect network resources. First, it identifies a possible occurrence of

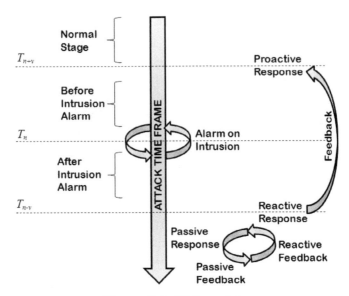

Figure 6.2: IRS model.

a DDoS attack with high confidence based on prediction analysis and takes appropriate actions to block such potential malicious incidents. Second, it receives feedback from passive and reactive response components, analyzes them, and takes necessary actions to prevent future and current attacks.

Stage II: Post-attack Stage

In this stage, i.e., during the time interval T_n to $T_{n+\gamma}$, the reactive response model becomes active and plays an important role to minimize damage to resources. During this post-attack stage, appropriate reactive countermeasures are taken based on the seriousness of the attack, and the level of confidence in its confirmation. If the confidence level is high and the attack sources are identified, it blocks the suspected source IPs from accessing victim host(s). The reaction process continues until $T_{n+\gamma}$.

Stage III: Investigation Stage

This stage starts at $T_{n+\gamma}$ and has no specific end interval. It continues until the incident has been completely investigated. It is mostly applicable to non-critical systems where the time interval for analysis and response generation is not strictly specified. Stage III waits, investigates, and learns from Stage II about the incident and then takes response actions. It also involves the passive component, collects its feedback and combines with the current stage, and prepares a feedback for reactive and proactive responses. The feedback between passive and reactive responses is bidirectional and hence it forms a feedback cycle, as shown in Figure 6.2.

Based on the above discussion, we summarize as follows.

- Intrusion response generation can be divided into two major zones: the active zone and the passive zone.

- The passive, proactive, and reactive responses are inter-related.

- Feedback items from both passive and reactive responses are combined and prepared as input for both reactive and proactive responses.

6.1.2 Development of IRSs: Approaches, Methods, and Techniques

In the past few years, several innovative IRSs have been developed. We classify these IRSs into two major groups [229] based on the *degree of automation*, as shown in Figure 6.3. Each group of IRSs is further categorized into subgroups using *five* other criteria. These are (i) the approach used for triggering responses, (ii) adaptability, (iii) promptness in response generation, (iv) ability to cooperate, and (v) versatility in reacting to unseen situations. We discuss various approaches used to develop IRSs in the next section, following the taxonomy given in Figure 6.3.

6.1.2.1 Based on the Degree of Automation

Classification schemes based on the degree of automation have been introduced by several researchers [229], [224], [44], [199].

Following these authors, we classify IRSs into three distinct categories on the basis of degree of automation, viz., *manual, semi-automatic*, and *automatic*. These categories can also be differentiated according to the level of participation and expertise of the human analysts or system administrators involved in generating appropriate courses of action based on IDS alerts.

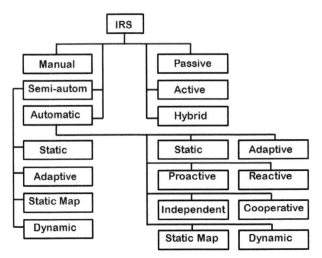

Figure 6.3: A taxonomy of IRSs.

Manual IRS: In a manual IRS, the system administrator or security analyst has a major role to play. It is an IRS with the lowest degree of automation. The system administrator manually decides an appropriate set of response actions from a pre-specified (i.e., already defined) set of responses based on the alert information received from the IDSs. The correctness or relevance of the responses generated by such an IRS mostly depend on (i) the experience of the administrator and (ii) the content in the attack information received from the IDSs.

Semi-automatic IRS: This category of IRSs is situated between manual and automatic IRSs. In other words, the participation of the system administrator in this IRS is more pronounced than in an automatic IRS, but less than in a manual IRS. It generates responses faster than a manual IRS using a decision support process with low involvement of the system administrator. Such IRSs are generally more effective due to (i) easy implementability, (ii) high adaptability, (iii) easy configurability, and (iv) low rate of false alarms.

Automatic IRS: The aim of an automatic IRS is to react immediately on identification of an intrusion using a fast decision-making process, without intervention of a system administrator or human analyst. The decision-making process of this type of IRS should be able to generate responses automatically based on attack information received from the IDS. In contrast to the other two categories of IRSs, an automatic IRS generates responses in a timely fashion, which is highly essential, especially for critical systems. However, with increasing sophistication in attackers' skills, implementation of such automatic IRSs in real life with zero false alarms is challenging.

6.1.2.2 Based on the Approach Used for Triggering Responses

An IRS may also act in an active or passive mode. In an active IRS, the system does not stop after notifying the administration with details of an attack, but also takes necessary action to minimize the damage by a DDoS attack and to prevent such attacks in the near future. In contrast, a passive IRS simply notifies the system administration about the attack.

(a) *Active IRS:* An active IRS is more involved in the defense process. It analyzes the alert information received from the IDSs and may take several response actions to minimize the damage by (i) blocking suspicious source IPs and ports, (ii) restoring the target system, (iii) blocking suspicious incoming / outgoing connections, and (iv) tracing the connection to isolate the attacker.

(b) *Passive IRS:* A passive IRS usually restricts itself to generation of alarms, notification of attack report with information about the victim, criticality of the attack, time of the attack, source IP information, and attack statistics. Depending on the situation, it may also enable (i) additional IDSs, (ii) network activity logging, (iii) trace connection for information gathering, and (iv) intrusion analysis tools.

(c) *Hybrid IRS:* This category of IRSs combines the advantage of both active and passive IRSs. Depending on the situation and the class of attack, such IRSs can act as dynamic IRSs, whereas in some other situations and for some non-critical attack classes, they act like static IRSs. In addition to performing like a static IRS, it also has the abilities of an active IRS such as (i) blocking suspicious ports, IP addresses, or connections, (ii) tracing connections to isolate attackers, and (iii) enabling or disabling additional firewall rules.

Cost-sensitive IRSs are examples of hybrid IRSs. The main goal of such IRSs is to minimize the damage due to attack at low response cost. To estimate response action cost and damage cost, it defines a cost-sensitivity assessment model taking into account a number of factors related to cost and risk. The main purpose of using this model is to balance these two factors. However, it is extremely difficult to estimate these two factors accurately. Such a system activates a passive or an active IRS module depending on how critical the system is. The number and nature of factors to consider to estimate damage and risk depends on the type of system and type of attack being handled. The dynamic module also needs to update the number and nature of cost factors and their values over time, which is a difficult task.

6.1.2.3   Based on Adaptability

IRSs can also be categorized based on their ability to adapt to changing situations. IRSs are referred to as adaptive, if they can update or adapt themselves during an attack. Otherwise, they are non-adaptive or static.

(i) *Non-adaptive or Static IRS:* A non-adaptive or static IRS is usually simple and easy to implement and deploy. However, it requires periodic upgrades by the system administrator based on feedback and past performance. Generally, during an attack period, such IRSs remain static. But if the performance of the IRS is not found to be effective, upgrade through human intervention becomes inevitable. Static IRSs are cost-effective and useful, especially in non-critical systems.

(ii) *Adaptive IRS:* In contrast to a static IRS, an adaptive IRS is able to update or adjust its response during an attack. In an adaptive IRS, adjustments to the system can take place in various ways, as indicated below:

- dynamic allocation or reallocation of resources dedicated to response generation due to augmentation in the IDS and
- recent performance evaluation of both the IDS and the IRS in terms of false alarms generated.

In the recent past, there have been several efforts to develop adaptive IRS. However, developing a generic IRS that can counter a wide range of attacks across multiple scenarios remains a challenge.

6.1.2.4   Based on Promptness in Response Generation

An IRS can act proactively or reactively. It may generate actions only after the attack is confirmed in a reactive IRS. In contrast, in a proactive IRS, the response system attempts to analyze the network behaviorally and tries to predict the occurrence of a DDoS attack probabilistically.

(i) *Proactive IRS:* This category of IRSs aims to ensure minimum damage to the system. It applies probabilistic analysis of network traffic and user–system behavior to estimate the probability of an attack in the near future. Such an IRS is usually strongly coupled with an IDS so that an instant response can be generated by the IRS once an attack is identified by the IDS. However, to foresee an attack based on statistical analysis before it actually takes place is not an easy task. Often, such systems generate a large number of false alarms. In addition, to be able to provide support for timely or real-time response generation without compromising accuracy in attack prediction remains an active area of research.

(ii) *Reactive IRS:* A reactive IRS generates responses only when occurrence of an attack is confirmed. So, such IRSs usually produce delayed responses since they follow a rigorous process to confirm an attack either (i) through a satisfactory matching against a relevant group of signatures with respect to a user threshold or (ii) by achieving a high confidence level based on the confidence matrix of the intrusion detection system. Hence, a reactive IRS often is not effective when systems are critical in nature.

6.1.2.5   Based on the Level of Cooperation

An IRS can generate response actions either independently or in cooperation with other IRSs. So, depending on the approach used by the IRSs to handle intrusion alerts, one can classify them as independent or cooperative.

Independent IRS: An independent IRS handles intrusion alerts independently by generating local response actions tailored to the attack information. For example, alerts received from a host-based intrusion detection system due to anomalies found in a server or host (single machine) may be handled by such an IRS by generating actions such as restarting the system, forcing shut down, and terminating processes.

Cooperative IRSs: Unlike an independent IRS, a cooperative IRS always decides on a set of response actions based on the combined effort of multiple IRSs. Such an IRS gathers feedback from several independent IRSs corresponding to autonomous systems (ASs), which are capable of responding to intrusion alerts locally, and then undertakes a global combination strategy suited to counter the attack. Such cooperative IRSs achieve very high precision and low response time, in comparison to an independent IRS in each individual AS acting alone. However, developing an unbiased combination strategy with proper coordination among a large number of ASs across an enterprise network is often difficult.

6.1.2.6 Based on Versatility in Reacting to Unseen Situations

One can classify IRSs based on their versatility in reacting to both known and unknown attack situations into two categories, viz., non-versatile or static mapping, and dynamic mapping.

(i) *Non-versatile or Static Mapping:* A non-versatile or static mapping IRS can be automatic or semi-automatic. It enumerates and uses a pre-defined set of responses. Response generation maps the alerts received from the IDSs into corresponding pre-defined responses. The alerts received on detection of a DDoS attack may trigger blocking of certain source IPs or may block some incoming packets. If the pre-defined set of response actions is exhaustive and the mapping is accurate, such static mapping IRSs are suitable for most systems. Such IRSs are easy to implement and maintain. However, a common difficulty with this type of IRS is that it offers a limited number of choices of response actions, which can be a serious vulnerability, since intruders can easily predict them. Further, such a system works effectively only when it is known how to raise an alert specific to an attack. Furthermore, a static mapping IRS cannot tune itself to the present state of the network and also cannot dynamically configure the decision table to cope with changes in the network environment.

(ii) *Versatile or Dynamic Mapping:* This category of IRSs is more sophisticated and technically more sound than its static versions,

as discussed above. Such IRSs follow an advanced response selection mechanism using multiple attack metrics such as attack
confidence and attack severity. Based on characteristics of the
attack, such IRSs select an appropriate set of responses that correspond to intrusion alerts in real time. To generate responses in
real time, such an IRS follows a fast rule-based or signature-based
approach. Three important advantages of this approach are: (i)
it is flexible in reconfiguring the rule base dynamically, (ii) it is
flexible in adjusting the attack metrics depending on the situation, and (iii) it can provide attack responses with high precision
and low false alarms. However, it suffers from limitations such as
(i) it is still vulnerable to attackers and (ii) it is costly to update
rules after appropriate conflict resolution.

6.1.3 Some Example Intrusion Response Systems

In this section, we introduce a few popular IRSs from both non-
commercial and commercial categories and discuss their features.

6.1.3.1 Cooperative Intrusion Traceback and Response Ar-
chitecture (CITRA)

CITRA [213] is a cooperative intrusion response system, which was initially developed to provide infrastructure to enable network anomaly
detectors, firewalls, routers, and other network components to work
cooperatively to trace the origin of attack sources as accurately as possible and block them. Later, it was extended to handle bandwidth
depletion attacks. It was enhanced by incorporating a cooperative approach using a network of nodes, each installed with the CITRA software to adapt in response to DDoS attacks. In the enhanced model,
each node in the network registers itself and coordinates with the rest
of the nodes through a dedicated component called the Discovery Coordinator (DC). Once an attack is detected, the nodes in the network use
the network audit data to trace back toward the origin of the attack.
During this traceback operation, it takes temporary action lasting only
2 minutes to minimize damage due to network flooding using traffic
rate limiting. Traffic rate limiting overcomes the difficulties in packet
filtering. Within a 2−minute interval, CITRA comes up with a strategy to handle the attack using the discovery coordinator, following the
attack path, such that the components gather responses according to

the policy adopted to minimize the attack.

CITRA performs well if (i) parameters are appropriately chosen and (ii) bandwidth is adequate for legitimate traffic. For experimental evaluation, the authors created a test-bed using several subnets each with its own router enabled with CITRA. The authors establish that when the system is active, it allows uninterrupted viewing, although with poor quality. CITRA requires only 10 seconds to minimize the damage due to a denial-of-service attack. One can improve performance using more powerful hardware; however, quality is not guaranteed.

6.1.3.2   Distributed Management Architecture for Cooperative Detection and Reaction

Koutepas et al.'s approach [137] for detection and reaction to DDoS attacks is another cooperative IRS. The authors introduce an architecture to detect a DDoS attack and to locate its source using the concept of cooperative domains. These domains internally check whether DDoS attacks originate from within them and if so, generate alerts for other networks which may be affected. The authors use an optimal approach for multicast transmission of alerts to handle increased network congestion from the messages. It uses a minimal spanning-tree-based multicast approach to send messages only once from the source hosts and then replicates them whenever the path along the tree splits.

To determine the probability of an attack internally, there are entities in each domain which observe the alerts coming in from other domains and entities and the reports of local IDSs. These entities work in a cooperative manner and when an entity fails to work, another entity takes over the responsibility. The system checks the number of alerts, and if it exceeds a pre-defined user threshold, it takes appropriate actions following a *reaction table* stored at the entities. The reaction table specifies a set of response actions that can be taken at a certain state.

The claims made by the authors are not supported using experimental evidence. Theoretical analysis shows that unlike traditional traceback mechanisms, the system reacts faster and more efficiently. However, the heavy dependency on the multicast backbone may seriously limit the approach, if the attacker can successfully target this system backbone.

6.1.3.3 EMERALD

Neumann et al.'s [178] Event Monitoring Enabling Responses to Anomalous Live Disturbances (EMERALD) is a dynamic mapping system, enabling monitoring of events and generation of appropriate response actions. EMERALD uses established analytical techniques to primarily support, intrusion detection, and secondarily, automated response generation. Its architecture is highly reusable, interoperable, and scalable to large network infrastructures [8, 31]. Its modular structure and effective tool sets enable timely generation of response actions.

From a structural point of view, EMERALDS's primary entity is the monitor, which has a well-specified interface to receive and send event data and analytical results from third-party security services. A monitor typically interacts with the environment in two modes, viz., (i) in passive mode, by reading network packets or logged activities or (ii) in active mode, by scanning or probing to supplement normal event gathering. It deploys multiple interacting monitors within each administrative domain. The monitors are empowered to analyze a target event stream signature analysis as well as using profile-based statistical analysis for anomaly detection. Further, each monitor includes a countermeasure decision engine, referred to as EMERALD resolver instance, to fuse or aggregate alerts from its associated analysis engines and to invoke response handlers to protect resources from malicious activities. Because of its ability to aggregate alerts received in a distributed environment, EMERALD is an effective intrusion response generator. EMERALD's tiered organization of monitors and coordinated exchange of alert information help achieve timely generation of response actions to minimize damage. Its resolvers can perform the following two major activities.

- Request and receive intrusion reports from other resolvers at lower layers of the analysis hierarchy, enabling the monitoring of and response to malicious activity on a global basis.

- Invoke real-time countermeasures in response to malicious or anomalous activity reports produced by the analysis engines.

With each valid response method, EMERALD includes evaluation metrics to help identify the circumstances following certain criteria for detachment of the method. Typically, two criteria are used.

(i) Confidence of the analysis engine that the attack is real.

(ii) The severity of the attack.

By combining these metrics, the resolver formulates an appropriate response policy for its monitors. The authors claim that EMERALD is effective because of its strong analytical base and tiered organization of monitors in both anomaly detection and timely generation of response actions.

6.1.3.4   CSM

CSM [263] is an effective dynamic mapping system that can (i) detect intrusions in a large network environment, and (ii) select response actions based on computed confidence information about the attack. CSM works in a cooperative manner to detect intrusive behavior based on the feedback of the individual anomaly detection monitors, referred to as Security Managers. These monitors not only observe, but also play other roles in the detection of an attack. CSM does not depend on a centralized component to detect the occurrence of an attack. Whenever a security manager, i.e., a monitor, senses suspicious behavior, it performs anomaly detection for its own users. Once any anomalies are detected, each Security Manager reports it to the connection originating Security Manager for the host. By doing so, an added advantage is that a Security Manager can update itself about the activities as the user travels from one host to another in a distributed environment.

Once an intrusion is detected, a dedicated component, which can be referred to as the intruder-handler (IH), is activated to decide the set of response actions. The decision of the IH mainly depends upon the severity of the attack, as perceived. Initially, the IH simply notifies the occurrence of the attack to the system manager. In subsequent steps, it gradually notifies other trailing security managers for this user. In addition, two other important actions are taken: (i) killing the recent session of the identified intruder, and (ii) blocking the account of the suspected user to gain control. CSM initiates the process of response generation, only when (i) attack evidence is strong and (ii) damage is presumed to be severe, if immediate response action is not taken.

6.1.3.5 Adaptive, Agent-Based IRS (AAIRS)

AAIRS, introduced by [44], is a dynamic mapping agent-based automated IRS. It was introduced by the same research group, that developed CSM. In this system, several IDSs monitor a computer system and if any anomalous behavior or attack is detected, generate intrusion alarms. AAIRS gathers alert information through interface agents and builds a model of false alarms and missed alerts received from the detectors to compute an attack confidence metric. This metric, along with the intrusion statistics sent to a *master analysis* (MA) agent to classify the situation either as an existing incident or as a novel attack using a decision-making process that uses a set of parameters, such as the target application and target port. The decision-making process used in AAIRS is also adopted by another system called ADEPTS [81].

When MA identifies an unseen intrusion, it generates a new analysis agent to handle the intrusion. The agent uses the *response taxonomy* agent to analyze the incident and to generate appropriate abstract response actions. The abstract response actions are forwarded to the *tactics agent* for implementation using a *Response Toolkit*. The tactics agent decomposes the abstract response actions into specific actions and then implements them invoking appropriate components from the Response Toolkit. AAIRS provides response adaptation using three components:

(i) an interface agent, to adapt by modifying the confidence metric associated with each IDS,

(ii) an analysis component, to receive additional incidence reports, which may lead to reclassification of the type of attacker and/or type of attack, and

(iii) a tactics agents, to implement the planned steps using multiple techniques and to adapt by choosing alternate steps, if necessary.

All these components keep track of success metrics on their plans and actions and use the most successful ones in subsequent instances of an attack.

6.1.3.6 ALPHATECH

Armstrong et al. introduce a lightweight autonomous defense system (ADS), called α-LADS [14] using a partially observable Markov decision process (PO-MDP). It is a host-based defense system developed by a company called Alphatech, which was later acquired by BAE systems [14], [15], [139]. α-LADS is a prototype autonomous defense system developed using the PO-MDP stochastic controller. The main focus of this work is to develop and analyze the controller and to evaluate its performance experimentally.

The two main goals of α-LADS at an abstract level are (i) to select a correct set of responses in the face of an attack, and (ii) not to take any actions if any attack has not occurred. α-LADS has a stochastic feedback controller, which receives input from an anomaly sensor, called *CylantSecure*, and attempts to compute the attack occurrence probability for the system. If the probability is high, it invokes actuators to react to the perceived attack. The authors refer to the system as partially observable for two reasons: (i) the alerts generated by the intrusion detecting sensors may be inaccurate or false, and (ii) the response actions taken by the system may not bring back the system to a functional state.

To evaluate the performance of α-LADS, the authors used data from a worm attack on a host and developed a Markov state model for the attack scenario. Two intrusion detector sensors were chosen to receive observations. One sensor was used to monitor activities on the IP port, whereas the other was used to monitor processes operating on the host computer. The authors calibrated both sensors against activities which represent typical usage of a computer system. For validation, the authors used training data generated by combining both stochastic HTTP and FTP accesses in addition to random issuances of commands. From the first experimentation, it was concluded that the prototype ADS built on a feedback controller performs better in the presence of legitimate system activities than a static controller. From the second experiment, it was established that α-LADS was able to respond to unseen attacks as well. In other words, when α-LADS was trained with a worm attack on the FTP server, it was able to counter similar worm attacks. Further, α-LADS could also counter every single instance of unknown attacks.

6.1.3.7   SITAR

The design of this intrusion-tolerant system relies on redundancy [14]. Its major architectural components are proxy servers which help (i) validate both incoming and outgoing network traffic, and (ii) detect failures within and among application servers. SITAR mitigates undesirable effects from successful intrusion attempts using redundant and diverse internal components. It introduces diversity in internal component selection by manually choosing different server codes such as Apache and Internet Information Server for Web servers, and by selecting multiple OSs such as Linux, Solaris, and Microsoft. The main motive behind using multiple servers is that an intruder can mutually compromise only one server at a time with a single intrusion attempt. Detailed architecture of SITAR is given in Section 6.2.1.

6.1.4 Discussion

Following the discussion on intrusion reaction systems, we summarize below.

- An IRS has its own independent existence in most IDSs and is responsible for generating response activities.

- Adaptive and dynamic IRSs are able to counter most types of DDoS attacks and minimize damage to network resources.

- In a proactive IRS, responses are generated prior to occurrence of an attack using probabilistic analysis of network behavior. In contrast, in a reactive IRS, response actions are taken only after confirmation of the attack based on analysis of alert information received from the IDSs.

- Reactive and proactive IRSs can work together to minimize damage to resources from both known and unknown intrusions.

6.2 DDoS Tolerance Approaches and Methods

In a DDoS tolerance system, the defender aims to defend a network and its resources from malicious attacks using a fault-tolerant design approach. Abandoning the conventional aim of preventing all intrusions, intrusion tolerance instead uses mechanisms that prevent intrusions from causing system security failure. Classical fault tolerance techniques can be useful for tolerating intrusion and error detection-and-recovery, or error masking techniques can be applied to maintain data integrity or service availability in spite of intrusions. However, such fault tolerance techniques are usually harmful to data confidentiality due to the redundancy that they imply. Figure 6.4 provides a

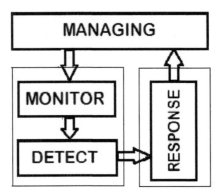

Figure 6.4: Intrusion tolerance system: a generic view.

generic view of an intrusion tolerance system. The managing system, the monitoring component, and the detection component are similar to those in an IDS, but the reaction component uses tolerance techniques. In the reaction component, intrusion tolerance techniques try to prevent intrusions from causing system failure.

A tolerance system aims to provide reliable services and survivability to legitimate users of a network under DDoS attack by limiting the possible damage caused by the attacks. Typically, a tolerance mechanism does not depend on a specific DDoS detection or prevention system, or even may not be aware of occurrence of an attack in a network. Without even distilling the anomalous traffic from legitimate ones, an intrusion tolerance system (ITS) attempts to minimize the damage caused by a DDoS attack.

In designing an intrusion tolerant system, most researchers are guided by three basic principles: (i) *redundancy*, to avoid any single point of failure, (ii) *diversity*, to alleviate common weaknesses using software (e.g., operating systems) of different kinds in the servers, and (iii) *reconfiguration* of the services, components and servers to ensure that services are continually provided only to legitimate users, even in an attack situation.

In the recent past, several novel approaches have been introduced [256], [136], [187], [205], [184], [253], [84] to provide tolerance support to the network community. One can classify these approaches into three broad categories [180]: (i) multi-level IDS-based, (ii) middleware algorithm-based and (iii) recovery-based. In addition to these, researchers have also developed tolerance mechanisms by successful combination of these approaches to provide the best possible tolerance services. Such approaches can be categorized as hybrid approaches. In this chapter, we discuss a few prominent and representative methods from these three categories only.

6.2.1 Multi-Level IDS-Based Approaches

In this approach, ITS developers improve defense capability by incorporating multiple levels of detection to achieve high reliability and survivability. The basic idea behind the design is that only through fast, accurate, and reliable DDoS detection, one can trigger an appropriate recovery mechanism, and hence can ensure continuity of operation.

SITAR [256] is one such architecture, introduced to work with distributed services, especially for commercial off-the-shelf (COTS) servers. The main idea behind the design of SITAR is that *effects* are given more importance than *causes*, because the network or a system must first survive in an attack situation before it can identify whether the cause was an attack or an accidental failure. SITAR relies on both redundancy and diversity. Figure 6.5 shows the conceptual framework of the SITAR service architecture. The basic building blocks shown within the dashed-line box are the major contributions of the authors of SITAR. The block at the bottom in the figure includes the COTS servers. The thin downward directed lines show requests, whereas the thick and dashed upward directed lines represent responses and control, respectively. SITAR uses intrusion vulnerable servers, but is able to provide intrusion-tolerant services. Typically, information flow occurs in such an architecture as follows.

Proxy servers shown at the top are the public access points for the intrusion-tolerant services. The policy enforced by these servers decides which COTS servers (CS) are responsible and how the service is rendered. On behalf of the original request, a new request is generated by the PS (Proxy Server) as shown by the thin downward directed line and submitted to the appropriate COTS server. During this process, relevant BMs (Ballot Monitors) and AMs (Acceptance Monitors) also get involved by message passing. While responses are generated by the CSs (shown by thick upward directed lines), they are initially processed by the AMs after validity check and then forwarded to the BMs with checksum results. The BMs finally decide the response on behalf of the CSs based on majority voting or by a Byzantine agreement process.

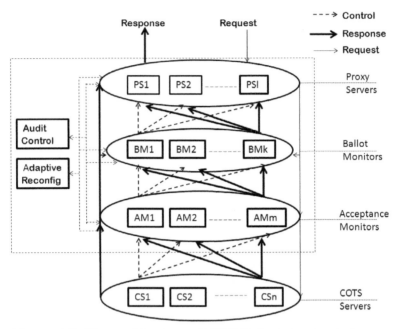

Figure 6.5: The architecture of SITAR for intrusion tolerance.

The AR (Adaptive Reconfiguring) module is responsible for evaluating intrusion threats and cost/performance impact based on trigger information received from all other modules, and it generates new reconfigurations for the system. SITAR also maintains a backup AR to safeguard against a single point of failure, because at any time any of the individual components may be compromised. AC (Audit Control) is responsible for auditing the behavior of the various components of an ITS. A detailed security analysis of SITAR is reported in [255].

SITAR's advantages include its scalability and ability to provide tolerance services by means of redundancy and diversity. It is able to handle unknown attacks and zombies responsible for unpredictable behavior during DDoS attacks using existing intrusion-vulnerable servers. When an attack (external or internal) is detected, SITAR is able to reconfigure compromised servers. However, SITAR has its own limitations. (i) It has high computational complexity, (ii) acceptance tests are specific to applications and require specific configurations, and (iii) adaptive recovery is executed, only when intrusion is detected.

In addition to SITAR, several other significant ITSs have been developed. DPASA (Designing Protection and Adaptation into a Survivability Architecture) [187] is one such system developed by Pal et al. This system, also commonly known as DPASA Survivable JBI, integrates concrete defense mechanisms to prevent, detect, and respond to known and unknown intrusions, that cannot be prevented. DPASA is designed to protect assets and resources using multiple zones and layers to contain external attacks. In this architecture, the innermost zone is the host, which manages security defense. Proxy servers are responsible for intercepting incoming traffic from outer zones. Like SITAR, it also detects intrusions using its own network intrusion detection system (NIDS).

The Willow architecture [136] is another significant proposal that seeks to protect critical applications in a distributed computing environment. The architecture includes components (i) to identify faults due to malicious activities, (ii) to analyze system vulnerabilities, and (iii) to perform reconfiguration, once malicious activities are identified. The reconfiguration component of this architecture performs a key role. For identification of intrusions, it monitors application hosts using distributed intrusion-detection sensors. It is able to sense network states effectively, can analyze changes, and can estimate required changes to the configuration. Like SITAR, the Willow architecture also performs reconfiguration, only when intrusion is detected. The cost of processing in this architecture is high.

An adaptive intrusion-tolerant architecture, referred to as DIT (Dependable Intrusion Tolerance), was introduced by Valdes et al. [250] to provide alert information when intrusions take place. This adaptive architecture is composed of a cluster of mediating proxies and a monitoring system. The cluster is not only able to detect intrusions but also able to identify anomalies using an agreement protocol. Like other IDS-based tolerance methods discussed above, DIT also requires a significant amount of processing to analyze, monitor, and detect intrusions and anomalies.

Similarly, HACQIT (Hierarchical Adaptive Control of Quality of Service for Intrusion Tolerance) is another significant contribution to the area of intrusion tolerance. This intrusion-tolerant service, introduced by Reynolds and Just [205], delivers critical user services allowing performance degradation at most 25%. It tries to minimize redundancies working with other R&D and COTS efforts, and develop new capabilities. HACQIT uses active defenses and diversity in design to augment standard fault-tolerant ability. It alleviates repeatable errors by preventing use of out-of-band control systems, once errors are detected. Depending on the situation and feasibility, it introduces COTS-supplied design diversity (e.g., various operating systems, DBMSs, and server applications) to enhance fault-tolerant abilities. HACQIT's advantages include the following: (i) it can use diversity effectively for intrusion detection, enhancing tolerance, (ii) it is able to prevent repeated attacks from succeeding, for any server on the Internet, and (iii) it can provide recovery from intrusions by continuous on-line repair. However, two common disadvantages of HACQIT are: (i) it requires a significant amount of additional cost in hardware and software, and (ii) it demands high administrative overhead.

ITSI (Intrusion-Tolerant Server Infrastructure), introduced by O'Brien, Smith, Kappel, and Bitzer, [184] is another useful development in intrusion tolerance system design, with its ability to detect intrusions at the network layer. It detects and isolates intrusions, blocks them from spreading freely from one host to another, and continues to provide services to legitimate users. For identification of intrusions, it uses smart NICs and after detection of an intrusion, it helps fast recovery from the intrusion. Like the other systems, ITSI also suffers from the need for additional computing cost and administrative overhead.

6.2.2 Middleware Algorithm-Based Approaches

The systems developed under this category are mostly focused on developing special middleware algorithms such as threshold cryptography, voting algorithms, and fragmentation redundancy scattering (FRS) to harden resilience.

MAFTIA (Malicious and Accidental Fault Tolerance for Internet Applications), introduced by Verissimo [253] is a pioneer middleware algorithm-based approach, suitable for constructing large-scale dependable distributed applications. It is able to handle both accidental and malicious faults. Though it incorporates IDS sensors, it does not focus on building IDS capability. Instead, it relies on authority and transaction management services that are developed on a platform of common services that provide voting algorithms and k-threshold cryptography. The MAFTIA architecture can be viewed in terms of three crucial dimensions, i.e., *hardware*, *local support*, and *distributed software*, as shown in Figure 6.6. The hardware dimension includes the host and network devices comprising the physical system. The local support services are provided by the operating system (OS) and runtime platform

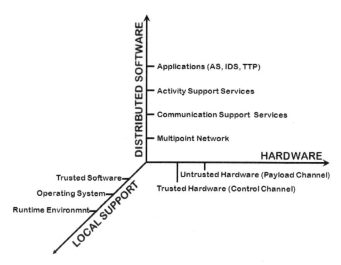

Figure 6.6: Three crucial dimensions of MAFTIA.

within each node, which may vary from host to host. The distributed software provides authorization, intrusion detection, and trusted third parties. The MAFTIA operational framework is shown in Figure 6.7. It is able to provide an effective defense against both known and unknown threats. The MAFTIA technology has now been incorporated into product and service offerings from IBM. However, like all other systems, it introduces additional cost for processing and management overhead.

PASIS (Perpetually Available and Secure Information System [84]) is another significant effort by researchers to provide effective tolerance services. It is designed with two primary goals, to provide for availability and confidentiality. It is a distributed framework for building perpetually available secure systems. The PASIS architecture is based on three fundamental technologies, viz., (i) *decentralized storage systems*, to avoid single point of failure, (ii) *threshold data encoding*, to provide information availability and confidentiality, and (iii) *dynamic self- management*, for automatic and instantaneous data maintenance to achieve reliable and survivable storage. The client-side agents of PASIS establish communication with the storage nodes for reading and writing information. PASIS hides its decentralized nature from the client system. A threshold secret-sharing scheme is used to encode and disperse data in survivable storage systems. The authors believe that to increase intrusion tolerance capability, one must increase the number

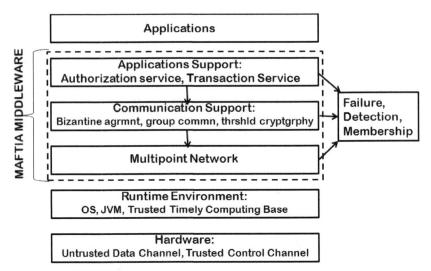

Figure 6.7: MAFTIA: a middleware algorithm-based tolerance architecture.

of replicas and threshold values. The agents responsible for automated monitoring and repairing are helpful in providing self-maintenance features. The three major benefits provided by PASIS are the following. (i) *Confidentiality*: It reveals 0% information if one storage node is compromised and 4.4%, when 3 nodes are compromised. (ii) *Availability*: It ensures that the probability that PASIS cannot serve a read request is extremely low, given that any node fails with a probability 0.001. (iii) *Performance*: It shows performance comparable to conventional systems for reading large objects. The two major limitations of PASIS are that (i) development of PASIS libraries and agent software for relevant client platform is costly, but it is a one-time cost and (ii) processing overhead is high.

OASIS [71], i.e., Organically Assured and Survivable Information System, is another significant addition to developments in ITS. It is a US DARPA program, with a major focus on providing defense capabilities against sophisticated attacks to allow continued operation in the presence of known and future cyber attacks. The three major objectives of the OASIS program are: (i) to develop ITS using potentially vulnerable components, (ii) to analyze and specify the cost benefits of ITSs, and (iii) to provide evaluation and validation support for any ITS. The program has financed 30 intrusion tolerance projects. ITUA (Intrusion Tolerance by Unpredictable Adaptation) [186] is one among these projects. It is a middleware algorithm-based approach that provides effective tolerance service. ITUA is a distributed object framework that adaptively protects applications at the object level using protocols for group communication and cryptography. It is a collection of several mechanisms based on redundancy, Byzantine fault tolerance and adaptive response that supports tolerance of network attacks. A schematic view of the ITUA architecture is shown in Figure 6.8. The architecture enables (i) isolation of compromised resources, (ii) recovery from failure, and (iii) graceful degradation. It provides cryptographic support for authentication and consensus-based message signing. It uses intrusion-tolerant gateways to protect object–object communication. ITUA manages a number of redundant hosts organized in a decentralized manner in the security domain without implicit trust to provide continuous tolerance support against network intrusions.

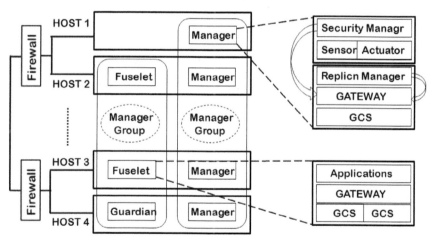

Figure 6.8: ITUA architecture.

6.2.3 Recovery-Based Approaches

Unlike the two previous types of architectures, recovery-based architectures assume that once a system becomes online, it may be compromised at any moment. So, periodic restoration of the system to a good known state is an essential requirement.

Self-Cleansing Intrusion Tolerance (SCIT)[108] is an effective and well-known recoverable intrusion tolerance system that uses a periodic recovery policy and maintains service availability using redundant servers. It is composed of an SCIT controller and several redundant servers, as shown in Figure 6.9. The SCIT server can exist in any of four different states, viz., *active, grace period, cleansing period,* and *live spare period.* In the *active* state, the server is online and accepts requests from the outer world. When the server is in the *grace* period, it does not communicate with the outer world and only processes tasks for requests that were received during the active period. In the *cleansing* period, the server is offline and it recovers system configuration files, service files, and so on. Finally, the server waits to be active in the *live spare* period.

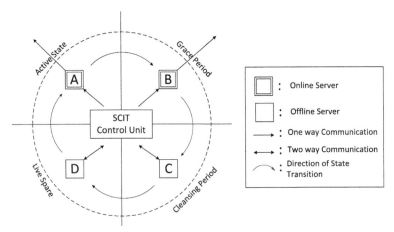

Figure 6.9: SCIT architecture.

The group of identical servers employed by SCIT may have some diversity. It applies round-robin cleansing among this group of servers to restore the system to its pristine image. The SCIT model has several significant advantages. It is applicable to any open server on the Internet, such as Web and Domain Name System servers. The architecture is simple and does not rely on intrusion detection. The core component of SCIT is its controller. The responsibility of the controller is to manage server rotation in and out of cleansing mode. The controller algorithm managing the server rotation takes into account the group cardinality, a server's cleansing-cycle time, and the number of required online servers. The implementation of this algorithm is based on virtualization technology. It assumes that the interfaces between the controller and the group of servers to be protected are trusted.

Huang et al. develop several remediation mechanisms [109], [106], [107], [105], [104] based on the Self-Cleansing Intrusion Tolerance (SCIT) architecture, to counter a wide range of unknown attacks. Typically, in an SCIT-based mechanism, multiple servers are configured to provide various services such as Web services, email services, or DNS services. The SCIT cluster architecture permits an individual server to perform different roles at different points of time without compromising the quality of service that the cluster is supposed to provide. Within the SCIT framework, a server always begins its lifecycle with the cleansing role and then gradually proceeds with one or more online service roles. As we cannot expect an individual online server to remain online for an infinite period of time, such cleansing operations are performed periodically. It minimizes the opportunities an attacker gets to exploit any vulnerabilities in a server by limiting the maximum duration a server is exposed online. In addition, due to periodic cleansing, it limits the possibility that attackers are able to set up a foothold to be exploited later to launch future attacks. In [107], [105], the authors introduce an initial hardware enhancement for an SCIT-based DNS system. Similarly, in [104], the authors introduce a cluster-wide self-cleansing intrusion tolerance management approach.

However, the operations and mechanisms of SCIT could also be compromised by unknown attacks, and hence the cleansing operation and role rotation may also be disrupted. It is definitely possible in case of software implementation of the SCIT mechanism. To overcome, the authors introduce a hardware-based generic SCIT framework, referred to as SCIT/HES [16]. The two main motivations behind the design of the hardware SCIT mechanism are the following. (i) Considering the growing complexities and newer vulnerabilities that continually arise, a software implementation can be potentially corrupted through communications. (ii) Online servers cannot be expected to be online indefinitely; they can be corrupted at any point of time, since all possible vulnerabilities are not known. SCIT/HES is a scalable hardware framework that attempts to alleviate the shortcomings of the software components in SCIT and to enforce and guarantee the six security primitives of SCIT. These are given below.

(i) The servers are reset and cleansed periodically.

(ii) Files, which are critical for successful server operation, are loaded only from read-only and secure devices.

(iii) The initial transition of a server is from the clean (ready) state to the assigned online service role.

(iv) Execution of critical security operations takes place only during the offline clean state.

(v) Online servers are isolated from internal network and trusted storage.

(vi) Secure controllers are isolated.

In addition to the above, SCIT/HES also addresses three other important issues viz., *scalability, generality,* and *removal of a single point of failure.* A schematic view of SCIT/HES high-level architecture is shown in Figure 6.10. In this figure, for simplicity, the detailed interactions between the central controller and a particular server X is shown. A similar setup is applicable for other servers in the SCIT cluster. The authors also show that their hardware architecture not only guarantees security properties but also is economical and easy to administer.

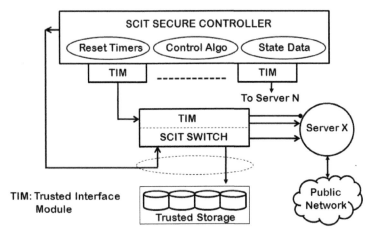

Figure 6.10: SCIT/HES architecture for a single server X.

In addition to the SCIT-based family of recovery-based architectures, several other significant efforts have also been made by researchers. Aung et al. [18] introduce a cluster recovery model with a software *rejuvenation* methodology with two approaches, i.e., a stochastic approach and a Markov decision process approach. The model's analysis is effective in deciding which vulnerable application component processes lead to longevity flaws and to choose them for rejuvenation. The authors consider the service daemon processes as better candidates, as these processes are expected to run forever. Rejuvenation is a cost-effective approach, and it ensures high availability of services, provided analysis and tuning of its parameters are properly carried out. However, proper estimations of the mean time between failures, vulnerable component processes, base longevity interval, survivability, downtime cost due to scheduled rejuvenation and unexpected failures, and availability, are extremely difficult and costly tasks.

Another significant tolerance service provided under this category is FOREVER (Fault/intrusiOn REmoVal through Evolution & Recovery) [190]. The main objective of this service is to eliminate faults and intrusions by effective use of evolution and recovery techniques. The service is able to enhance the resilience of the replicated systems, which may be affected by malicious attacks. To guarantee availability, FOREVER coordinates the recovery of different replicas. For this coordination, it requires three distinct services: (i) *perfect failure detection* to detect whether the application replicas are alive or not, (ii) *clock synchronization* to ensure that the recovery time schedule for each replica is precise, and (iii) *total order multicast* to update the same recovery schedule on every FOREVER monitor without compromising the availability of the intrusion-tolerant application. For effective implementation of these services, a major requirement is that the wormhole subsystem be synchronized. FOREVER is known for another important feature, the introduction of diversity after a successful recovery operation is over. In other words, a recovered system is made different from its previous form or incarnation. However, generation of diversified forms after successful recoveries must be done carefully. An appropriate tradeoff to achieve enhanced resilience is another major issue with FOREVER.

In addition to the above three distinct categories of tolerant support services, several other significant efforts have been made by researchers in the past few years to provide best possible tolerance services. *Fireflies*, introduced by Johansen et al. [124] is one such effort. Fireflies is a scalable protocol that supports intrusion-tolerant network overlays. A network overlay provides the necessary routing functionality such as multicast routing, content-based routing, and resilient routing, which are not supported by the Internet directly. Members considered by Fireflies are in three states: *correct, stopped,* and *Byzantine*. Fireflies allows members identified as *correct* to execute protocols such as *Gossip* and *Ping*, whereas *Byzantine* members are not within the jurisdiction of the protocol. *Stopped* members are not allowed to execute the protocol. Gossip is a simple group communication protocol where each member picks a random member from its view and exchanges state information. Pinging is used by a member to detect failures of other members. Both correct and Byzantine members are also categorized as "live", and they can switch between states at any point in time. To support intrusion-tolerant network overlays, the Fireflies protocol depends on three sub-protocols: (i) an *adaptation pinging* protocol that makes the probability of a wrong failure detection independent of message loss, (ii) an intrusion-tolerant *gossip* protocol that helps communication among the correct members within a probabilistic time bound, and (iii) a *membership* protocol, responsible for implementation of membership details by using accusations and rebuttals provided by Fireflies. This protocol provides its correct members with a membership view of all the members found correct over a long period, and at the same time eliminate all members found stopped for a long duration.

6.2.4   Discussion

Based on the discussion on the design and analysis of various intrusion tolerance systems in this chapter, we make the following observations.

- An ITS provides reliable services and survivability to legitimate users of a network under DDoS attack by minimizing the damage caused by the attacks.

- Three basic principles that guide ITS developers are (i) redundancy, which helps avoid any single point of failure, (ii) diversity, to overcome common weaknesses of different types of servers, and (iii) reconfiguration, to ensure that services are provided only to legitimate users during an attack.

- Intrusion-tolerant systems can be categorized into three distinct types, viz., multi-level IDS-based, middleware algorithm-based, and recovery-based.

- Designers of multi-level ITSs improve defense capability by incorporating multiple levels of detection mechanism to achieve high reliability and survivability. In contrast, in a middleware algorithm-based ITS, developers mostly focus on developing special middleware to harden resilience. However, in a recovery-based ITS, developers assume that an online system can be compromised at any moment, hence, periodic restoration of the system to a good state is absolutely necessary.

6.3 Chapter Summary

We end the discussion on intrusion reaction and tolerance, and systems that support these goals, by making the following summary observations.

- Unlike passive IRSs, an active IRS analyzes alert information received from IDSs and takes response actions to minimize the damage that can be caused by attacks.

- In contrast to static IRS, an adaptive IRS can update or adjust response selection during an attack period itself.

- Proactive IRSs analyze network traffic and user-system behavior using probabilistic approaches and aim to ensure minimum damage to systems. However, though the response actions generated by reactive IRSs are mostly accurate, they are slow and hence not suitable for critical systems.

- Static mapping IRSs are suitable for most systems if the set of response actions is exhaustive and the mapping mechanism is accurate.

- Dynamic mapping IRSs are flexible and can handle changing network configurations.

- An IRS should be able to handle unpredictable attack scenarios, in addition to known ones.

- Existing intrusion-tolerant systems can be classified into three distinct categories, i.e., multi-level IDS-based, middleware algorithm-based, and recovery-based.

- *Multi-level IDS-based* ITS designers assume that only through fast, accurate, and reliable DDoS detection, one can trigger an appropriate recovery mechanism, and hence can ensure continuity of operation.

- Designers of *middleware algorithm-based* ITSs develop special middleware algorithms such as threshold cryptography, voting algorithms, and fragmentation redundancy scattering (FRS) to harden resilience.

- A *recovery-based* ITS designer assumes that an exposed system can be compromised at any moment. So, periodic restoration of the system to a known good state is absolutely necessary.

- Most ITSs have been designed to provide continued services in the presence of both known and unknown adversaries. But, they are able to do so only with significantly high (i) computing cost and (ii) administrative and management overhead.

- Although in the recent past, a good number of intrusion-tolerant systems under various categories have been proposed, an efficient ITS that addresses the following two issues properly, is still yet to be built.

  (a) Providing IDS-based, real-time, intrusion-tolerant services with low administrative and management overhead to obviate the necessity of a separate NIDS for DDoS detection.

  (b) Developing an ITS with low additional computing cost that allows continuity of operation in any known or unknown adverse situation.

Chapter 7

Tools and Systems

7.1 Introduction

With continuing growth in the number of network users, the number of malicious network activities also keeps on increasing. As a consequence of security threats posed by such malicious activities, network systems are often compromised. Network attacks attempt to bypass security mechanisms of a target network by exploiting its vulnerabilities. An attacker usually attempts to disrupt a network system or a server by launching various types of attacks using attack tools. Today, one can easily download a sophisticated attack tool such as LOIC [196] or HOIC from the Web, and can disrupt a network system using such a tool.

At the receiving end, for smooth administration of a network of systems, the administrators also require tools to monitor and analyze network traffic so that they are prepared to defend their networks. To build a proper line of defense, network engineers or administrators must have a good understanding of the psychology and behavior of the attackers.

A network security tool is usually developed with multiple objectives in mind, such as attack generation, packet or flow capture, network traffic monitoring and analysis, and visualization of traffic behavior. With increased sophistication and complexity of attacks, constant vigilance and sophistication have become absolutely necessary. In this chapter, we provide a comprehensive and structured presentation of a number of network security tools, along with salient features, the purposes for which they were designed, and their effectiveness in the context of what they were designed for. We also give a glimpse of how one can develop one's own tool to launch DDoS attacks of various types as well as to monitor and analyze network traffic.

If we analyze the intentions or motives of an attacker based on observed attack patterns or behaviors, we see six distinct classes of attackers in general. The first class of attackers, whom we call ordinary attackers, is comprised of individuals who discover that there are tools available on the Web to generate attacks, become curious, and experiment with them and execute such tools causing attacks without pre-meditated malice. There is another class of individuals who may be knowledgeable about systems as well as attacks, and their intention may be simply to create nuisance in the network to annoy or vex people they dislike or for fun. On the other hand, there is a third class of dangerous hackers who attack a network intentionally for profit. This class of attackers attacks networks to capture or sniff important and useful information. A fourth class of attackers are those who attack a network to degrade network performance or to challenge the security system to express political views. A fifth class of attackers consists simply of terrorists intent on causing maximum harm. Finally, governments across the world have become involved in cyberattacks and cyber-espionage causing large-scale intrusions in government and corporate networks in enemy or even friendly countries.

To launch an attack successfully, the attacker must be aware of weaknesses or vulnerabilities in the target network. The weaknesses can be assessed by scanning the network in an information gathering step. Once the vulnerability information has been gathered, the attacker attempts to exploit identified weakness(es) of the security system for successful launch of an attack. In recent times, a large number of attack launching tools and systems to generate network attacks have become available in the public domain. One can use these tools to launch an attack on any of the network layers in the TCP/IP network model; however, most target network and transport layers.

In the recent past, a large number of highly sophisticated attacks have evolved making the task of defending networks burdensome. However, an appropriate use of tools and systems can simplify the task significantly. This necessitates a good understanding of the characteristics and capabilities of these tools and systems, and how they are used. This chapter presents a large number of tools in three major categories: (a) information gathering tools, (b) attack launching tools, and (c) capture, visualization, and monitoring tools. The lack of a consistent description of attack-related tools has often made it difficult to understand the network security literature. Therefore, before we describe the tools, we introduce a taxonomy of relevant network security tools.

7.2 Types of Network Security Tools

As discussed in the previous section, attackers generally target Websites or databases or organizational networks by first gathering information on their weaknesses. Attackers choose appropriate tools for the class of attack they desire to launch and based on the weaknesses discovered at the target site or networks already assessed, they make use of the tool(s). Based on the features they possess, purposes for which they are designed and used, we classify existing tools as shown in Figure 7.1. Sub-categories are introduced under each basic category considering differentiating characteristics within a class of tools. In the next few sections, we introduce some well-known tools that are useful to an attacker and discuss each briefly. We also present comparisons among the tools by category to provide readers with a better overall understanding.

7.2.1 Information Gathering Tools

The first step an attacker takes before launching an attack is to understand the environment where the attack is to be launched. To do so, attackers initially gather information about the network such as the number of machines, types of machines, operating systems, versions of various software systems, and so forth. Once relevant information is gathered, attackers try to assess weaknesses in the target Website or network using various tools. In this section, we discuss information gathering tools [101], [206] under two major categories, i.e., sniffing tools and network mapping and scanning tools.

7.2.1.1 Sniffing Tools

An efficient sniffing tool is capable of capturing, examining, analyzing, and visualizing packets or frames traversing the network. Such a tool also helps extraction of additional packet features for subsequent analysis. Most sniffing tools also help understand the underlying protocols

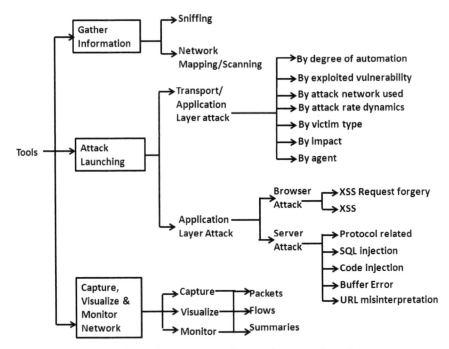

Figure 7.1: Taxonomy of attack-related tools.

and accordingly, include protocol parameters during visualization. We list some popular packet sniffing tools and briefly describe them.

(a) *Tcpdump*: This is a premier packet analyzer for security professionals. It enables the analyst to capture, save, and view packet data. This tool also can be used by a third-party software such as *Wireshark*.

(b) *Ethereal*: This is a multi-platform sniffer and traffic analyzer. This tool includes two libraries: (i) *GTK+*, a GUI-based library and (ii) *libpcap*, a packet capture and filtering library. Ethereal is capable of reading *tcpdump* output and can apply tcpdump filters to select and display records conditionally. It allows decoding of a large number (≥ 400) of protocols. Further, this tool is useful in identifying and inspecting a network attack.

(c) *Net2pcap*: This is a simple tool to transform packet traffic into a pcap file. It does not use any library during the transform. Further, it is partially dependent on *libc*, a Linux library utility. The command % *tcpdump -w capfile* almost does the same thing as

Net2Cap. Finally, it can capture and help analyze traffic in a hostile environment.

(d) *Snoop*: This is a Linux tool almost similar to *tcpdump*. However, its file format differs from the *pcap* format, and is defined in RFC 1761. Its provision of writing to an intermediate file avoids packet loss. Further, it allows one to filter, read, and interpret packet data. To observe traffic between two systems, say X and Y, we simply need to write % *snoop* X, Y.

(e) *Snort*: This is a lightweight, yet powerful misuse detection tool. Snort is flexible and runs on multiple platforms. To capture traffic and to detect misuse, one simply needs to pick up the appropriate commands.

(f) *Angst*: This is a Linux and OpenBSD-based active packet sniffer. It allows one to capture data by injecting data into switched networks. *Angst* is able to flood a network using random MAC addresses, by causing switches to transmit packets toward all ports.

(g) *Ngrep*: This provides a filtering facility on payloads of packets. This tool has the sniffing functionality of tcpdump. It uses the libpcap library.

(h) *Ettercap*: This is an effective sniffer that supports multiple platforms. *Ettercap* can also be used as an active hacking tool. It uses an *ncurses* interface, and is able to decode several protocols. Further, this tool can collect passwords in multiple situations, such as when killing connections and injecting packets or commands into live connections.

(i) *Dsniff*: This is a collection of tools that enable active sniffing on a network. This tool can perform man-in-the-middle attacks against SSHv1 and HTTPS sessions. Further, it is capable of sniffing switched networks by actively injecting data into the network.

(j) *Cain & Able*: This is a multipurpose sniffer that runs on Windows NT, 2000, and XP. It allows for password recovery for a number of protocols. One can also launch man-in-the-middle attacks for SSHv1 traffic using this tool.

(k) *Aimsniff*: This is a simple tool to capture the IP address of an AOL Instant Messenger user. Once the connection is established successfully, it is able to capture the IP address easily.

(l) *Tcptrace*: This is a very effective and powerful tcpdump file analyzer that can generate connection-specific information. This tool is capable of accepting input files generated by several capture tools. Further, it supports graphical presentation of traffic characteristics for analysis.

(m) *Tcptrack*: This tool can sniff and display TCP connection information. *Tcptrack* can watch passively for connections on the network interface and can keep track of their state and display a list of connections. It displays source IP, source port, destination IP, destination port, connection state, idle time, and bandwidth usage.

(n) *Nstreams*: This is a visualizer and analyzer for network streams generated by users between several networks, and between networks and the outside. This tool can optionally output the *ipchains* or *ipfw rules*. It parses the outputs generated by tcpdump or tcpdump with the *-w* option.

(o) *Argus*: This tool runs on several operating systems and can process either live packet data or captured traffic files. *Argus* can output status reports on flows detected in a stream of packets. It also obtains information on almost all packet parameters such as reachability, availability, connectivity, duration, rate, load, loss, and jitter.

(p) *Karpski*: This is a user-friendly tool, with limited sniffing and scanning capabilities. It can include protocol definitions dynamically. This tool can also serve as an attack launching tool against addresses on a local network.

(q) *IPgrab*: This tool supports network debugging at the data link, network, and transport layers. It is able to provide detailed header field information for all network layers.

(r) *Nast*: This can sniff packets in normal or promiscuous mode for analysis. It uses *libnet* and *libpcap* for sniffing. *Nast* captures and stores header and payload information in ASCII/ASCII-hex format.

(s) *Aldebaran*: This is an advanced libpcap-based TCP sniffing and filtering tool. This tool provides partial header information without flag details. It also monitors data sent by connections to sniff passwords. It uses libpcap rules to sniff packet headers and payload contents and can transmit captured data to another host via UDP. In addition, it can encrypt, analyze, and report the desired packet statistics.

(t) *ScoopLM*: This is a Windows-based sniffer to capture LM and NTLM authentication information. Such captured information can later be used by a tool like *BeatLM* to crack authentication data.

(u) *Gulp*: This is a robust tool that can capture and store voluminous network traffic from the network firehose. It overcomes the packet loss problem of tcpdump by using multiple CPUs during capture. It writes data as a *pcap* file.

(v) *Nfsen*: This tool is used to capture network flow data and to display the data graphically. It can visualize protocol specific flows in a graphical format.

(w) *Nfdump*: This tool enables one to collect and process *Netflow* data. It can read *Netflow* data and can organize them based on time. It is capable of analyzing a single file or several concatenated files for a single run. The tool generates output in either ASCII text or binary form.

In Table 7.1, we summarize these commonly used sniffing tools with important features along with the sources from which they can be downloaded.

From the above discussion, it is perhaps transparent that different sniffing tools are designed with different purposes in mind. So a network defender or an attacker must judge the importance and effectiveness of a tool based on his/her requirements and relevance to the task at hand. To clarify, let us consider a few example cases. Cain & Able is capable of password cracking, but is not suitable for capturing live network traffic. Similarly, one can use tcpdump and libpcap for capturing all information in a packet and to store it in a file. On the other hand, we cannot use *Nfsen* or *Nfdump* for packet traffic capture, but they are effective in flow traffic capture and analysis. Similarly, *Gulp* is very useful for packet traffic capture, but not for Netflow capturing.

Table 7.1: Some sniffing tools and their features.

Tool name	Protocols	Features	Sources
Ethereal	TCP/HTTP /SMTP	Powerful packet capture; provides user-friendly interface.	www.ethereal.com.
Tcpdump	TCP/UDP /ICMP	Powerful packet capture; less intrusive than Ethereal.	www.tcpdump.org
Net2pcap	TCP/UDP /ICMP	A Linux-based packet capture tool; it is also auditable.	www.secdev.org
Snoop	TCP/UDP/ ICMP/Telnet /FTP	A robust packet capture tool; no packet loss; supports >12 options.	www.softpanorama.org
Snort	TCP/UDP /ICMP	A Linux- and Windows-based lightweight, yet robust tool.	www.snort.org
Angst	HTTP/POP	An aggressive Linux-based sniffer; easy to use.	www.angst.sourceforge.net
Ngrep	TCP/UDP /ICMP	A Linux and Windows-based packet capture tool; can handle large data.	www.ngrep.sourceforge.net
Ettercap	TCP/UDP	An effective Linux and Windows-based sniffer; can be used for man-in-middle attack.	www.ettercap.sourceforge.net
Dsniff	FTP/Telnet/ HTTP/POP/ SMTP	A Unix-based password sniffer.	www.naughty.monkey.org
Cain & Able		A Windows NT/XP-based password recovery tool.	www.oxid.it
Aimsniff	TCP/HTTP /UDP	A Linux-based packet capture tool.	www.sourceforge.net
Tcptrace	TCP	A commonly used Linux-based TCP packet traffic analyzer.	www.tcptrace.org/
Tcptrack	TCP	A Linux-based TCP connection analyzer.	www.rhythm.cx
Nstream		A Linux and Windows-based traffic analyzer.	www.hsc.fr/cvs.nessus.org
Argus	TCP/UDP	A Linux and Windows-based audit data analyzer.	www.qosient.com/argus/
Karpski	TCP/UDP	A Linux-based packet analyzer.	www.softlist.net
IPgrab		A Linux-based packet analyzer.	www.ipgrab.sourceforge.net/
Nast	TCP/UDP	A Linux-based traffic analyzer.	www.nast.berlios.de
Gulp	TCP/UDP /ICMP	A Linux-based packet capture tool; supports visualization.	staff.washington.edu/corey
Libpcap	TCP/UDP /ICMP	A Linux and Windows-based packet capture tool.	www.tcpdump.org
Nfsen	TCP/UDP	An effective Linux-based flow capture tool; supports user-friendly visualization of net flow data.	www.nfsen.sourceforge.net
Nfdump	TCP/UDP	A Linux-based flow capture tool; an effective traffic analyzer.	www.nfdump.sourceforge.net

7.2.1.2 Network Mapping/Scanning Tools

Network scanning or mapping activities are useful to both network defenders and attackers. Using a network scanning tool, one can identify active hosts on a network. Based on scanned information, an attacker can assess vulnerabilities in the target Website or network and subsequently can attack them. An efficient scanning tool supports four types of port scans: (i) one-to-one, (ii) one-to-many, (iii) many-to-one, and (iv) many-to-many as shown in Figure 7.2. Such a tool provides an overall status report regarding network hosts, ports, IP addresses, etc. We present some commonly used scanning tools, their features, and sources in the rest of the section.

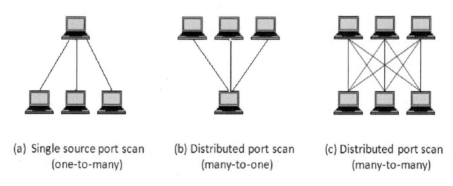

(a) Single source port scan   (b) Distributed port scan   (c) Distributed port scan
       (one-to-many)   (many-to-one)   (many-to-many)

Figure 7.2: Types of port scans.

(a) *Nmap*: Nmap facilitates network exploration and security auditing. Nmap is capable of scanning large networks fast, especially from single hosts. It uses raw IP packets and can effectively identify a large number of useful parameters such as available hosts, services offered by the hosts, OSs running, and use of packet filters or firewalls. Nmap is not only useful in scanning and gathering useful network parameters, but also helpful for network administrators in security audits and other routine tasks such as maintaining network inventory, managing service upgrade schedules, and monitoring host or service uptime.

(b) *Amap*: This tool can identify applications running on a specific port by sending trigger packets, which typically leads to an application protocol handshake. It is capable of detecting an application protocol, without depending on the TCP or UDP ports to which it is bound. In general, network daemons respond to the correct handshake (e.g., SSL) only. Amap considers the responses and attempts to find matches. It supports TCP and UDP protocols, regular and SSL-enabled ASCII and binary protocols, and supports a wide range of options to control its behavior.

(c) *Vmap*: This version of the mapper tool enables one to identify the version of a daemon by fingerprinting its characteristics, based on its responses to bogus commands.

(d) *Unicornscan*: This is an asynchronous scanner as well as a payload sender. This scalable and flexible tool collects information quickly. For fast response, it uses a distributed TCP/IP stack and provides a user-friendly interface to introduce a stimulus into a TCP/IP-enabled device or network and measure the response. The main features of this tool include asynchronous protocol-specific UDP scanning, asynchronous stateless TCP scanning with wide variations in TCP flags, and asynchronous stateless TCP banner grabbing.

(e) *Ttlscan*: Ttlscan sends TCP SYN packets to each port of the host using *libnet* and *libpcap* utilities to identify a host. It sniffs the response from the host and uses it to identify hosts with services by forwarding packets to another host behind a firewall. It reads specific header parameters such as TTL, window size, and IPID to identify the OS and its various versions running on a host behind the firewall.

(f) *Ike-scan*: This tool is able to discover, fingerprint, and test IPSec VPN servers based on the IKE protocol. Ike-scan works in Linux, Unix, Mac OS, and Windows environments under the GPL license.

(g) *Paketto*: This set of tools is useful to assist in manipulating TCP/IP networks based on non-traditional strategies. They can provide tapping functionality within the existing infrastructure and also extend protocols beyond their original intention. Example tools include (i) *Scanrand*, which facilitates fast discovery of network services and topologies, (ii) *Minewt*, which serves as user space for a NAT/MAT router, (iii) *Linkcat*, which offers a Ethernet link to stdio, (iv)*Paratrace*, which helps trace network paths without spawning new connections, and (v) *Phentropy*, which uses *Open-*

QVIS to render arbitrary amounts of entropy from data sources in 3-D phase space.

In Table 7.2, we show the basic features of the tools discussed in this section and the sources from which they can be obtained. Almost all these tools are Linux based.

Table 7.2: Some scanning tools and their features.

Tool's name	Protocol	Features	Sources
Nmap	TCP/UDP	A Linux and Windows-based scanning tool; provides several options.	www.insecure.org
Amap	TCP/UDP	A Linux and Windows-based scanning tool.	www.freeworld.thc.org
Vmap	TCP/UDP	A Unix-based version mapping tool.	www.tools.l0t3k.net
Unicornscan	TCP/UDP	A Linux and Unix-based scanning tool.	www.unicornscan.org
Ttlscan	TCP	A Linux-based effective scanning tool.	www.freebsd.org
Ike-scan	TCP/UDP	A Linux and Unix-based scanning and host discovery tool.	www.stearns.org
Paketto	TCP	A Linux-based scanning tool	www.packages.com

From our experience, we feel that for scanning a large network, Nmap is the best choice. This tool not only provides several options for scanning a large network, but also has the ability to determine identities of active hosts and ports, host operating systems, protocols, timing and performance, firewall evaluation, and spoofing. It is a popular multi-functional tool with most network administrators. Although Amap and Vmap are similar tools, they do not support most functions of Nmap. Most DDoS attackers use Namp to find vulnerabilities of a host to compromise it for constructing botnets during attack generation using the agent handler architecture.

7.2.2   Attack Launching Tools

During the past decade, a large number of attack launching tools have come into existence with various levels of sophistication, and have been made available on the Web. One can easily download these tools and can use them for malicious activities. Some example tools can be used for Trojan propagation, probe attack, buffer overflow attacks,

DoS/DDoS attacks, and application layer attacks. Some DDoS attack tools are very effective in disrupting the services of a network or a Website instantly. Some tools are used in wired networks to capture and exploit valuable information while others are used in wireless networks. We discuss these tools under three main categories, viz., Trojans, transport and network layer attack tools, and finally, application layer attack tools.

7.2.2.1   Trojans

A Trojan is a malicious file whose executables are powerful enough to break the security system of a computer or a network. Generally, when a user attempts to open the file, the Trojan is executed and damaging action is performed. The four possible sources from which victims usually download a Trojan are (i) the Internet, (ii) an FTP archive, (iii) via peer-to-peer file exchange using IRC, and (iv) Internet messaging. Typically, Trojans are of seven distinct types. We introduce each type with examples.

(a) *Remote Access Trojans*: This type of malware program uses back doors to control a target machine with administrative privilege. One can download this type of Trojan invisibly with a user request for a game program or an email attachment. Once the attacker compromises a machine, the Trojan uses this machine to compromise more machines to construct a botnet for launching a DoS or DDoS attack. An example of this type of Trojan is *Danger*.

(b) *Sending Trojans*: This type of Trojan is very dangerous and can silently provide confidential data about the victim to the attacker. It attempts to install a keylogger to capture and transmit sensitive information such as passwords, credit card information, log files, email addresses, and IM contact lists to the attacker based on recorded keystrokes. Examples of this type of Trojan are *Bad-trans.B email virus* and *Eblast*.

(c) *Destructive Trojans*: This is another dangerous Trojan type and is often programmed to infect a computer by automatically deleting some essential executable programs, configuration, and DLL (dynamic link library) files. Such a Trojan acts either (i) as per the instructions of a back-end server, or (ii) based on pre-installed or pre-programmed instructions, to strike on a specific day and at a specific time. Two examples of this type are *Bugbear virus* and *Goner worm*.

(d) *Proxy Trojans*: This Trojan type attempts to use a victim computer as a proxy server. It compromises a computer and attempts to perform malicious activities such as fraudulent credit card transactions and launching of malicious attacks against other networks. Examples of proxy Trojans are *TrojanProxy:Win32* and *Paramo.F.*

(e) *FTP Trojans*: This type of Trojan attempts to open port 21 and establish a connection from the victim computer to the attacker using File Transfer Protocol (FTP). An example of an FTP Trojan is *FTP99cmp*.

(f) *Security Software Disable Trojans*: These Trojans can destroy defense or protection mechanisms such as antivirus programs or firewalls. Typically, an attack mastermind combines such a Trojan with another type of Trojan as a payload. Two common examples are *Trojan.Win32.KillAV.ctp* and *Trojan.Win32.Disable.b.*

(g) *DoS Trojans*: This is another type of dangerous Trojan that attempts to flood a network instantly with useless traffic so that it cannot provide any service. Some examples of this category of Trojan are *Ping-of-death* and *Teardrop*.

7.2.2.2   Transport and Network Layer Denial-of-Service Attacks

Denial of service is a common class of attacks. This class of attacks is caused by an explicit attempt by an intruder to prevent or block legitimate users of a service from using desired resources. Some common examples of this class of attacks are *SYN Flooding, Smurf, Fraggle, Jolt, Land,* and *Ping-of-death*. Such an attack may occur in both centralized as well as in a distributed setting.

Denial of service in a distributed setting, also referred to as *Distributed Denial-of-Service* (DDoS) attack, is a coordinated attempt on the availability of services of a victim system or a group of systems or on network resources, launched directly or indirectly from a large number of compromised machines on the Internet. Typically, a DDoS attacker adopts two approaches: (i) $m:1$, i.e., many compromised machines attack a single victim machine, or (ii) $m:n$, i.e., many compromised

Table 7.3: Types of trojans.

Trojan	Features of Trojan Types	Examples
Remote Access	A malware program; uses back doors to control the target machine with administrative privilege; downloadable invisibly with a user request for a program (game or an email attachment); uses a compromised machine to compromise more machines to create a botnet for DoS /DDoS attack.	*Danger*
Sending	Captures and provides sensitive information such as passwords, credit card information, log files, email addresses, and IM contact lists to the attacker; attempts to install a keylogger to capture and transmit all recorded keystrokes to the attacker.	*Eblast*
Destructive	Very destructive for a computer; can be programmed to delete automatically some essential executable programs, configuration and DLL (dynamic link library) files to infect a computer; can act based on the instructions of a back-end server; also can act based on pre-installed or programmed instructions, to strike on a specific day, at a specific time.	*Bugbear virus*
Proxy	Attempts to use a victims computer as a proxy server; compromises a computer and attempts to perform malicious activities such as fraudulent credit card transactions; can launch malicious attacks against other networks.	*Paramo.F*
FTP	Attempts to open port 21 for file transfer; establishes a connection from the victim computer to the attacker using the File Transfer Protocol (FTP).	*FTP99cmp*
Security software Disable	Attempts to destroy or to thwart defense mechanisms or protection programs such as antivirus programs or firewalls; can be combined with another type of Trojan as a payload.	*trojan.Win32. Disable.b*
DoS	Floods a network instantly with useless traffic so that it cannot provide any service.	*Teardrop*

machines attack many victim machines, making it very difficult to detect or prevent. A DDoS attacker normally initiates such a coordinated attack using either an architecture based on agent handlers or Internet Relay Chat (IRC). The attacking hosts are usually personal computers with broadband connections to the Internet. These computers are compromised by viruses or Trojan programs called *bots*. These compromised computers are usually referred to as *zombies*. The actions of these zombies are controlled by remote perpetrators often through (i) *botnet commands* and (ii) a control channel such as IRC.

Generally, a DDoS attack can be launched using any one of seven distinct ways. (i) *By degree of automation*, where the attack-generation phases such as recruit, exploit, infect, and use are performed in three possible ways, i.e., manually, automatically, and semi-automatically. (ii) *By exploited vulnerability*, where the attacker exploits the vulnerability of a security system to deny the services provided by that system. A semantic attack exploits a specific feature or implementation bug of some protocols or applications installed in the victim machine to overload the resources used by that machine. An example of such attacks is the TCP SYN attack. (iii) *By attack network used*, where an attacker uses either an agent handler network or IRC network to launch a DDoS attack. (iv) *By attack rate dynamics*, where the attacker varies the attack rate depending on the number of agents used to generate the DDoS attack. Depending on the fluctuations used, such attacks can be increasing rate, constant rate, fluctuating rate, and subgroup attacks. (v) *By victim type*, where the attackers attempt to paralyze different types of victims. Victims may be of four types: application attack, host attack, network attack, and infrastructure attack. (vi) *By impact*, where an attack is characterized based on the impact it has created. It can be either disruptive or degrading. (vii) Finally, *by agent*, where an attacker launches DDoS attacks using a constant agent set or a variable agent set.

Many DoS and DDoS attack-generation tools have been developed and made publicly available. Some of those tools and their features are presented next.

(a) *Jolt*: This tool attacks a target machine running Windows 95 or NT by sending a large number of fragmented ICMP packets in such a manner that the target machine fails to reassemble them for use, and as a consequence, it freezes up and cannot accept any input from the keyboard or mouse. The damage caused by this tool is not very serious and one can recover from this attack with a simple reboot.

(b) *Bubonic*: This tool attacks a Windows 2000 machine by randomly sending a large number of TCP packets with random settings. As a consequence, the load in the target machine significantly increases and the machine fails to accept any input, and finally it crashes.

(c) *Targa*: This tool comprises 16 different DoS attack programs. One can launch these attacks individually as well as in a group and can damage a target machine or a network instantly.

(d) *Blast20*: This TCP service stress tool is able to quickly identify potential weaknesses in the network servers. An example use of this tool is shown below.
   % blast targetIP port start_ size end_size /b (i.e., begin text) "GET/SOME TEXT" /e (i.e. end text) "URL"
   The command is used to send attack packets of size minimum *start_size* bytes to maximum *end_size* bytes on a server address at the specified target IP.

(e) *Crazy Pinger*: This tool launches an attack by sending a large number of ICMP packets to a victim machine or to a large remote network.

(f) *UDPFlood*: This tool can flood a specific IP address at a specific port instantly with UDP packets. The flooding rate, maximum duration and maximum number of packets can be specified when launching this tool. It can also be used for testing the performance of a server.

(g) *FSMax*: This is a server stress testing tool. To test a server in evaluating buffer overflows that may be exploited during an attack, it accepts a text file as input and using the input, a sequence of tests is conducted on a server to assess the ability of the server.

(h) *Nemsey*: The presence of this tool implies that a computer is insecure, and is infected with malicious software. It attempts to launch an attack with an attacker-specified number of packets of attack-specific sizes including information such as protocol and port.

(i) *Panther*: This UDP-based DoS attack tool can flood a specified IP at a specified port instantly.

(j) *Slowloris*: This tool creates a large number of connections to a target victim Web server by sending partial requests, and attempts to hold them open for a long duration. As a consequence, the victim servers maintain these connections as open, consuming their maximum concurrent connection pool, which eventually compels them to deny additional legitimate connection attempts from clients.

(k) *BlackEnergy*: This Web-based DDoS attack tool, which is an HTTP-based botnet, uses IRC-based command and control.

(l) *HOIC*: This is a very effective DDoS tool that focuses on creating high-speed multi-threaded HTTP flooding. It can simultaneously flood up to 256 Websites. The built-in scripting system in this tool allows the attacker to deploy boosters, which are scripts designed to thwart DDoS countermeasures.

(m) *Trinoo*: Trinoo uses a master host and several broadcast hosts to launch a DDoS attack. It issues commands using a TCP connection to the master host, and the master instructs the broadcast hosts via UDP, to flood a specific target host IP address at random ports with UDP packets. To launch an attack using this tool, an attacker should have prior access to the host to install a Trinoo master or broadcast server, either bypassing or by compromising the existing security system.

(n) *Shaft*: This is a variant of Trinoo that provides statistics on TCP, UDP, and ICMP flood attacks. This helps the attackers identify the victim machine's status (e.g., completely down or alive), or to decide termination of zombie additions to the attack.

(o) *Knight*: This IRC-based tool can launch multiple DDoS attacks for a SYN attack, UDP flood, and urgent pointer flood on Windows machines.

(p) *Kaiten*: This is an IRC-based attack tool, capable of launching multiple attacks, such as UDP and TCP flood, SYN attacks, and PUSH+SYN attacks. It uses randomized source addresses.

(q) *RefRef*: RefRef exploits SQL injection vulnerabilities by using features included in MySql SELECT permissions to create a denial-of-service attack on the associated SQL server. It works with a Perl translator and attempts to exhaust server resources by sending malformed SQL queries carrying payloads.

(r) *LOIC*: This is a very effective DDoS attack tool that works via IRC. It supports multiple protocols and operates in three modes of attack: TCP, UDP, and HTTP. LOIC creates a large number of threads to launch an attack and it exists in two versions: binary and Web-based.

(s) *Hgod*: This Windows XP-based tool can be used to spoof source IP addresses, and specify protocol and port numbers during an attack.

By default, it is used for TCP SYN flooding. An example use of this tool against 192.168.10.10 on port 80 with a spoofed address of 192.168.10.9, is shown below.

%hgod 192.168.10.10 80 -s 192.168.10.9

(t) *TFN*: TFN, a variant of Trinoo, is another effective DDoS attack launching tool. It is composed of a client host and several daemon hosts. TFN can launch ICMP flood, UDP flood, SYN flood, and Smurf attacks. TFN2K is a variant of TFN, which includes some special features such as encryption and decryption, and the ability to launch stealth attacks to crash a specified target host using DoS attacks and to communicate shell commands to daemons.

(u) *Stacheldrath*: This is a hybridization of TFN and Trinoo. It includes some additional features such as encrypted transmission between components and automatic updating of daemons.

Out of a large and increasing pool of DoS/DDoS attack tools, we have discussed only a select few. Most tools are freely available on the Internet and are powerful enough to crash networks and Websites. However, among these, LOIC and HOIC are very effective in launching a DDoS attack within a short duration of time. LOIC is capable of generating attack packets involving TCP, UDP, and HTTP protocols, whereas HOIC supports only the HTTP protocol. Although TFN, Trinoo, and Stachaldraht are effective in launching DDoS attacks, these tools require substantial customization to use on an experimental testbed. Further, they are not as powerful as LOIC. However, it must be noted that use of these tools to launch an attack in a public network is unethical and a crime.

7.2.2.3   Application Layer Attack Tools

Application layer DDoS attacks are usually low-rate DDoS attacks and they are more subtle than the transport or network layer attacks since they use legitimate protocols and legitimate connections. Hence, detection of application layer attacks is more difficult. An application layer attack tool generally uses legitimate HTTP requests from legitimately connected network machines to overwhelm a Web server [271]. The attack itself may be a session flooding attack, a request flooding attack, or an asymmetric attack [201, 276]. We discuss four basic types of application layer attacks.

Table 7.4: Some attacking tools.

Tool's name	Platform	Protocol	Sources
Jolt	Windows	ICMP	http://www.flylib.com/books/ en/ 3.500.1.136/1/
Burbonic	Linux/Windows	TCP	http://www. packetstormsecurity.org/
Targa	Linux	TCP/UDP/ICMP	http://www. packetstormsecurity.org/
Blas20	Linux/Windows	TCP	
Crazy Pinger	Linux/Windows	ICMP	http://www.softwaretopic. informer.com
UDPFlood	Windows	UDP	http://www.foundstone.com
FSMax	Windows		http://www.brothersoft.com
Nemsey	Windows	TCP	http://packetstormsecurity.org/
Panther	Windows	UDP	http://www. bestspywarescanner.net
Slowloris	Windows	HTTP	http://www.ha.ckers.org/ slowloris/
Blackenergy	Linux/Windows	TCP/UDP/ICMP	http://www.airdemon. net
HOIC	Windows/Linux	HTTP	https://www.rapidshare.com
Shaft	Linux/Windows	TCP/UDP/ICMP	
Knight	Windows	TCP/UDP	http://www.cert.org
Kaiten	Windows	TCP/UDP	http://www.mcafee.com
RefRef	Windows		http://www.hackingalert.net/ 2011/10/ completeguideto-refrefdostool.html
Hgod	Windows	TCP/UDP/ICMP	http://www.flylib.com/books/ en/ 3.500.1.136/1/
LOIC	Linux/Windows	TCP/UDP/ICMP	http://www.sourceforge.net
Trinoo	Linux/Windows	UDP	http://www.nanog.org
TFN	Linux/Windows	TCP/UDP/ICMP	http://www.codeforge.com
TFN2K	Linux/Windows	TCP/UDP/ICMP	http://www.goitworld.com
Stachaldraht	Linux/Windows	TCP	http://www. packetstormsecurity.org
Mstream	Linux/Windows	TCP	http://www.ks.uiuc.edu/ Research/namd/ doxygen/MStream_ 8Csource.html
Trinity	Linux/Windows	TCP/UDP	http://www.garykessler. net/library/ ddos.html

(a) *HTTP-related attacks*: In this type of application layer attack, the attacker sends a massive number of HTTP requests to overwhelm the target site in a very short period of time. Some well-known tools of this type are *Code Red Worm* and its mutations, *Nimda Worm* and its mutations, and *AppDDoS*.

(b) *SMTP-related attacks*: In this attack, the attacker uses the SMTP protocol to transmit email over the Internet. The attacker attempts to flood a mail server using the Simple Mail Transfer Protocol. Some commonly used attack tools of this category are SMTP Mail Flooding, SMTP worms and their mutations, Extended Relay attacks, and Firewall Traversal attacks.

(c) *FTP-related attacks*: In this attack, the attacker establishes a legitimate FTP connection with the victim and then sends attack packets to it. Examples include FTP bounce attacks, FTP port injection attacks, passive FTP attacks, and TCP segmentation attacks.

(d) *SNMP-related attacks*: This class of attacks aims to change the configuration of a system and then monitor the state or availability of the system. Examples of this category of attacks include SNMP flooding attacks, default community attacks, and SNMP put attacks.

7.2.2.4   Additional Attack Tools

In addition to the large number of tools reported above, there are plenty of others that have direct or indirect use in attack launching or defending. In this section, we discuss a few more tools that will further help improve awareness of students and security researchers.

(a) *Ping*: This pioneering tool helps check the connectivity status of a computer or a router on the Internet. It performs a simple task by sending a ping request to a particular host to test its connectivity or reachability on an IP network. In reply, it displays the response of the destination and how long it takes to receive a reply. Ping uses the ICMP protocol, which has low priority and slower speed than regular network traffic.

(b) *Hping2*: This is a variant of Ping with additional features. It sends custom TCP/IP packets to a target and displays reply messages received from the target. It handles fragmentation and arbitrary packet size and can also be used to transfer files. Hping2 is capable of testing firewall rules, port scanning, testing-protocol-based network performance, and path MTU discovery.

(c) *Hping3*: It is an effective variant of Hping2. It can handle fragmentation and arbitrary packet size like Hping2. Hping3 can also find the sequence numbers of reply packets from the source port. It starts with a base source port number and increases this number for each packet sent. The base source port number is random. The source port number may also be kept constant for each sent packet.

(d) *Traceroute*: Traceroute is useful in finding the route between two systems in a network. This tool can show all intermediate routers from the source end to the destination end. Using this tool, one determines how systems are connected to each other or how IPs connect to the Internet to provide services. The traceroute program is available on most computers including most Unix systems, Mac OS, and Windows 95.

(e) *Tctrace*: This is almost similar to traceroute, although it uses TCP SYN packets to trace. Tctrace enables one to trace through firewalls if one knows a TCP service that is allowed to pass from the outside.

(f) *Tcptraceroute*: Tcptraceroute is another effective tool to find the path that a packet traverses to reach the destination. It sends either UDP or ICMP ECHO request packets using a TTL field that is incremented on each hop until the destination is reached. A difficulty with this tool is that widespread firewall usage may filter Tcptraceroute packets, as a result of which, it may not be able to complete the path to the destination.

(g) *Traceproto*: Traceproto is another variant of Traceroute, which allows the user to choose the protocols to be traced. It normally allows one to trace TCP, UDP, and ICMP protocols. One can also use this tool to test and bypass firewalls, packet filters, and check if ports are open. Traceproto is also referred to as a traceroute substitute written in C.

(h) *Fping*: Fping is a powerful tool to determine whether a host is active or not. It uses the ICMP protocol and can scan any number of hosts or a file containing a list of hosts. Unlike other similar tools, after trying one host, Fping does not wait until it times out or replies; rather it sends out a ping packet and moves on to the next host in a round-robin fashion. Once a host replies, it is

noted and removed from the list of hosts to check. If a host does
not respond within a certain time limit and/or retry limit, Fping
considers it unreachable. Fping is used in scripts and its output
can be easily parsed.

(i) *Arping*: This is a Unix tool to test whether an IP address is in use
or not. It performs the task by sending ARP request messages to
a destination host in a LAN.

Table 7.5: Additional relevant tools.

Tool Name	Protocol	Features	Sources
Ping	ICMP	A Linux and Windows-based user-friendly host discovery tool with.	www.download.cnet.com
Hping2	TCP/UDP/ ICMP	A Linux-based port scanner; supports several options.	www.hping.org.
Hping3	TCP/UDP/ ICMP	A Linux-based port scanner; powerful for network testing.	www.hping.org.
Traceroute	TCP/UDP/ ICMP	A Linux, Solaris and Windows-based user-friendly route discovery tool.	www.brothersoft.com
Tctrace	TCP	A Linux-based user-friendly route discovery tool.	www.tcptrace.org/
Tcptraceroute	TCP	A Linux and Solaris-based DNS lookup tool; very effective in route discovery.	www.michael.toren.net/
Traceproto	TCP/UDP/ ICMP	A Linux route discovery tool; effective in firewall testing.	www.traceproto.sourceforge. net
Fping	ICMP	A Linux and Windows-based target host discovery tool. more effective than ping.	www.softpedia.com
Arping	ARP	A Linux-based tool to send ARP request.	www.linux.softpedia.com

7.2.3   Network Monitoring Tools

Monitoring network traffic is an essential activity for network administrators who want to observe, analyze, and identify anomalies occurring
in the network. To support such activities of the network administrator
and to assist in meaningful interpretation of the outcomes of their analysis, network monitoring and analysis tools have an important role to
play. Widespread malicious attempts to compromise the confidentiality, integrity, and access control mechanisms of a system or to prevent
legitimate users of a service from accessing requested resources, have

led to an increased demand for useful tools to visualize network traffic in a meaningful manner to support subsequent analysis. We introduce some tools in two distinct categories, *visualization* and *analysis*.

7.2.3.1 Visualization and Analysis Tools

An effective network traffic (both packet traffic and network flow) visualization tool can be of significant help to the network administrator in monitoring and analysis tasks. Appropriate visualization not only supports meaningful interpretation of analysis results, but also assists the system administrator in identifying anomalous patterns. It also helps in taking appropriate action to mitigate attacks before they propagate and infect other parts of the network. Some visualization tools are presented below.

(a) *Tnv*: This is a time-based traffic visualization tool that discovers packet details and links among local and remote hosts. Tnv assists in learning normal patterns in a network, investigating packet details, and network troubleshooting. It is able to provide multiple services such as (i) opening and reading libpcap files, (ii) capturing live packets, and (iii) saving captured data in a MYSQL database.

(b) *Network Traffic Monitor*: This tool supports scanning and presentation of detailed traffic scenarios from the inception of an application. It allows analysis of traffic details.

(c) *Rumint*: This Windows-based tool allows one to visualize live captured traffic as well as saved *pcap* traffic data.

(d) *EtherApe*: EtherApe is a Unix tool that allows one to sniff live packet data and to monitor captured data in the Unix environment.

(e) *NetGrok*: This is an effective real-time network monitoring tool that creates a graphical layout and a tree map to support visual organization of the network data. It supports capture of live packets and trace, and assists in filtering activities.

(f) *NetViewer*: This is an effective visualization tool that not only allows observation of captured live traffic data in aggregate, but also helps identify network anomalies. NetViewer also supports visualization of useful traffic characteristics to support tuning of defense mechanisms.

(g) *VizNet*: This monitoring tool helps visualize the performance of a network based on bandwidth utilization.

We have presented here a few visualization tools, most of which also support analysis of network traffic. Not all tools are useful for all kinds

Table 7.6: Some visualization tools and their features.

Tool's name	Protocol	Features	Sources
Tnv	TCP/UDP/ ICMP	-A Linux and Windows-based traffic visualizer; -supported by all OSes.	www.tnv.sourceforge.net
Traffic Monitor 1.02	TCP/UDP/ ICMP	-A Windows-based live traffic monitoring tool; -user-friendly display.	www.monitor-network-traffic.winsite.com
Rumint	TCP/UDP/ ICMP/IGMP	-A Windows-based live traffic visualizer; -flexible and user-friendly.	www.rumint.org
EtherApe	TCP	-A Linux and Unix-based flow visualizer; -simple but powerful.	www.brothersoft.com
Netgrok	TCP/UDP/ ICMP	-A Windows-based real-time traffic visualizer; -user-friendly and supports multiple platforms.	www.softpedia.com
Netviewer	TCP/UDP	-A Windows-based traffic analyzer; -can be used for defense.	www.brothersoft.com
VizNet	TCP/UDP	-A Windows-based traffic analyzer and visualizer.	www.viznet.ac.uk

of monitoring and analysis tasks. EtherApe in Unix or NetViewer in Windows are two useful visualization tools. However, for real-time visualization of live traffic for intrusion detection, NetViewer is the best choice due to its additional ability to detect anomalous traffic. A network administrator requires support for real-time visualization of live traffic as well as for identification of abnormal behavior of network traffic and subsequent generation of alert messages to inform the administrator.

7.3   Observations

In the preceding sections, we have discussed several tools, their salient features, purposes for which they were designed, and sources from

Table 7.7: Category-wise information for some important tools.

Category	Tool Name	Effectiveness	Source
Trojans	NukeNabbler	Malicious executables;	community.norton.com
	AIMSpy	Breaks security of	www.securitystronghold.com
	NetSpy	systems or networks.	www.netspy-trojan-horse.downloads
Information Gathering Tools	ASS	Gathers network info.	www.manpages.ubuntu.com
	NMap	Assesses weaknesses of	www.nmap.org
	p0f	systems or networks.	www.lcamtuf.coredump.cx/p0f.shtml
	MingSweeper		www.hoobie.net/mingsweeper
	THC Amap		www.freeworld.thc.org/thc-amap
	Angry IP Scanner		www.angryziber.com/w/Download
DoS attack tools	Targa	Prevents legitimate users from accessing resources.	www.security-science.com/ www.softpedia.com
	Burbonic		
	Blast20	Coordinated attempts are more devastating.	seomagz.com/2010/03/dos-denial- of-service-attack-tools-ethical-hacking-session-3/
Spoofing attack tools	Engage Packet Builder		www.engage-packet-builder.software. informer.com/
	Hping	Allows attackers to sniff, receive, craft, and	www.hping.org
	Nemesis	inject varieties of	www.nemesis.sourceforge.net
	PacketExcalibur	packets.	www.linux.softpedia.com
	Scapy		www.softpedia.com
Spoofing Attack Tools in Wireless	libpcap	Robust packet sniffer.	www.sourceforge.net/projects/ libpcap
	Kismet	Can capture and store	www.linux.die.ne
	libnet	packet information fast.	www.libnet.sourceforge.net
	libdnet		www.libdnet.sourceforge.net/
	libradiate		www.packetfactory.net/projects/libradiate
App Lyr Attack Tools	HOIC	Attempts to flood the	www.rapidshare.com
	LOIC	Webserver by sending	www.softpedia.com
	RefRef	valid HTTP requests.	www.softpedia.com

which they can be obtained under three main categories, i.e., information gathering, attack launching and capture, and visualization and monitoring. It is clear from the discussion that a network defender or an attacker cannot expect to get all the desired features in a single tool. So, for both a network defender as well as an attacker, an appropriate selection of tools is highly essential. This requires an adequate knowledge of the pros and cons of each tool. To acquire appropriate hands-on experience, we suggest that the user assess the abilities of the tools of interest practically on a testbed. A testbed will also help in the design and development of suitable security tools. To provide practical guidance, we discuss a step-by-step procedure for developing a multi-purpose network security tool in the next section. Our tool, referred to as TUCANNON+, provides support for information gathering, DDoS attack launching as well as for visualization of live attack and normal traffic. TUCANNON+ is able to launch all types of DDoS attacks using a large number of threads.

7.4   TUCANNON+: DDoS Attack-Generation and Monitoring Tool

DDoS attack tools, such as Trinoo [60], TFN [60], TFN2k [60], and others, are easily downloadable from the Internet. However, these tools need substantial customization to generate a coordinated DDoS attack in a testbed environment. We believe that to develop good defense solutions as part of network security research, one has to develop one's own testbed and DDoS attack-generation and network monitoring tools. In this section, we discuss the development of an experimental prototype of a DDoS attack-generation and monitoring tool, referred to as TUCANNON+, which supports not only generation of DDoS attacks of various types but also provides a facility to visualize the captured traffic patterns for analysis. TUCANNON+ is composed of two modules: (i) an attacker's module, which is installed in the attacker's network, and (ii) a defender's module, which is installed in the victim's network. A simplified TUIDS testbed for implementation and validation of the experimental prototype is shown in Figure 7.3.

The TUIDS testbed was developed in the Network Security laboratory of Tezpur University. It includes multiple networks and the hosts are divided into several VLANs. Each VLAN is attached to an L3 switch or an L2 switch inside the testbed. One can attack from both

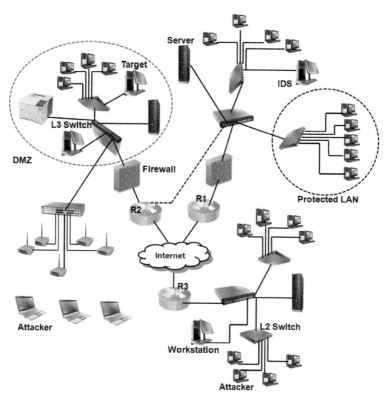

Figure 7.3: TUIDS testbed architecture with DMZ for TUCANNON+.

wired or wireless networks (may be with reflectors), but the victim or target is inside the network (shown in dotted oval). The attackers can use the TUCANNON+ tool to launch attack traffic of all types, such as constant-rate, increasing-rate, pulsing-rate, and subgroup attacks including all the three protocols, i.e., TCP, UDP, and ICMP.

The attack module within TUCANNON+, which comprises two sub-modules, the *Server* sub-module and the *Client* sub-module, can be operated from any node specified as the attacker in the testbed, whereas the monitoring module of TUCANNON+ includes four sub-modules, viz., capture/read, packet and flow traffic organizer, statistics generator, and visualizer, can be operated in the victim's network (shown in dotted oval) to observe packet traffic for analysis. Below, we discuss the development of these two modules of the experimental prototype testbed.

7.4.1   TUCannon: Attack-Generation Module

The attack module, viz., TUCannon in TUCANNON+ adopts the direct DDoS attack strategy depicted in Figure 7.4. It can generate DDoS attack types such as the constant-rate attack, increasing-rate attack, pulsing attack, and subgroup attack, as defined in [170]. The two sub-modules of TUCannon are described next.

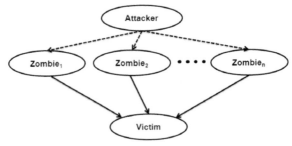

Figure 7.4: Direct attack strategy adopted by TUCannon.

(i) The first sub-module, referred to as the *server module*, is used by the attacker to establish communication and to send instructions to the bots. This module uses a graphical user interface to easily specify parameters such as protocol type, attack pattern type, and number of threads.

(ii) The other sub-module, referred to as the *client* module, is a program that is executed in each bot or compromised machine. This module is responsible for accepting commands from the server module and launching the attack accordingly.

Now we discuss the logic structure of each of these sub-modules in detail.

7.4.2   Server Sub-module of TUCannon

Based on the protocol used, we classify the attack types as follows.

(a) *TCP floods*: A stream of packets with various flags (SYN, RST, ACK) are sent to the victim machine. TCP SYN flood works by exhausting the TCP connection queue of the host, denying legitimate connection requests. TCP ACK floods can cause disruption at the nodes corresponding to the host addresses of the floods as well. TFN [60] is a popular DDoS tool for this type of attack.

(b) *ICMP floods (e.g., ping floods)*: A stream of ICMP packets is sent to the victim host. A variant of the ICMP flood attack is the Smurf attack, in which a spoofed IP packet consisting of an ICMP ECHO_REQUEST is sent to a directed broadcast address. TFN [60] is able to launch this DDoS attack type also.

(c) *UDP floods*: A huge number of UDP packets are sent to the victim host. Trinoo [60] is a popular DDoS tool that uses UDP floods as one of its attack payloads.

The server sub-module communicates with the machines that are configured as bots in the testbed. This server program is developed with a user interface through which one can easily specify and control different properties of the attack traffic. Such properties are the protocol type (TCP, UDP and ICMP), the attack pattern (constant-rate attack, increasing-rate attack, and pulsing attack) and the type of source IP (actual IP of the machine or randomly generated valid but spoofed IP address), the number of threads (where each thread executes one copy of the slave program inside a single bot machine), and the range of ports of the victim to send the traffic. After the master starts, it waits for slaves to connect to it. Figure 7.5 is a snapshot of the GUI of the server sub-module. We discuss the various components of the interface next.

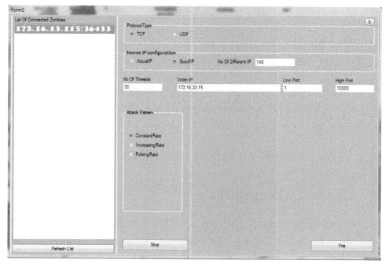

Figure 7.5: GUI of TUCannon server sub-module.

(a) *List of zombies:* After the attacker starts the server program, it waits for the client programs to connect to it. As soon as a client program connects to the server, the client's IP address is shown on the left side panel of the interface as shown in Figure 7.5.

(b) *Protocol type:* To launch an attack, the attacker selects the type of protocol by selecting one of the radio buttons.

(c) *Source IP configuration:* These options are used to specify whether the attack packet carries the actual source IP address or a spoofed one. For spoofed source IP addresses, the attacker can also specify the number of different unique spoofed IP addresses used in the attack. This option allows the attacker to spread the required attack traffic over a specified number of source IP addresses.

(d) *Number of threads:* The number of machines in our testbed is very limited. Hence, to increase the amount of traffic, each client program sends traffic using multiple threads. The number of threads used by each client can be specified by the attacker through this input. This feature is used by the attacker to control the traffic rate in the attack.

(e) *Victim IP:* This input field is used by the attacker to specify the IP address of the victim machine.

(f) *Low port and high port:* The attacker can specify the range of ports to which traffic is sent via these inputs.

(g) *Attack pattern:* As mentioned earlier there can be four different traffic patterns. The attacker can select a pattern from this list.

(h) *Fire:* When the attacker clicks this button, the attack command and the specified input are sent to all clients currently connected to the server.

(i) *Stop:* The attacker can stop the attack by clicking this button.

7.4.3 Client Sub-module

This sub-module is responsible for sending the attack traffic as specified by the commands sent from the master. When the client sub-module starts, it connects to the server whose IP address is specified as input to the client program. Once connection is established with the server, it waits for commands from the server. On receipt of commands, the client module takes actions accordingly.

7.4.4 Scalability of TUCannon

TUCannon is able to generate attack traffic ranging from 50,000 traces with all possible attack patterns, viz., increasing rate, pulsing rate, constant rate, and subgroup attack.

7.4.5 Speed of TUCannon

TUCannon is able to generate a full (i.e., 95–100%) attack within a very short time due to its efficient logic structure. In the above testbed, it can generate a full bursty attack within a second.

7.4.6 Reflector Attack

TUCannon is also able to launch indirect or reflector attacks. In a reflector attack, the attacker instructs the zombies to send attack traffic to a set of innocent machines with the source IP address spoofed as the victim's IP address. When an innocent machine receives these spoofed requests, it sends a reply to the source IP address carried by the request packet. As a result, the victim receives a huge number of response messages, which may exhaust the victim's resources. A typical indirect attack is shown in Figure 7.6. To perform an indirect attack, the user

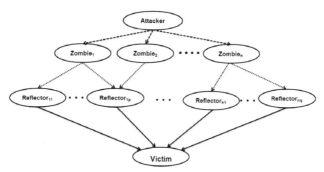

Figure 7.6: Reflector attack.

interface of TUCannon allows the attacker to send a list of innocent IP addresses to the zombies. The zombies then use these innocent servers as reflectors to perform an indirect attack.

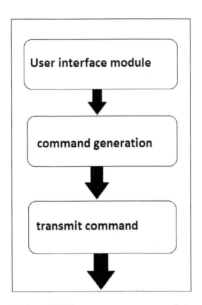

Figure 7.7: TUCannon server architecture.

7.5 TUCannon Architecture

In this section we discuss the design of TUCannon. As mentioned, TUCannon comprises of two different sub-modules, server and client. The architectures of these two components is shown in Figure 7.7 and Figure 7.8, respectively.

We use a modular structure for both components so that any further enhancements can be performed to accommodate new features with the least modification of the corresponding module.

7.5.1 Server Architecture

The server component of TUCannon consists of three modules as shown in Figure 7.7. The *user interface module* is responsible for providing the user with a sophisticated but easy-to-understand user interface from which the user can specify attack parameters such as the protocol, number of threads, source IP type, destination port range, victim address, and attack pattern (constant, pulsing, increasing, and subgroup). The user can also specify the attack mode as direct or indirect. In case of an indirect attack, the user is provided with a user interface to transmit the IP addresses of the reflectors to the zombies.

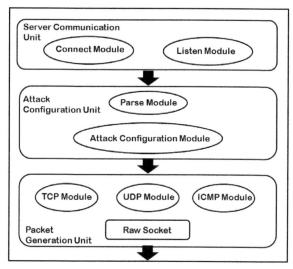

Figure 7.8: Client architecture of TUCannon.

The *command-generation module* extracts the input specified by the user and generates a command string that is recognizable by the client (i.e., a zombie). Once the command is constructed based on the user specification, the *transmit module* transmits the command to the list of zombies connected to the server.

7.5.2 Client Architecture

The modular architecture of the client component is shown in Figure 7.8. The client program consists of three units, the *server communication unit*, the *attack configuration unit*, and the *packet-generation unit*. The server communication unit consists of two modules. The *connect module* is responsible for connecting to the server at a fixed port as soon as the client program is started. After connection establishment, the *listen module* takes control and waits for commands from the server.

When the listen module receives a command from the server, it is passed to the *attack configuration unit*. The attack configuration unit consists of a *parser* and a *configuration* module. The *parser* module parses the received command to extract the user-specified parameters. The configuration module then configures parameters of the zombie such as the protocol, the number of threads, the source and destination IP addresses of the attack packets, and the number of threads to generate packets. After configuration of the parameters, packets are

generated accordingly by activating a *TCP, UDP,* or *ICMP module*
based on the protocol specified by the user. The generated packets are
then injected into the network using a raw socket.

7.6   TUMonitor

TUMonitor is a GUI-based packet and flow traffic monitoring tool,
which allows one to observe a set of selected features such as packet
count per interval, protocol-specific packets per interval, TCP flag specific packets per interval, and the number of unique source IP addresses
within a given interval of time. TUMonitor can also accept arithmetic
expressions involving a subset of the features as input to monitor a specific network traffic pattern. For example, a user of this tool might be
interested in observing the percentage of SYN packets over all TCP-
specific packets; this percentage can vary widely under a TCP SYN
flooding attack with a very high probability. The tool is also useful for
a student or researcher to understand traffic under different conditions.
Certainly, TUMonitor is not an IDS; however, a network administrator
can use this tool to keep an eye on the traffic passing through the monitoring point. For example, the network administrator can monitor the
difference between the number of SYN and (FIN+RST) packets. As
suggested by [257], a sudden hike in the value of the above-mentioned
observed traffic attribute could be a strong sign of a TCP SYN flooding DDoS attack. Similarly, a drastic increase in the fraction of ICMP
or UDP traffic may also raise suspicion or the sudden increase in the
number of unique source IP addresses might be a point of concern for
the network administrator.

7.6.1   TUMonitor: An Overview

TUMonitor provides support to a network administrator or a network
security researcher not only in observing traffic patterns in a network,
but also aids in network defense building. It allows the user to capture
and read both packet and flow traffic. It is also able to organize, gather,
and visualize network traffic statistics using user-specified traffic features. We discuss the support provided by TUMonitor below.

(a) *Selection of Capture Type:* TUMonitor provides options to either
    listen to live network traffic or to open already existing captured
    traffic traces stored in a particular directory. It allows capturing

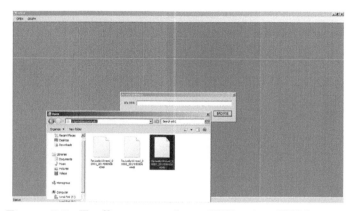

Figure 7.9: Traffic capture from NIC using TUMonitor.

of packets as well as extraction of flow information using a selected subset of features. In its beginning screen, it allows the user to select any of these options. For flow information, one can extract it from the router or from the stored packet information.

(b) *Selection of Traffic Source:* After selecting the capture type, the user is asked to specify either the available network interfaces or the path of the directory from which captured traffic traces can be read, based on the selection made by the user. In both cases, TUMonitor will support visualizing the input packets for a given interval of time, as a graph to the user. Two sample screen shots for these two features are shown in Figures 7.9 and 7.10.

(c) *Specify and Visualize Traffic Features:* TUMonitor provides an option, called IOGraph, for a user (i) to specify a set of features and

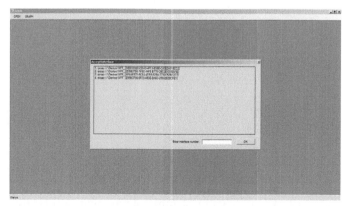

Figure 7.10: Traffic reading from file in TUMonitor.

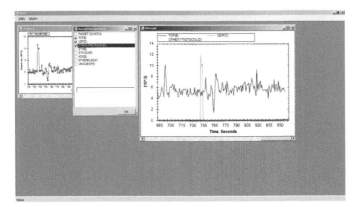

Figure 7.11: Traffic feature selection in TUMonitor.

(ii) to visualize their graph form for a given interval of time in several windows. A sample screen shot related to feature selection is shown in Figure 7.11.

Another screen-shot, shown in Figure 7.12, exhibits the facility TUMonitor provides to visualize multiple graphs at a time. By using this facility, one can specify multiple feature types and can monitor the attack and normal traffic patterns for a given interval of time in multiple windows.

(d) *Arithmetic Expression as Input:* TUMonitor also supports a special provision to monitor packet and Netflow traffic patterns by writing an arithmetic expression in an expression textbox for a given interval of time. Figure 7.14 shows an example of such a fa-

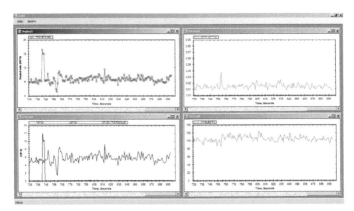

Figure 7.12: Visualization of multiple graphs in TUMonitor.

cility. It shows the percentage of SYN packets over all TCP packets. Here, each feature is represented by a letter. For example, packet count is represented by the letter A, the number of TCP packets is represented by B, and so on. The user can write any valid *infix* arithmetic expression using these letters as space holders in the given textbox to obtain the corresponding graph.

7.6.2 TUMonitor Architecture

In this section, we provide the modular architecture of TUMonitor. Figure 7.13 depicts the architecture of TUMonitor. The four basic sub-modules that comprise the TUMonitor module are described below.

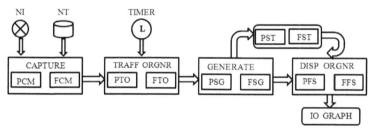

Figure 7.13: TUMonitor architecture.

(a) *Capture/Read Sub-module:* This sub-module is responsible for sniffing live traffic from the network interface (NI) or from stored traces (NT). It uses a user-specified file to store the captured data. It is dependent on two dedicated components, called PCM and FCM. PCM is used to collect packets from live traffic or to read from a specified file. It forwards the packet information to a packet traffic organizer (PTO). For the purpose of packet capture, it uses the *pcap.net* library [1]. Similarly, for extracting flow information, FCM provides two options, viz., to collect directly from router or to extract from packets already captured. Once flow information is successfully extracted, FCM forwards it to a flow organizer, called the flow traffic organizer (FTO).

(b) *Traffic Organizer Sub-module:* As we mentioned earlier, TUMonitor keeps track of protocol-specific packet counts, TCP flag-specific packet counts, as well as the number of unique source IPs for a given interval of time. To facilitate this, it includes two components called PTO and FTO. PTO, i.e., the packet organizer, main-

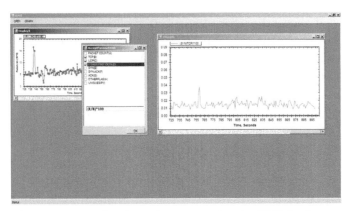

Figure 7.14: Arithmetic expression in TUMonitor.

tains counters for different features and updates them upon the arrival of new packet information. Similarly, FTO organizes flow information extracted from two different sources and maintains it.

(c) *Traffic Statistics Generator Sub-module:* This sub-module is dedicated to generation of statistical information from both packet traffic and flow information. Like the previous sub-modules, it is also composed of two generator components, i.e., a packet statistics generator (PSG) and a flow statistics generator (FSG). For packet statistics generation, the PSG maintains a timer, that ticks after each specified interval. On each tick, it extracts the value of each counter and inserts it into an in-memory table, where each row corresponds to the statistics at a particular interval and each column represents the value of the corresponding feature at a different interval. The FSG follows similar logic to generate flow statistics from the extracted flow information.

(d) *Feature Display Organizer Sub-module:* This visualization support module provides options for selecting features or for entering an arithmetic expression for visualization of either packet traffic (using PFS) or flow information (using FFS). Once a request is submitted based on specified features or an expression is submitted, the display unit creates a new thread. The thread in turn reads (and evaluates in case of an expression) the specied features for each interval from the in-memory statistics table and plots the graph in a separate window.

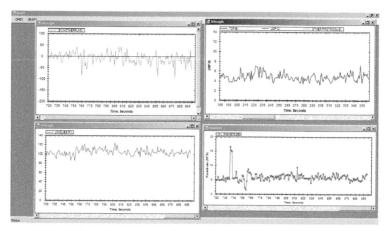

Figure 7.15: Visualization under normal conditions in TUMonitor.

7.6.3   Visualization with TUMonitor

To demonstrate the working of TUMonitor, the testbed discussed in
the previous section (as shown in Figure 7.3) is used. The monitoring
tool can be installed at the edge router of the victim subnet, marked
as the *victim zone*, shown in the right oval. One can generate DDoS
attacks of different specification using TUCannon and can visualize and
monitor the patterns of different selected features under these attacks
using TUMonitor. For easy understanding, a demonstration showing
monitoring of packet count, the number of different protocol packets,
the number of unique source IP addresses, and an arithmetic expression
SYN–(FIN+RST), which can be considered the parameters for DDoS
detection, as given in [257], is shown in Figures 7.15, 7.16, and 7.17.
In this demonstration, a DDoS attack was launched targeting a victim
machine using TUCannon by sending a huge number of packets with
randomly spoofed source IP addresses. Figure 7.16 shows a screen-
shot of a TCP flooding traffic, whereas in Figure 7.17, a screen-shot
of UDP flooding attack is shown.

   An executable version of TUCANNON+ is available at   http://
agnigarh.tezu. ernet.in/~dkb/resources.html.

7.7   DDoS Defense Systems

In this section, we present some well-known academic and commercial
defense systems for DDoS detection, prevention, tolerance, and reac-

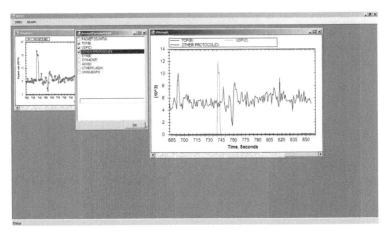

Figure 7.16: Visualization of TCP flooding in TUMonitor.

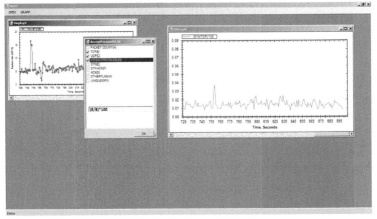

Figure 7.17: Visualization of UDP flooding in TUMonitor.

tion. We present architectures and pros and cons analysis of several detection, prevention, tolerance, and reaction systems.

7.7.1   Systems that Respond to Intrusion

We can define intrusion as a way to create an abnormal state in a system or a computer network, due to which, normal services are affected undesirably. Thus, maintaining a system or a network in a fully normal or pseudo-normal state is the aim of a defense system. Defense experts, analysts, and researchers provide methodologies, approaches, architectures, and systems with such goals. In this section, some commonly

used and well-known architectures and systems are described for the
benefit of our readers.

7.7.1.1 Architectures of Some Well-Known Defense Systems

We have already discussed in *Chapter 4* that an intrusion detection
system (IDS) monitors and analyzes a network or system for malicious
activities, or policy violations, or abnormal traffic behavior. If any
threat is detected, the IDS alerts the system or network administrator.
In Figure 7.18, the architecture of a successful IDS, referred to as the
Bro cluster architecture [33], is shown.

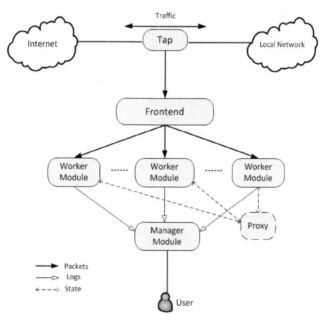

Figure 7.18: Bro IDS cluster architecture [33].

This Unix-based open-source, passive network traffic analyzer in-
spects network traffic for detection of any abnormal behavior. Bro
adopts a signature-based approach to detect known attacks and events,
such as failed connection attempts, using a set of predefined attack signatures. Bro generates neutral events after analyzing live or recorded
traffic. To handle events, it uses policy scripts or actions such as sending an email, raising an alert, executing a system command, updating
an internal metric, and even calling another Bro script.

In addition, a virtual machine introspection-based architecture for host-based IDS, proposed by Garfinkel and Rosenblum [85], is shown in Figure 7.19. Unlike most traditional host-based IDSs, this detection system observes hardware status, events, and software states of hosts and offers a more robust view of the system than HIDS. The virtual machine monitor (VMM) is responsible for hardware virtualization and also offers isolation, monitoring, and interposition properties.

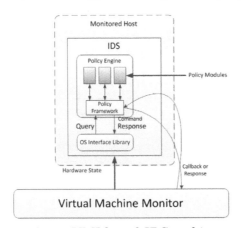

Figure 7.19: VMI-based IDS architecture.

As noted in *Chapter 5*, an intrusion prevention system (IPS) is developed as an advanced version of IDS. Though, both IDS and IPS monitor network traffic and/or system activities for malicious activity, an IPS is able to actively prevent intrusions that are detected by (i) dropping malicious packets, (ii) generating an alarm, (iii) blocking traffic from the offending source IP addresses, and/or (iv) resetting the connection. In Figure 7.20, a network-based architecture called Javvin [118] is shown. It can be seen in the figure that every specific zone is protected by an IPS system. The IPS is organized in layers and works in a coordinated manner to provide defense against intrusion.

Jia and Wang [121] introduce a method to support designing and analyzing an intelligent IPS model based on a dynamically distributed cloud firewall linkage as shown in Figure 7.21. The authors have established the significance of their model considering several important issues of cloud security. Their model can detect, intercept, and handle a good number of the latest attacks such as computer viruses and malicious Websites. The model sends best the possible solutions to users for proactive defense in their network.

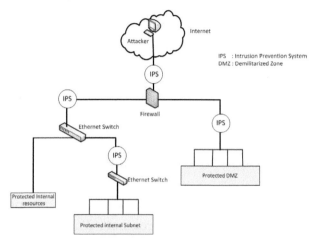

Figure 7.20: Network-based intrusion prevention system.

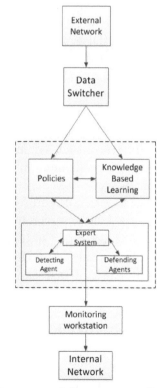

Figure 7.21: Architecture of dynamic intelligence cloud firewall.

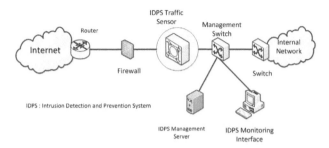

Figure 7.22: An example architecture of IDPS [211].

An intrusion detection and prevention system (IDPS) combines both detection and prevention approaches. The detection module of the system first monitors and analyzes the captured traffic in a network. If it identifies any abnormality, the prevention module drops or blocks the unwanted traffic actively. The defense system introduced by Scarfone and Mell [211], the architecture of which is shown in Figure 7.22, is an example of such an IDPS.

It introduces the concept of deploying IDPS sensors inline. The main motivation is to enable the sensors to stop attacks by blocking network traffic at an early stage. Inline sensors are deployed in the network just like other devices such as firewalls. They segregate the external networks and the borders between different internal networks.

We mentioned in   *Chapter 6* that an intrusion response system (IRS) automatically executes a predefined and preconfigured set of responsive actions based on the type of attack. A distinguishing feature of an automated IRS is that it does not require any human intervention, unlike an IDS where there is a delay between intrusion detection and response. EMERALD (Event Monitoring Enabling Responses to Anomalous Live Disturbances)[195] is a successful IRS. It is a distributed and scalable system that keeps track of malicious activities through and across large networks. The highly distributed nature of surveillance, attack isolation, and automated response generation, make EMERALD more attractive and useful as an IRS. Figure 7.23 shows the architecture of EMERALD. The monitors contribute to a streamlined event analysis system that combines signature analysis with statistical profiling to provide localized real-time protection of the most widely used network services on the Internet.

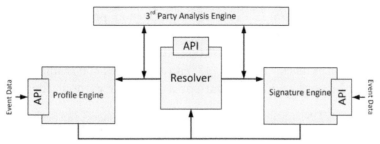

Figure 7.23: EMERALD architecture.

7.7.2 Some Commercial and Academic Defense Systems

In this section, we present some commercially available and academic defense systems introduced in the past two decades.

(i) *AlienVault*: This is an open source security information and event management system, designed to provide security, intrusion detection and prevention [10]. It is available for both commercial and non-commercial sectors. It runs on a Debian Linux core, and hence can be deployed on VMware virtual machines or Amazone EC2 cloud or directly in hardware. A sensor component collects log information and helps detect intrusions. File integrity monitoring, log normalizations and SIEM event correlation are also performed.

(ii) *ArcSight Enterprise Security Manager*: This is a security event manager system [13]. Every event that occurs is analyzed and correlated to maintain an exact priority of security risks and compliance violations. Example events include login, logoff, file access, and database query. The correlation engine is very powerful and it can go through millions of log records to detect critical incidents to resolve the matter at home. The correlation engine communicates with security administrators to report critical incidents.

(iii) *CA-Host-Based IPS*: This tool [41] provides five services in a host-based environment. These are endpoint firewall, operating system security, intrusion detection, intrusion prevention, and application control. It is deployed and managed from a central location via a single, intuitive console to improve endpoint security.

(iv) *Checkpoint IPS-1*: This is an intrusion prevention system for both clients and servers, that uses the gateway firewall technique. Blocking of traffic is based on source, destination, and port information. Checkpoint IPS [47] can also check the traffic content. It can be deployed as software or as a sensor without the firewall.

(v) *Cisco IDS*: Cisco IDS [43] is a network-based detection system. It uses a signature-oriented database to trigger intrusion alarms. The sensors monitor real-time traffic packets. Alarms are transmitted through the command-and-control interface to the director platform. The director platform manages software configuration, log creation and display of alarms.

(vi) *Cisco Security Monitoring, Analysis, and Response System (MARS)*: This system [241] identifies threats on the Cisco network by learning the environment structure including topology, configuration, and behavior. It helps the mitigation procedure by visualizing the attack path and identifying the source of the threat. Management and response are simple due to integration with Cisco Security Manager software.

(vii) *DeepNines IPS*: This is an intrusion prevention system [66] that is deployed in the network layer. Specifically, it is deployed at critical points in the network architecture, like in front of the router, and acts as the first line of defense. Its capabilities include inspection using multiple methods, provision of an intelligent firewall, fragmentation control, policy checking, signature-based IPS, adaptive rate control, etc.

(viii) *Enterasys Intrusion Prevention System*: The Enterasys Intrusion Prevention System [72] ensures confidentiality, integrity, and availability of business, critical resources with industry-leading intrusion prevention capabilities. It has the ability to gather records of an attacker's activity, remove the access of the illegitimate user to the network, and reconfigure the network to resist penetration. Enterasys IPS offers an extensive range of detection capabilities, host-based and network-based deployment options, and seamless integration with the Enterasys Secure Networks architecture.

(ix) *FlowMatrix*: Flow Matrix [80] by Akma Labs is a free security tool that provides network behavior analysis and anomaly detection. It is a non commercial network-based detection system.

(x) *IBM Proventia Desktop Endpoint Security*: IBM Proventia Desktop [216] is an automatic endpoint security system. It tries to reduce the risk from known and unknown attacks by providing multilayered security in a single host. It can be managed simply, and it also helps prevent data theft.

(xi) *IBM Proventia Network IPS Series*: Having access to high-speed Internet, large enterprises and telecommunication providers require an optimized platform with both high security and high performance. IBM Proventia Network IPS [112] Series provides a network-based solution. It is a next-generation firewall solution that combines a firewall and an intrusion prevention system into a single module.

(xii) *IBM Tivoli Security Operation Manager*: This system [38] autonomously monitors and analyzes the data collected throughout the IT infrastructure to detect intrusions or any threats. It also provides optimization, incident recognition, investigation, and response. By monitoring and administering security policies, it helps users gain knowledge of threats to mitigate them before they turn into unwanted incidents.

(xiii) *iPolicy Intrusion Detection/Prevention*: The network-based iPolicy Intrusion Detection/Prevention Firewall [116] combines an intrusion detection engine and an intrusion prevention engine that delivers comprehensive, high-performance, real-time attack detection and prevention. The Detection component uses multiple detection techniques to detect intrusion to form a real-time high-speed detection engine. It applies signature-based detection to identify known attacks, and the iPolicy IDS/IPS signature database has over 2000 entries. An application-aware protocol anomaly engine detects anomalies and a statistical traffic anomaly engine provides the ability to detect suspicious behavior and Distributed Denial-of-Service (DDoS) attacks.

(xiv) *TippingPoint IDS/IPS*: TippingPoint IDS/IPS [113] provides an advanced security solution for protection of resources from both known and unseen attacks. It is equipped with (i) a strong set of application layer functionalities with user awareness and (ii) abilities to investigate input/output content. It is scalable and dynamic, and works with applications, network, and data. It uses

adaptive intelligence to protect resources from new and advanced
threats at the application layer in real time.

(xv) *StoneGate IPS*: StoneGate IPS[117] is a proactive defense system to block malicious traffic automatically before any damage
occurs. Its SSL inspection feature monitors encrypted Web traffic
and prevents disruption to business network traffic. The sensor
appliances protect up to two line segments. It has a bypass interface pair for each inline segment and two standard Ethernet interfaces. These standard interfaces are used as capture interfaces to
detect intrusion and one of them is used for traffic management.

(xvi) *Strata Guard IPS*: Strata Guard[234] is a high-speed intrusion
detection/prevention system with greater than 4 GB throughput
with up to 8 interfaces. Beyond blocking intrusions, it enforces
network audits and usage policies and blocks a peer-to-peer file
sharing, instant messaging, chat, prohibited browsing activity,
and worm propagation. Strata Guard detects anomalous events
like spoofed attack source addresses, performs TCP state verifi-
cation and rough services running on the network. Strata Guard
takes the powerful, open-source Snort IDS engine and makes it
practical for protecting corporate-scale networks. A hardened
Linux OS installs with Strata Guard. Through its multilayered
Dynamic Attack Qualification technologies, Strata Guard elimi-
nates false positives. Its multi-node, multi-user management capabilities allow for enterprise-wide deployments and provide appropriate levels of control for all users requiring access to secure
data.

(xvii) *Snort IDS*: Snort IDS [183] is a network-based open source intrusion detection system. Using packet sniffing, it monitors the
network traffic in real time, checking the payload of each packet
closely for any suspicious anomalies. Snort is based on libpcap,
a tool which is widely used in TCP/IP packet sniffing and analysis. Through protocol analysis, content searching, and matching,
Snort detects attack methods, including denial-of-service, buffer
overflow, CGI attacks, stealth port scans, and SMB probes. If
any detection of attack occurs, Snort sends a real-time alert to
syslog.

(xviii) *SecureNet IDS/IPS*: SecureNet System [215] performs critical deep packet analysis and is endowed with application awareness. It can be deployed actively for intrusion prevention and passively for intrusion detection. In both cases, the system gathers unsurpassed knowledge about traffic in the network removing all guesswork involved with establishing perimeter defense. Intrusion prevention deployments can be configured to block or pass network traffic on failure.

(xix) *Samhain*: Samhain [2] is a host-based intrusion detection system that provides file integrity checking and log file monitoring and analysis, in addition to rootkit detection, port monitoring, and detection of rough or hidden processes. It has been designed to monitor multiple hosts with different operating systems with centralized management. It can be applied in a standalone environment also.

(xx) *Radware's DefensePro*: Radware's DefensePro [67] appliances are designed to be in front of the firewall and provide security against intrusion. They provide prevention and DoS protection for networks and individual servers. They use behavioral analysis for the networks and generate real-time signatures.

(xxi) *PHPIDS*: PHPIDS [193] is a open source Web-based application for intrusion detection. It has the ability to find intrusion data coming from the client side to PHP Web applications. It speeds up PHP application development by reducing the time and money needed to spend on security. Cross-site scripting, SQL injection, header injection, directory traversal, remote file execution, local file inclusion, and Denial-of-Service are detected using PHPIDS by checking input variables like POST, GET, SESSION and COOKIE.

(xxii) *OSSEC*: OSSEC [32] is comprised of a central manger and agents. The central manager monitors everything that is received from agents. All rules and decoders are stored centrally in the manager to make it easy to deploy for a large number of agents. The agents are small programs installed on the systems that are to be monitored. The agents collect the information in real time and forward to the manager to analyze.

(xxiii) *McAfee Host Intrusion Prevention for Desktop*: It is a commercial host-based intrusion prevention system [162] for the endpoint desktop. McAfee Host Intrusion Prevention for Desktop reduces patching frequency and protects data confidentiality, and simplifies regulatory compliance.

(xxiv) *McAfee IntruShield IDS*: The complete McAfee IntruShield IDS (McAfee) [163] is a combination of network appliances and software. This combination is built for accurate detection and prevention of intrusions, denial-of-service attacks, and network misuse. McAfee combines real-time detection and prevention for a comprehensive and effective network security system.

(xxv) *Osiris*: Osiris [185] came into being as a few Perl scripts which eventually evolved into a extensive and sophisticated package. The architecture is geared toward central management with encrypted communications. The hosts naturally require a client to be installed, which is a drawback of any HIDS, but otherwise nothing is stored on the host. The central manager does the heavy lifting. This is not unlike an application that needs to be installed on every computer on the LAN, something that is done all the time, but it is still overhead.

(xxvi) *Juniper IDP*: Juniper IDP [225] products provide comprehensive inline network security from worms, Trojans, spyware, keyloggers, and other malware. By accurately identifying application traffic, the network security solutions ensure continuous availability of critical applications. It is a network-based commercial system.

(xxvii) *Netfence Gateways*: Netfence [266] gateways combine all functions needed in modern network security infrastructure and are primarily used as classic perimeter security systems. They are also the central entities for branch office networking and Unified Threat Management infrastructures. Its flexible structure enables it to meet customer requirements such as the number of users, performance, and NICs. Netfence gateways can also be used in virtualized environments and support VMware ESX as a platform.

(xxviii) *DC&A*: This [78] is a static proactive intrusion response system that provides a delayed response. The time is delayed until the attack is confirmed. If a response system acts in a proactive manner, we can consider it as a prevention-type process. By delaying the response, intrusion handling is performed after the intrusion occurs and it includes actions to restore system state.

(xxix) *CSM*: Cooperating Security Managers (CSM) [264] performs intrusion detection by delaying the response until the observed abnormality matches an intrusion pattern. It reports the match to the functions in a distributed environment autonomously without requiring a designated central site or server to perform the analysis of network audit data.

(xxx) *BMSL-Based Response*: Behavioral Monitoring Specification Language (BMSL) [31] enables concise specifications of event-based on security-relevant properties. This action can be represented by invocation of a response function, assignment to a state variable, or a set of rules for process isolation. This intrusion response system provides a response in delayed time with autonomous activity.

(xxxi) *SoSMART*: The SoSMART model [174] uses Case-Base Reasoning (CBR) for an adaptation mechanism that matches current system state to the previously identified situations as intrusive. The use of CBR is to define incident and response pairings that can recognize situations that may require response and associate response actions according to the situations.

(xxxii) *pH*: Somayaji and Forrest developed the pH system [224] to detect and respond to intrusion. The detection component is comprised of a normal behavioral profile of N-gram sequences of system calls. Sequences of calls deviating from the normal behavior are considered anomalous and can be either aborted or delayed.

(xxxiii) *Lee's IRS*: Lee et al. [145] proposed an approach to intrusion response based on a cost-sensitive modeling of the intrusion detection and response. The authors define three cost factors: *operational cost* of processing and analyzing data for detection of intrusion, *damage cost* to assesses the amount of damage due to attack, and *response cost* to characterize the cost of reaction to intrusion.

(xxxiv) *SARA*: Survivable Autonomic Response Architecture (SARA) [147] was developed to coordinate fast automatic response against intrusion. It comprises several components that work as *sensors* for information gathering, *detectors* for analysis of sensored data, *arbitrators* in selection of appropriate response actions, and *responders* for implementation of response. These components can be sequenced among participating machines to provide the strongest defense.

(xxxv) *CITRA*: The Cooperative Intrusion Traceback and Response Architecture (CITRA) [214] was developed to provide a cooperative agent-based solution. The architecture uses neighborhood structure to propagate information about a detected intrusion to the source of the attack and submit to the centralized authority. The centralized authority, the Discovery Coordinator, determines an optimal system response. It is also responsible for coordinating a global response.

(xxxvi) *TBAIR*: The TBAIR (Tracing-Based Active Intrusion Response) [259] framework attempts to trace back to the intrusion source host and dynamically choose a suitable response, such as remote blocking of the intruder, isolation of the contaminated hosts, etc. Its operation is based on the idea of Sleepy Watermark Tracing (SWT) [260].

(xxxvii) *Network IRS*: Toth and Kruegel [246] proposed a method by considering costs and benefits of the response actions, and by modeling dependencies among services in a system. Such modeling reveals priorities at response targets and can evaluate the impact of different response strategies on dependent services and the system.

(xxxviii) *Specification-Based IRS*: Balepin et al. [21] developed a system, where a hierarchy of local resources is represented using a directed graph. The system follows a cost-sensitive and cooperative approach. Nodes of the directed graph are system resources and graph edges represent dependencies among the resources. A list of response actions is attached with each node. These actions can be performed to restore the working state of the resource in case there is an attack.

(xxxix) *ADEPTS*: Foo et al. presented a proactive approach [81] to mount a response. The system they proposed employs an intrusion graph (I-Graph) to build an attack model of goals and consequently to determine possible spread of the intrusion. Integrating IDS map alarms to IGraph nodes indicates the attack spread based on alarm confidence values. Finally, appropriate response actions are performed according to the identified attack goals.

(xl) *FLIPS*: Locasto et al. introduce a hybrid adaptive intrusion prevention system [154] called FLIPS (Feedback Learning IPS). Host-based FLIPS uses both signature matching and anomaly-based classification. Its goal is to detect and prevent code injection attacks. It uses an intermediate emulator to detect injected malicious attack code and does not generate attack signatures.

(xli) *FAIR*: Papadaki and Furnell proposed a cost-sensitive response system [188]. The system assesses the statics and dynamics of the attack. To manage important characteristics of an attack, a database is used to analyze them. The characteristics include targets, applications, vulnerabilities, and so on. For the evaluation of the dynamic context of an attack, they apply some interesting ideas. The two main features of this model are (i) the ability to easily propose different orders of responses for different attack scenarios, and (ii) the ability to adapt decisions in response to changes in the environment.

(xlii) *Kheir's IRS*: Kheir et al. developed a dependency graph [134] to calculate the confidentiality, integrity impacts, and the availability impacts. Each resource present in the dependency graph is defined with a 3D CIA vector. The 3D CIA vector values are cost values and these are quickly updated either by active monitoring to estimate them or by extrapolation using the dependency graph.

(xliii) *OrBAC*: Kanoun et al. were the first to provide a risk-aware framework [131] to activate and deactivate response methodologies in regard to intrusion. It consists of an online model and its architecture. The success possibility of an ongoing threat or an actual attack, the cumulative impacts and the response are considered before activating or deactivating a strategic response. The main contribution of the proposed model is to determine when a strategic response should be deactivated and how.

(xliv) *IRDM-HTN*: Mu and Li reported a hierarchical task network planning model [176] to defend intrusions. In this system, every response has an associated static risk threshold. The value is calculated by its ratio of positive to negative effects. When the risk index is more than the response static threshold, the required response is deployed. They also proposed a response selection window, where the most effective responses are selected to repel intrusions.

(xlv) *Strasburg's IRS*: Strasburg et al. [233] presented a host-based framework for the assessment of sensitive cost and selecting intrusion response. They introduce a set of measurements that characterize the potential costs associated with the intrusion-handling method. They provide a theory for intrusion response evaluation with respect to the risk of potential intrusion damage, the effectiveness of the response action, and the response cost for a system.

(xlvi) *Jahnke*: Jahnke et al. presented a graph-based approach [119] against intrusion. The graph is used for modeling the effects of attacks against resources. The effects of the response measures are taken into account to measure reaction to the attacks. Using metrics from the graph, it may (a) be possible to quantify relevant properties of a response method after its execution, and (b) be easier to estimate these properties for all available response methods before deploying them.

(xlvii) *DIPS*: Haslum et al. proposed a real-time intrusion prevention method [97]. This model is cost-sensitive. It involves in a dynamic risk assessment process based on a fuzzy model. Fuzzy logic is used to estimate risk.

(xlviii) *Stakhanova's IRS*: Stakhanova et al. [228] reported a cost-sensitive preemptive intrusion response model. This model detects anomalous behavior in software monitoring system behaviors such as system calls. It uses two levels of classification to detect intrusion. In the first step, if normal and abnormal patterns are available, the model determines what kind of pattern is triggered when a series of system behaviors are observed. If the monitored sequences do not match normal or abnormal patterns, the system uses machine learning techniques to determine whether the system is normal or abnormal.

(xlix) *Tanachaiwiwat's IRS*: Tanachaiwiwat et al. propose a response model [238] against intrusion using a cost-sensitive method. They report that verifying the effectiveness of a response is necessary. They consider IDS efficiency, alarm frequency (per week), and damage cost to select the best strategy. The alarm frequency gives the number of alarms triggered per attack, and cost estimates the amount of damage that could be caused by the attacker.

7.7.3 Discussion

After studying different architectures and systems, whether they are commercial and non-commercial, we can state the security problem in a network against intrusion in a general way. The success of a defense system in a network depends on the following points.

- The defense system should be generic in nature to confront any anomalous activity.

- The defense system should be deployed on the basis of potential intrusion activities observed and their nature.

- A dynamic solution in real time with a low false positive rate and low false negative rate is preferred.

- Scalability of the defense system and incremental updating as new anomalies become apparent should be possible.

- The design should be independent of the underlying communication protocol.

7.8 Chapter Summary

Based on a detailed discussion of a large number of tools in this chapter, we summarize the following.

- Existing information-gathering tools can scan a network successfully in one-to-one and one-to many scenarios. However, most existing tools are unsuitable for coordinated scanning (i.e., $m:1$ and $n:m$ mappings) with varying source and destination IP addresses that are obtained dynamically.

- An integrated tool with support for capture, preprocessing, analysis, and visualization of both flow and packet data is desired. Existing tools (e.g., Wireshark, Nfsen, and Nfdump) can support either flow capture and presentation or packet analysis and presentation, but not both.

- Most DDoS attack tools are network layer specific, protocol specific, or traffic pattern specific. They do not provide enough flexibility, and require substantial customization before using on a testbed or in practice in the real world.

- Most existing DDoS attack tools are restricted to a limited number of attack scenarios and cannot be customized to use in additional attack scenarios.

Chapter 8

Conclusion and Research Challenges

8.1 Conclusion

In the previous chapters, we provided an extensive presentation of machine learning methods followed by detailed discussions of current state-of-the-art research in DDoS attack detection, prevention, reaction, mitigation, and tolerance. In particular, Chapter 2 is dedicated to causes, evolution, and classification of DDoS attacks. To practically understand how attackers plan and mount DDoS attacks, we discussed the development of a testbed with accompanying tools to launch DDoS flooding attacks of random packet intensity (low-rate to high-rate) using a random number of compromised nodes in Chapter 7. Although in past years, network security researchers have presented several innovative and practical solutions to detect, protect from, react to, mitigate, and tolerate DDoS attacks, there are still many challenges to overcome to safeguard networks from growing threats of this sophisticated attack. With the increased complexity in the technology used by intruders to launch attacks and with the growing evolution of high-speed network technology, we believe that future attackers are always designing more effective attack launching tools to inflict maximum damage. Our intention is to help improve the know-how of network security researchers and practitioners about design trends in attacks tools; our purpose is neither to educate anyone in the design of attack launching tools themselves nor to teach how to counter DDoS attack mitigation techniques or methods. It is only possible for a defender to protect a network by filtering malicious traffic when the defender has in-depth knowledge of the various ways an attacker can attempt to intrude into the network.

8.1.1 Source IP Spoofing

Source IP spoofing is an effective technique used widely by DDoS attackers. Although many researchers deem source IP spoofing to be of low relevance and low usefulness in the context of current botnet-based DDoS attacks, many attackers still prefer to use it because it is inexpensive and effective at the same time. It is also costly to hire a botnet and manage it properly. Even though ingress and egress filters are considered very effective in filtering traffic with invalid IP addresses, attackers still manage to bypass such protection mechanisms using appropriate source IP spoofing schemes. Thus, providing a foolproof solution against source IP spoofing still remains an important research issue.

8.1.2 Degree of Randomization

Most attackers believe that a high degree of randomization of header fields such as port addresses (source and destination) and sequence numbers along with partial or complete spoofing of source IP addresses, are enough to mount a successful DDoS attack. But it is not really true! It is actually easier for a defender to distill anomalous traffic from legitimate traffic when the degree of randomization is high. A believable and effective tool should generate traffic with addresses within a probable range. Any traffic with an arbitrary address (beyond a safe range) may generate an obvious anomaly. Therefore, we believe that sophisticated attackers are likely to develop and use tools that generate attack traffic with careful and partial source IP spoofing, and randomization of other header fields without violating the likely range. Network defenders must be able to counter such efforts of attackers.

8.1.3 Isolation vs. Combination

Most flooding tools, such as the UDP flooding of *Agabot*, generates attack traffic by exploiting packet size randomization, source IP spoofing, or randomization of other header fields. None of the tools are designed by carefully combining all the relevant features. So, we believe that the next generation of attackers is likely to develop attack tools that combine all such features with greater sophistication and are able to generate flooding attacks that work with a wide range of protocols. Therefore, network defenders must think ahead now to develop methods to detect such efforts at feature combination.

8.1.4 Realistic TCP SYN Flooding

Improper balance between SYN and ACK packets and unusual service requests are the major actions that give away TCP SYN flooding attacks. Knowing this, in each round of flooding, a sophisticated attack tool is likely to generate SYN and ACK packets with the proper balance to avoid quick detection as anomalous traffic. An expert attacker is unlikely to generate any service requests for unusual IP protocol types, other than the most commonly used TCP or UDP. The use of other protocols is quite likely to lead to anomalies in the traffic and hence make it easily detectable. So, proper understanding of the protocols and associated typical services in the context of a specific network are important for a malfeasant who wants to develop an effective attack tool. Network defenders must be prepared to apprehend such expert attacks.

8.1.5 Removal of Unique Characteristics

A knowledgeable attacker is likely to avoid generating any traffic with unique characteristics that stand out (such as the use of unusual or unrealistically spoofed addresses for source IPs and ports, or unlikely values for other parameters, e.g., packet size, service type, and granularity in delay setting), because they will help detect such traffic as anomalies. Therefore, an advanced attack tool will probably have a mechanism to filter out traffic with easily discoverable characteristics before sending traffic to cause flooding. A defense mechanism must be prepared to handle traffic that is not very far from normal.

8.1.6 Low-Cost and Limited Bandwidth Attack

An attacker who plans to launch a DDoS attack using mobile botnet technology must work with limited bandwidth and battery backup. So, to develop an attack tool on a mobile botnet, a sophisticated attacker will have to be able to generate many variations of attack classes under these constraints. It is imperative that a defender should also be looking out for the same variations.

Another one of our observations is that most existing DDoS defense methods are very specific and are developed to counter a specific class of DDoS attacks, particular to a group of layer-specific protocols. Such methods are mostly validated either using a restricted network environment or on a set of synthetic datasets. A generic DDoS defense system that is able to detect and block several or most classes of DDoS attacks using various protocols and at all network layers, is still a dream. We also have observed that most DDoS detection and protection methods depend on multiple user parameters and the performance of the methods is highly sensitive to the values of these parameters. It is quite likely that defenders must develop heuristic method(s) that can estimate values of these parameters more accurately. Similarly, although several source-end defense systems have been introduced, developing a cost-effective and real-time source-end defense system that can work with all protocols is not yet a reality.

8.2   Research Challenges

Based on our extensive experience, we have identified a few important research challenges for network defenders who want to be well prepared for tomorrow's DDoS attacks. We enumerate them below.

8.2.1   Developing a Generic DDoS Defense Mechanism

As far as we know, a generic DDoS defense system that can identify any class of DDoS attacks that can occur in a real network environment, regardless of protocol and network layer, does not exist. Designing such a defense system with generic features, but one that is able to identify DDoS anomalies in real time without compromising QoS is a very challenging task, if it is at all possible to do so. Maybe a generic architecture with plugins for various specific attacks is the way to go, or maybe a more integrated solution is a better choice.

8.2.2   Integration of Packet/Flow Monitoring and Detection

At this time, there is no integrated monitoring-cum-defense tool that supports monitoring as well as detection of both high-rate and low-rate DDoS attacks in real time. It may be possible to develop a soft computing solution that can adapt to a variety of attack situations such as Cormelt and Crossfire attacks. Thus, it is time to develop a security solution that provides plugins for comprehensive protection in real time.

8.2.3 Developing DDoS-Tolerant Architecture

An efficient, practical, and robust defense architecture that uses minimum resources but can withstand all classes of DDoS flooding attacks does not currently exist. Thus, designing an architecture that can tolerate DDoS flooding and is able to offer high-quality services even in the worst case of flooding, is the ideal goal of DDoS research.

8.2.4 Developing a Cost-Effective Source-End Defense

Developing a cost-effective and adaptive source-end defense system that uses minimum computational resources and can block all classes of DDoS attacks regardless of protocols remains a big challenge. Such a defense mechanism should be able to adapt itself when a new type of DDoS attack is identified.

8.2.5 Developing an Efficient Dynamic Firewall

Designing a firewall with the ability to dynamically update a ruleset, assisted by efficient filtering (e.g., ingress/egress filtering), to block forged IPs without compromising quality of service is another research challenge. When a new type of DDoS attack is identified, the ruleset needs to be updated and it needs to become effective without delay or interruption.

8.2.6 Hybridization Issues to Support Real-Time Performance with QoS

Developing an appropriate hybridization of source-end and victim-end defense mechanisms, that uses an optimal set of dynamic rules to recognize as well as block both known and unknown DDoS attacks without compromising quality of service (QoS), is an important research issue. The hybridization should be cost-effective and should be able to perform well in real time.

8.2.7 Heuristics for Accurate Estimation of Defense Parameters

Developing an effective heuristic method to accurately estimate the width of local and global packet windows and the corresponding user thresholds that fit the network environment and can identify all classes of DDoS attacks without false alarms, is a challenging task. The methods should not be biased to a specific or a handful of network scenarios.

8.2.8 Developing a Robust and Cost-Effective Proximity Measure

Designing a robust proximity measure to help accurately distill out anomalous traffic (high-rate as well as low-rate traffic) from normal traffic in real time by working with a small number of attributes, is a challenge that needs to be overcome.

8.2.9 Standard for Unbiased Evaluation of Defense Solutions

Developing an appropriate measure to evaluate the effectiveness of a solution for DDoS attack detection is an absolute current necessity. A measure should consider all possible aspects of a defense system such as accuracy, reliability, adaptability, scalability, timeliness, and consistency, for unbiased evaluation of the system.

8.2.10 Large-Scale Testbed for Defense Validation

To validate tolerance, timeliness, accuracy, reliability, and scalability of a defense system, development of a large-scale testbed with a large combination of both virtual and physical nodes is essential. Developing such a testbed to allow (i) launching of all possible types and classes of DDoS attacks that are both high-rate and low-rate, and (ii) evaluating the defense system for its ability to identify attacks from the normal traffic in real time, is a problem that is difficult but needs to be addressed.

Bibliography

[1] http://pcapdotnet.codeplex.com/.

[2] The SAMHAIN file integrity /host-based intrusion detection system. SAMHAIN Labs. 2010. http://www.la-samhna.de/samhain/.

[3] Eggheads.org-eggdrop development, 1993.

[4] Worldwide Infrastructure Security Report, vol x. *pages.arbornetworks.com/rs/arbor/images/WISR2014_EN2014.pdf, Arbor Networks, Ann Arbor, Michigan, USA, Tech. Rep 10* (2014).

[5] ABDI, H. The Kendall rank correlation coefficient. *Encyclopedia of Measurement and Statistics. Sage, Thousand Oaks, CA* (2007), 508–510.

[6] ABLIZ, M. Internet denial of service attacks and defense mechanisms. *University of Pittsburgh, Department of Computer Science, Technical Report* (2011).

[7] ABRAHAM, A., AND JAIN, R. Soft computing models for network intrusion detection systems. In *Classification and clustering for knowledge Discovery*. Springer, 2005, pp. 191–207.

[8] AHMED, H. A., MAHANTA, P., BHATTACHARYYA, D. K., AND KALITA, J. K. Shifting-and-scaling correlation based biclustering algorithm. *IEEE/ACM Transactions on Computational Biology and Bioinformatics (TCBB) 11*, 6 (2014), 1239–1252.

[9] AKELLA, A., BHARAMBE, A., REITER, M., AND SESHAN, S. Detecting DDoS attacks on ISP networks. In *Proceedings of*

the *Twenty-Second ACM SIGMOD/PODS Workshop on Management and Processing of Data Streams* (2003), Citeseer, pp. 1–3.

[10] ALIENVAULT, L. Alienvault technical documentation. https://www.alienvault.com/document.

[11] ALWIS, H. A., DOSS, R. C., HEWAGE, P. S., AND CHOWDHURY, M. U. Topology based packet marking for IP traceback. In *Proceedings of the (ATNAC) Australian Telecommunication Networks and Applications Conference* (2006), University of Melbourne, pp. 224–228.

[12] ANUAR, N. B., PAPADAKI, M., FURNELL, S., AND CLARKE, N. An investigation and survey of response options for intrusion response systems (IRSs). In *Information Security for South Africa (ISSA), 2010* (2010), IEEE, pp. 1–8.

[13] ARCSIGHT: ENTERPRISE SECURITY MANAGER. http://www.arcsight.com.

[14] ARMSTRONG, D., CARTER, S., FRAZIER, G., AND FRAZIER, T. Autonomic defense: Thwarting automated attacks via real-time feedback control. *Wiley Complexity, Special Issue on "Resilient and Adaptive Defense of Computing Networks" 9* (2003), 41–48.

[15] ARMSTRONG, D., FRAZIER, T., CARTER, S., AND ALPHATECH, I. A controller-based autonomic defense system. *DARPA Information Survivability Conference and Exposition, 2003. Proceedings 2* (2003), 21–23.

[16] ARSENAULT, D., SOOD, A., AND HUANG, Y. Secure, resilient computing clusters: Self-cleansing intrusion tolerance with hardware enforced security (SCIT/HES). In *Proc. of the 2nd International Conference on Availability, Reliability and Security (ARES'07)* (IEEE Press, 2007), pp. 1–8.

[17] ATZORI, L., IERA, A., AND MORABITO, G. The Internet of things: A survey. *Computer Nnetworks 54*, 15 (2010), 2787–2805.

[18] AUNG, K. M. M., PARK, K., AND PARK, J. S. A rejuvenation methodology of cluster recovery. In *Proceedings of the Int'nl Symposium on Computer Computing and Grid* (2005), IEEE Press, pp. 90–95.

[19] BACHER, P., HOLZ, T., KOTTER, M., AND WICHERSKI, G. Know your enemy: Tracking botnets. The Honeynet Project. https://www.honeynet.org/papers/bots, 2005.

[20] BAILEY, M., COOKE, E., JAHANIAN, F., XU, Y., AND KARIR, M. A survey of botnet technology and defenses. In *Proc. Cyber security Applications and Technology Conference for Homeland Security* (2009).

[21] BALEPIN, I., MALTSEV, S., ROWE, J., AND LEVITT, K. Using specification-based intrusion detection for automated response. In *Recent Advances in Intrusion Detection* (2003), Springer, pp. 136–154.

[22] BECK, M. S., AND PLASKOWSKI, A. *Cross Correlation Flowmeters, Their Design and Application.* CRC Press, 1987.

[23] BEVERLY YANG, B., AND GARCIA-MOLINA, H. Designing a super-peer network. In *Data Engineering, 2003. Proceedings. 19th International Conference on* (2003), IEEE, pp. 49–60.

[24] BHATTACHARYYA, D. K., AND KALITA, J. K. *Network Anomaly Detection: A Machine Learning Perspective.* CRC Press, Taylor and Francis, USA, 2013.

[25] BHATTACHARYYA, D. K., AND KALITA, J. K. *Network Anomaly Detection: A Machine Learning Perspective.* Chapman and Hall, CRC Press, Taylor & Francis Group, June, 2013.

[26] BHUYAN, M. H., BHATTACHARYYA, D. K., AND KALITA, J. K. An empirical evaluation of information metrics for low-rate and high-rate ddos attack detection. *Pattern Recognition Letters 51* (2015), 1–7.

[27] BHUYAN, M. H., KASHYAP, H. J., BHATTACHARYYA, D. K., AND KALITA, J. K. Detecting distributed denial of service attacks: Methods, tools and future directions. *Computer Journal 57*, 4 (2014), 537–556.

[28] BLUMAN, A. G. *Elementary Statistics.* Brown Melbourne, 1995.

[29] BLUMENTHAL, L. M. *Theory and Applications of Distance Geometry*, vol. 347. Oxford, 1953.

[30] BORGAONKAR, R. An analysis of the Sssprox botnet. In *Emerging Security Information Systems and Technologies (SECURWARE), 2010 Fourth International Conference on* (2010), IEEE, pp. 148–153.

[31] BOWEN, T., CHEE, D., SEGAL, M., SEKAR, R., SHANBHAG, T., AND UPPULURI, P. Building survivable systems: An integrated approach based on intrusion detection and damage containment. In *DARPA Information Survivability Conference and Exposition, 2000. DISCEX'00. Proceedings* (2000), vol. 2, IEEE, pp. 84–99.

[32] BRAY, R., CID, D., AND HAY, A. *OSSEC Host-Based Intrusion Detection Guide*. Syngress, 2008.

[33] BRO, I. http://www. bro-ids. org, 2008.

[34] BRODER, A., AND MITZENMACHER, M. Network applications of bloom filters: A survey. *Internet Mathematics 1*, 4 (2004), 485–509.

[35] BRONIATOWSKI, M. Estimation of the Kullback-Leibler divergence. *Mathematical Methods of Statistics 12*, 4 (2003), 391–409.

[36] BRONIATOWSKI, M. *Estimation of the Kullback-Leibler Divergence, Chapter: Mathematical Methods of Statistics*. Princeton University Press, 2003.

[37] BUCKLAND, S. T., ANDERSON, D. R., BURNHAM, K. P., AND LAAKE, J. L. *Distance Sampling*. Wiley Online Library, 2005.

[38] BUECKER, A., AMADO, J., DRUKER, D., LORENZ, C., MUEHLENBROCK, F., TAN, R., ET AL. *IT Security Compliance Management Design Guide with IBM Tivoli Security Information and Event Manager*. IBM Redbooks, 2010.

[39] BURCH, H., AND CHESWICK, B. Tracing anonymous packets to their approximate source. In *LISA* (2000), pp. 319–327.

[40] BUSH, R., AND MEYER, D. Some Internet architectural guidelines and philosophy. https://tools.ietf.org/html/rfc3439. December, 2002.

[41] CAHIPS. CA Host-Based Intrusion Prevention System. http://store.ca.com/business/hips.

[42] CAIDA. Cooperative association for Internet data analysis. http://www.caida.org, 2011.

[43] CARTER, E. *CCSP Self-study: Cisco Secure Intrusion Detection System.* Cisco Press, 2004.

[44] CARVER, C., HILL, J., SURDU, J. R., AND POOCH, U. W. A methodology for using intelligent agents to provide automated intrusion response. In *Proceedings of the IEEE Systems, Man, and Cybernetics Information Assurance and Security Workshop, West Point, June 6-7* (2000), pp. 110–116.

[45] CENTER, C. C. Cert advisory ca-1996-01 UDP Port Denial-of-Service attack. https://www.cert.org/historical/advisories/ca-1996-01.cfm?. February, 1996.

[46] CENTER, C. C. Cert advisory ca-1996-21 TCP SYN flooding and IP spoofing attacks, 1996.

[47] CHECK POINT IPS-1. http://www.checkfirewalls.com.

[48] CHEN, C. On information and distance measures, error bounds, and feature selection. *Information Sciences 10*, 2 (1976), 159–173.

[49] CHEN, Q., LIN, W., DOU, W., AND YU, S. CBF: a packet filtering method for DDoS attack defense in cloud environment. In *Dependable, Autonomic and Secure Computing (DASC), 2011 IEEE Ninth International Conference on* (2011), IEEE, pp. 427–434.

[50] CHEN, T., AND REN, J. Bagging for Gaussian process regression. *Neurocomputing 22*, 7–9 (2009), 1605–1610.

[51] CHEN, W.-H., HSU, S.-H., AND SHEN, H.-P. Application of SVM and ANN for intrusion detection. *Computers and Operations Research 32*, 10 (2005), 2617–2634.

[52] CHEN, X., AND HEIDEMANN, J. Flash crowd mitigation via adaptive admission control based on application-level observations. *ACM Transactions on Internet Technology (TOIT) 5*, 3 (2005), 532–569.

[53] CHEN, Y., AND HWANG, K. Collaborative detection and filtering of shrew DDoS attacks using spectral analysis. *Journal of Parallel and Distributed Computing 66*, 9 (2006), 1137–1151.

[54] CHEN, Z., CHEN, Z., AND DELIS, A. An inline detection and prevention framework for distributed denial of service attacks. *Computer Journal 50* (2007), 7–40.

[55] CHENG, J., YIN, J., WU, C., ZHANG, B., AND LIU, Y. DDoS attack detection method based on linear prediction model. In *Emerging Intelligent Computing Technology and Applications*. Springer, 2009, pp. 1004–1013.

[56] CHIMPHLEE, W., ABDULLAH, A. H., NOOR MD SAP, M., SRINOY, S., AND CHIMPHLEE, S. Anomaly-based intrusion detection using fuzzy rough clustering. In *Hybrid Information Technology, 2006. ICHIT'06. International Conference on* (2006), vol. 1, IEEE, pp. 329–334.

[57] CHO, C., CABALLERO, J., GRIER, C., P. V., AND SONG, D. Insights from the inside: A view of botnet management from infiltration. In *Proc. Third USENIX Conf. Large-Scale Exploits and Emergent Threats: Botnets, Spyware, Worms, and More (USENIX LEET)* (2010).

[58] CHONKA, A., SINGH, J., AND ZHOU, W. Chaos theory based detection against network mimicking DDoS attacks. *Communications Letters, IEEE 13*, 9 (2009), 717–719.

[59] CLARK, P., AND NIBLETT, T. The CN2 induction algorithm. *Machine Learning Journal 3*, 4 (1989), 261–283.

[60] CRISCUOLO, P. J. Distributed denial of service: Trin00, tribe flood network, tribe flood network 2000, and stacheldraht CIAC-2319. Tech. rep., DTIC Document, 2000.

[61] CROUX, C., AND DEHON, C. Influence functions of the Spearman and Kendall correlation measures. *Statistical Methods & Applications 19*, 4 (2010), 497–515.

[62] DAINOTTI, A., PESCAPE, A., AND VENTRE, G. A cascade architecture for DoS attacks detection based on the wavelet transform. *Journal of Computer Security 17* (2009), 945–968.

[63] DAS, D., SHARMA, U., AND BHATTACHARYYA, D. An approach to detection of SQL injection attack based on dynamic query matching. *International Journal of Computer Applications 1*, 25 (2010), 28–34.

[64] DAS, D., SHARMA, U., AND BHATTACHARYYA, D. Detection of HTTP flooding attacks in multiple scenarios. In *Proceedings of the 2011 International Conference on Communication, Computing & Security* (2011), ACM, pp. 517–522.

[65] DECKER, A., SANCHO, D., KHAROUNI, L., GONCHAROV, M., AND MCARDLE, R. Pushdo/Cutwail botnet, 2009.

[66] DEEPNINES TECHNOLOGIES. Intrusion Prevention (IPS). http://softwaresolutions.fibre2fashion.com/company /deep-nines/productdetail.aspx?refno=1269.

[67] DEFENSEPRO, R. http://www.radware.com/products/defensepro-models/.

[68] DEPREN, O., TOPLLAR, M., ANARIM, E., AND CILIZ, M. K. An intelligent intrusion detection system (IDS) for anomaly and misuse detection in computer networks. *Expert Systems with Applications 29*, 4 (November 2005), 713–722.

[69] DESAI, N. Intrusion prevention systems: The next step in the evolution of IDS. *Retrieved October* (2009), 1–12.

[70] DUNN, J. C. A fuzzy relative of the isodata process and its use in detecting compact well-separated clusters. *Journal of Cybernetics 3* (1973), 32–57.

[71] ED., LALA, J. H. Organically assured and survivable information systems (oasis). In *Foundations of Intrusion Tolerant Systems, ISBN 0-7695-2057-X2003* (IEEE CS Press, 2003).

[72] ENTERASYS INTRUSION PREVENTION SYSTEM. http://www.ndm.net/ips/solutions/enterasys-networks.

[73] ERMAN, J., MAHANTI, A., ARLITT, M., COHEN, I., AND WILLIAMSON, C. Offline/realtime traffic classification using semi-supervised learning. *Performance Evaluation 64*, 9 (2007), 1194–1213.

[74] ESLAHI, M., SALLEH, R., AND ANUAR, N. B. Mobots: A new generation of botnets on mobile devices and networks. In *Computer Applications and Industrial Electronics (ISCAIE), 2012 IEEE Symposium on* (2012), IEEE, pp. 262–266.

[75] FARID, D. M., HARBI, N., BAHRI, E., RAHMAN, M. Z., AND RAHMAN, C. M. Attacks classification in adaptive intrusion detection using decision tree. In *World Academy of Science, Engineering and Technology, 63* (2010), pp. 86–90.

[76] FEINSTEIN, L., SCHNACKENBERG, D., BALUPARI, R., AND KINDRED, D. Statistical approaches to DDoS attack detection and response. In *DARPA Information Survivability Conference and Exposition, 2003. Proceedings* (2003), vol. 1, IEEE, pp. 303–314.

[77] FERGUSON, P., AND SENIE, D. Network Ingress Filtering: Defeating Denial of Service Attack which employ IP Source Address Filtering: RFC 2827. *Internet Engineering Task Force (IETF)* (2000).

[78] FISCH, E. A. Intrusion damage control and assessment: A taxonomy and implementation of automated responses to intrusive behavior. texas a & m university, 1996.

[79] FIU, F. MDK: The largest mobile botnet in china. *http://www.symantec.com/connect/blogs/mdk-largest-mobile-botnet-china* (2013).

[80] FLOW MATRIX: AKMA LABS. http://www.akmalabs.com, 2010.

[81] FOO, B., WU, Y.-S., MAO, Y.-C., BAGCHI, S., AND SPAFFORD, E. ADEPTS: Adaptive intrusion response using attack graphs in an e-commerce environment. In *Dependable Systems and Networks, 2005. DSN 2005. Proceedings. International Conference on* (2005), IEEE, pp. 508–517.

[82] FRANCOIS, J., AIB, I., AND BOUTABA, R. FireCol: A collaborative protection network for the detection of flooding DDoS attacks. *IEEE/ACM Transactions on Networking 20*, 6 (2012), 1827–1841.

[83] GADDAM, S. R., PHOHA, V. V., AND BALAGANI, K. S. K-means+ ID3: A novel method for supervised anomaly detection by cascading k-means clustering and ID3 decision tree learning methods. *IEEE Transactions on Knowledge and Data Engineering 19*, 3 (2007), 345–354.

[84] GANGER, G. R., AND KHOSLA, P. K. Pasis: A distributed framework for perpetually available and secure information systems. Tech. rep., DTIC Document, 2005.

[85] GARFINKEL, T., ROSENBLUM, M., ET AL. A virtual machine introspection based architecture for intrusion detection. In *NDSS* (2003), vol. 3, pp. 191–206.

[86] GAVRILIS, D., AND DERMATAS, E. Real-time detection of distributed denial-of-service attacks using RBF networks and statistical features. *Computer Networks 48*, 2 (2005), 235–245.

[87] GELENBE, E., AND LOUKAS, G. A self-aware approach to denial of service defence. *Computer Networks 51*, 5 (2007), 1299–1314.

[88] GOGOI, P., BHUYAN, M. H., BHATTACHARYYA, D. K., AND KALITA, J. K. Packet and flow-based network intrusion dataset. In *Proc. of the 5th International Conference on Contemporary Computing, Springer-Verlag* (Noida, India, 2012), pp. 322–334.

[89] GONG, R. H., ZULKERNINE, M., AND ABOLMAESUMI, P. A software implementation of a genetic algorithm based approach to network intrusion detection. In *Software Engineering, Artificial Intelligence, Networking and Parallel/Distributed Computing, 2005 and First ACIS International Workshop on Self-Assembling Wireless Networks. SNPD/SAWN 2005. Sixth International Conference on* (2005), IEEE, pp. 246–253.

[90] GOODRICH, M. T. Efficient packet marking for large-scale IP traceback. In *Proceedings of the 9th ACM Conference on Computer and Communications Security* (2002), ACM, pp. 117–126.

[91] GREENGARD, S. The war against botnets. *Communications of the ACM 55*, 2 (2012), 16–18.

[92] GU, Y., MCCALLUM, A., AND TOWSLEY, D. Detecting anomalies in network traffic using maximum entropy estimation. In *Proc*

of the 5th ACM SIGCOMM Conference on Internet Measurement (2005), USENIX Association, Berkeley, CA, USA, pp. 32–32.

[93] GUHA, S., RASTOGI, R., AND SHIM, K. Rock: A robust clustering algorithm for categorical attributes. In *Int'nl Conference on Data Engineering* (1999), pp. 512–521.

[94] HAN, J., AND KAMBER, M. *Data Mining: Concepts and Techniques.* Morgan Kaufmann Publishers, 2000.

[95] HANSON, R. S., AND CHEESEMAN, P. Bayesian classification theory. Tech. Rep. FIA-90-12-7-01, NASA Ames Research Center, AI Branch, 1991.

[96] HARRIS, B., AND HUNT, R. TCP/IP security threats and attack methods. *Computer Communications 22*, 10 (1999), 885–897.

[97] HASLUM, K., ABRAHAM, A., AND KNAPSKOG, S. Dips: A framework for distributed intrusion prediction and prevention using hidden Markov models and online fuzzy risk assessment. In *Information Assurance and Security, 2007. IAS 2007. Third International Symposium on* (2007), IEEE, pp. 183–190.

[98] HIGGINS, K. New massive botnet twice the size of storm. http://www.darkreading.com/attacks-breaches/new-massive-botnet-twice-the-size-of-storm/d/d-id/1129410. *Retrieved, May 13* (2008).

[99] HOLL, P. Exploring DDoS defense mechanisms. In *Proceedings of the Network Architectures and Services, March 2015* (2015), pp. 25–32.

[100] HOLZ, T., STEINER, M., DAHL, F., BIERSACK, E., AND FREILING, F. C. Measurements and mitigation of peer-to-peer-based botnets: A case study on storm worm. In *Proc. First Usenix Workshop Large Scale Exploits and Emergent Threats (LEET)* (2008).

[101] HOQUE, N., BHUYAN, M. H., BAISHYA, R., BHATTACHARYYA, D., AND KALITA, J. Network attacks: Taxonomy, tools and systems. *Journal of Network and Computer Applications* (2013).

[102] HRUSKA, J. New Mega-d Menace Muscles Storm Worm Aside. http://arstechnica.com., 2008.

[103] HUANG, H., ZHENG, Y., CHEN, H., AND WANG, R. Pchord: A distributed hash table for P2P network. *Frontiers of Electrical and Electronic Engineering in China 5*, 1 (2010), 49–58.

[104] HUANG, Y., ARSENAULT, D., AND SOOD, A. Closing cluster attack Windows through server redundancy and rotations. In *Proc. of the 2nd International Workshop on Cluster Security (Cluster-Sec06)* (Singapore, 2006).

[105] HUANG, Y., ARSENAULT, D., AND SOOD, A. Incorruptible system self-cleansing for intrusion tolerance. In *Proc. of the International Workshop on Information Assurance* (Phoenix, Arizona, 2006).

[106] HUANG, Y., ARSENAULT, D., AND SOOD, A. SCIT-DNS: Critical infrastructure protection through secure DNS server dynamic updates. *Journal of High Speed Networking 15*, 1 (2006), 1–19.

[107] HUANG, Y., ARSENAULT, D., AND SOOD, A. Securing DNS services through system self-cleansing and hardware enhancements. In *Proc. of the 1st International Conference on Availability, Reliability and Security (ARES'06)* (Viena, Austria, 2006).

[108] HUANG, Y., AND SOOD, A. Self-cleansing systems for intrusion containment. In *Proc. of the International Workshop on Self-Healing, Adaptive, and Self-Managed Systems (SHAMAN)* (2002).

[109] HUANG, Y., SOOD, A., AND BHASKAR, R. Countering web defacing attacks with system self-cleansing. In *Proc. of the 7th World Multiconference on Systems, Cybernatics and Informatics* (Orlando, Florida, 2003), pp. 12–16.

[110] HWANG, K., DAVE, P., AND TANACHAIWIWAT, S. Netshield: Protocol anomaly detection with data mining against DDoS attacks. In *Proc. 6th Int'nl Symposium on Recent Advances in Intrusion Detection* (Springer-Verlag, 2003), pp. 8–10.

[111] IANELLI, N., AND HACKWORTH, A. Botnets as vehicle for online crime. In *Proc. 18th Annual First Conference* (2006).

[112] IBM PROVENTIA NETWORK IPS SERIES. http://www.ibm.com.

[113] IDS/IPS, T. http://www.tippingpoint.com.

[114] INTELLIGENCE, M. Annual security report. *Symantec Corp* (2010).

[115] IOANNIDIS, J., AND BELLOVIN, S. M. Implementing pushback: Router-based defense against DDoS attacks.

[116] IPOLICY   INTRUSION   DETECTION/PREVENTION. http://www.ipolicynet.com.

[117] IPS, S. http://www.ndm.net/ips/stonesoft/stonegate-ips-1030.

[118] IPS: INTRUSION   PREVENTION   SYSTEM. http://www.javvin.com/networksecurity/ips.htmls, 2011.

[119] JAHNKE, M., THUL, C., AND MARTINI, P. Graph based metrics for intrusion response measures in computer networks. In *Local Computer Networks, 2007. LCN 2007. 32nd IEEE Conference on* (2007), IEEE, pp. 1035–1042.

[120] JALILI, R., IMANI-MEHR, F., AMINI, M., AND SHAHRIARI, H. R. Detection of distributed denial of service attacks using statistical preprocessor and unsupervised neural networks. In *Proc. of Int'nl Conference on Information Security Practice and Experience, Singapore, 11–14 April* (Springer-Verlag, 2005), pp. 192–203.

[121] JIA, T., AND WANG, X. The research and design of intelligent IPS model based on dynamic cloud firewall linkage. *International Journal of Digital Content Technology and its Applications 5*, 3 (2011), 304–9.

[122] JIAN-QI, Z., FENG, F., KE-XIN, Y., AND YAN-HENG, L. Dynamic entropy based DoS attack detection method. *Computers & Electrical Engineering 39*, 7 (2013), 2243–2251.

[123] JIN, S., AND YEUNG, D. S. A covariance analysis model for DDoS attack detection. In *Communications, 2004 IEEE International Conference on* (2004), vol. 4, IEEE, pp. 1882–1886.

[124] JOHANSEN, H., ALLAVENA, A., AND RENESSE, R. V. Fireflies: Scalable support for intrusion-tolerant network overlays. In *In*

the Proc of 1st ACM European Conference on Computer Systems (EUROSYS'06) (ACM, New York, USA, 2006), pp. 3–13.

[125] JOHN, J. P., MOSHCHUK, A., GRIBBLE, S. D., AND KRISHNA-MURTHY, A. Studying spamming botnets using Botlab. In *NSDI* (2009), vol. 9, pp. 291–306.

[126] JUNG, J., KRISHNAMURTHY, B., AND RABINOVICH, M. Flash crowds and denial of service attacks: Characterization and implications for CDNs and web sites. In *Proc. 11th Intl Conf. World Wide Web (WWW)* (2002), pp. 252–262.

[127] KABIRI, P., AND GHORBANI, A. A. Research on intrusion detection and response: A survey. *IJ Network Security 1*, 2 (2005), 84–102.

[128] KAILATH, T. The divergence and Bhattacharyya distance measures in signal selection. *Communication Technology, IEEE Transactions on 15*, 1 (1967), 52–60.

[129] KANG, M. S., LEE, S. B., AND GLIGOR, V. D. The crossfire attack. In *Security and Privacy (SP), 2013 IEEE Symposium on* (2013), IEEE, pp. 127–141.

[130] KANG, M. S., LEE, S. B., AND GLIGOR, V. D. The crossfire attack. In *IEEE Symposium on Security and Privacy (SP)* (2013), IEEE, pp. 127–141.

[131] KANOUN, W., CUPPENS-BOULAHIA, N., CUPPENS, F., AND DUBUS, S. Risk-aware framework for activating and deactivating policy-based response. In *Network and System Security (NSS), 2010 4th International Conference on* (2010), IEEE, pp. 207–215.

[132] KEIZER, G. Top botnets control 1 m hijacked computers. http://www.computerworld.com., 2008.

[133] KENDALL, M. G. Rank correlation methods, Oxford, England: Griffin Rank correlation methods, 1948.

[134] KHEIR, N., CUPPENS-BOULAHIA, N., CUPPENS, F., AND DEBAR, H. A service dependency model for cost-sensitive intrusion response. In *Computer Security–ESORICS 2010*. Springer, 2010, pp. 626–642.

[135] KIM, S., KIM, B., LEE, J., HWANG, C., AND J, L. Rule-based defense mechanism against DDoS attacks. In *Proceedings of the World Congress on Engineering 2008, vol 1* (WCE 2008, 2008), pp. 1–6.

[136] KNIGHT, J., HEIMBIGNER, D., AND WOLF, A. The willow architecture: Comprehensive survivability for large-scale distributed applications. In *Proc. Intrusion Tolerance System Workshop, Supplemental Vol. of the 2002 Int'l Conf. Dependable Systems and Networks* (IEEE Press, 2002), pp. C.7.1–C.7.8.

[137] KOUTEPAS, G., STAMATELOPOULOS, F., AND MAGLARIS, B. Distributed management architecture for cooperative detection and reaction to DDoS attacks. *Journal of Network and Systems Management 12* (2004), 73–94.

[138] KRAUSE, E. F. *Taxicab Geometry: An Adventure in Non-Euclidean Geometry.* Courier Corporation, 2012.

[139] KREIDL, O. P., AND FRAZIER, T. M. Feedback control applied to survivability: A host-based autonomic defense system. *IEEE Transactions on Reliability 53* (2004), 148–166.

[140] KULKARNI, A., AND BUSH, S. Detecting distributed denial-of-service attacks using Kolmogorov complexity metrics. *Journal of Network and Systems Management 14*, 1 (2006), 69–80.

[141] KUMAR, P. A. R., AND SELVAKUMAR, S. Detection of distributed denial of service attacks using an ensemble of adaptive and hybrid neuro-fuzzy systems. *Computer Communications 36*, 3 (2013), 303–319.

[142] LAPPAS, T., AND PELECHRINIS, K. Data mining techniques for (network) intrusion detection systems. *Department of Computer Science and Engineering UC Riverside, Riverside CA 92521* (2007).

[143] LAWRENCE, I., AND LIN, K. A concordance correlation coefficient to evaluate reproducibility. *Biometrics* (1989), 255–268.

[144] LEE, K., KIM, J., KWON, K. H., HAN, Y., AND KIM, S. DDoS attack detection method using cluster analysis. *Expert Systems with Applications 34* (2008), 16591665.

[145] LEE, W., FAN, W., MILLER, M., STOLFO, S. J., AND ZADOK, E. Toward cost-sensitive modeling for intrusion detection and response. *Journal of Computer Security 10*, 1 (2002), 5–22.

[146] LEITNER, M., LEITNER, P., ZACH, M., COLLINS, S., AND FAHY, C. Fault management based on peer-to-peer paradigms; A case study report from the Celtic project Madeira. In *Integrated Network Management, 2007. IM'07. 10th IFIP/IEEE International Symposium on* (2007), IEEE, pp. 697–700.

[147] LEWANDOWSKI, S. M., VAN HOOK, D. J., O'LEARY, G. C., HAINES, J. W., AND ROSSEY, L. M. Sara: Survivable autonomic response architecture. In *DARPA Information Survivability Conference & Exposition II, 2001. DISCEX'01. Proceedings* (2001), vol. 1, IEEE, pp. 77–88.

[148] LI, J., MIRKOVIC, J., WANG, M., REITHER, P., AND ZHANG, L. On the effectiveness of router-based packet filtering for distributed dos attack prevention in power-low internets. In *Proc. of the IEEE INFOCOM 2002* (2001), pp. 1557–1566.

[149] LI, K., HUANG, H., TIAN, S., AND XU, W. Improving one-class SVM for anomaly detection. In *Proc. of the Second International Conference on Machine Learning and Cybernetics* (Xi'an, 2003), pp. 3077–3081.

[150] LI, K., ZHOU, W., YU, S., AND DAI, B. Effective DDoS attacks detection using generalized entropy metric. In *Algorithms and Architectures for Parallel Processing*. Springer, 2009, pp. 266–280.

[151] LI, L., AND LEE, G. DDoS attack detection and wavelets. In *Proceedings. of the 12th International Conference on Computer Communications and Networks* (Dallas, Texas, USA, October 20-22, IEEE, 2003), pp. 421–427.

[152] LI, T., ZHOU, X., BRANDSTATTER, K., ZHAO, D., WANG, K., RAJENDRAN, A., ZHANG, Z., AND RAICU, I. ZHT: A lightweight reliable persistent dynamic scalable zero-hop distributed hash table. In *Parallel & Distributed Processing Symposium (IPDPS)* (2013).

[153] LIN, J. Divergence measures based on the Shannon entropy. *Information Theory, IEEE Transactions on 37*, 1 (1991), 145–151.

[154] LOCASTO, M. E., WANG, K., KEROMYTIS, A. D., AND STOLFO, S. J. Flips: Hybrid adaptive intrusion prevention. In *Recent Advances in Intrusion Detection* (2006), Springer, pp. 82–101.

[155] MA, X., AND CHEN, Y. DDoS detection method based on chaos analysis of network traffic entropy. *Communications Letters, IEEE 18*, 1 (2014), 114–117.

[156] MACESANU, G., CODAS, T., SULIMAN, C., AND TARNAUCA, B. Development of GTBoT, a high performance and modular indoor robot. In *Automation Quality and Testing Robotics (AQTR), 2010 IEEE International Conference on* (2010), vol. 1, IEEE, pp. 1–6.

[157] MACIÁ-FERNÁNDEZ, G., DÍAZ-VERDEJO, J. E., AND GARCÍA-TEODORO, P. Evaluation of a low-rate DoS attack against iterative servers. *Computer Networks 51*, 4 (2007), 1013–1030.

[158] MAHANTA, P., AHMED, H. A., BHATTACHARYYA, D. K., AND KALITA, J. K. An effective method for network module extraction from microarray data. *BMC Bioinformatics 13*, Suppl 13 (2012), S4.

[159] MAHONEY, M. V., AND CHAN, P. K. An analysis of the 1999 DARPA/Lincoln Laboratory evaluation data for network anomaly detection. In *Proc. of the 6th International Symposium on Recent Advances in Intrusion Detection* (2003), Springer, pp. 220–237.

[160] MARTINS, A. F., FIGUEIREDO, M. A., AGUIAR, P. M., SMITH, N. A., AND XING, E. P. Nonextensive entropic kernels. In *Proceedings of the 25th International Conference on Machine Learning* (2008), ACM, pp. 640–647.

[161] MAYMOUNKOV, P., AND MAZIERES, D. Kademlia: A peer-to-peer information system based on the XOR metric. In *Peer-to-Peer Systems*. Springer, 2002, pp. 53–65.

[162] MCAFEE. McAfee host intrusion prevention for desktop. http://www.mcafee.com.

[163] MCAFEE INTRUSHIELD IDS. http://www.ibm.com/support.

[164] MCHUGH, J. Testing intrusion detection systems: a critique of the 1998 and 1999 DARPA intrusion detection system evaluations as performed by lincoln laboratory. *ACM Transactions on Information and System Security 3*, 4 (November 2000), 262–294.

[165] MCMILLAN, R. Experts bicker over Conficker numbers, techworld, April 15. http://news.techworld.com., 2009.

[166] MICROHGJ, T. Worm SDbot. http://about-threats.trendmicro.com/archivemalware.aspx?language=us & name=wormsdbot, 2003.

[167] MIRKOVIC, J., DIETRICH, S., DITTRICH, D., AND REIHER, P. *Internet Denial of Service: Attack and Defense Mechanisms*. Prentice Hall, 2005.

[168] MIRKOVIC, J., PRIER, G., AND REIHER, P. Attacking DDoS at the source. In *Network Protocols, 2002. Proceedings. 10th IEEE International Conference* (2002), IEEE, pp. 312–321.

[169] MIRKOVIC, J., AND REIHER, P. A taxonomy of DDoS attack and DDoS defense mechanisms. vol. 34, *ACM SIGCOMM Computer Communication Review*, pp. 39–53.

[170] MIRKOVIC, J., AND REIHER, P. A taxonomy of DDoS attack and DDoS defense mechanisms. *ACM SIGCOMM Computer Communication Review 34*, 2 (2004), 39–53.

[171] MIRKOVIC, J., AND REIHER, P. D-ward: A source-end defense against flooding denial-of-service attacks. *IEEE Transactions Dependable and Secure Computing 2*, 3 (July 2005), 216–232.

[172] MIT LINCOLN LAB, I. S. T. G. DARPA intrusion detection data sets. http://www.ll.mit.edu/mission/communications/ist/corpora/ideval/data/2000data.html, March 2000.

[173] MIZRAK, A. T., CHENG, Y.-C., MARZULLO, K., AND SAVAGE, S. Fatih: Detecting and isolating malicious routers. In *Dependable Systems and Networks, 2005. DSN 2005. Proceedings. International Conference* (2005), IEEE, pp. 538–547.

[174] MNSMAN, S., AND FLESHER, P. System or security managers adaptive response tool. In *DARPA Information Survivability Conference and Exposition, 2000. DISCEX'00. Proceedings* (2000), vol. 2, IEEE, pp. 56–68.

[175] MOORE, D., SHANNON, C., BROWN, D. J., VOELKER, G. M., AND SAVAGE, S. Inferring Internet denial of service activity. *ACM Transactions on Computer Systems 24* (2006), 115–139.

[176] MU, C., AND LI, Y. An intrusion response decision-making model based on hierarchical task network planning. *Expert systems with applications 37*, 3 (2010), 2465–2472.

[177] MUKKAMALA, S., SUNG, A. H., AND ABRAHAM, A. Intrusion detection using an ensemble of intelligent paradigms. *Journal of network and computer applications 28*, 2 (2005), 167–182.

[178] NEUMANN, P. G., AND PORRAS, P. A. Experience with EMERALD to date. In *Workshop on Intrusion Detection and Network Monitoring* (1999), pp. 73 – 80.

[179] NGUYEN, H.-V., AND CHOI, Y. Proactive detection of DDoS attacks utilizing k-NN classifier in an anti-DDoS framework. *International Journal of Electrical, Computer, and Systems Engineering 4*, 4 (2010), 247–252.

[180] NGUYEN, Q. L., AND SOOD, A. A comparison of intrusion-tolerant system architectures. *IEEE Security & Privacy 9*, 4 (2010), 24–31.

[181] NO, G., AND RA, I. An efficient and reliable DDoS attack detection using a fast entropy computation method. In *Communications and Information Technology, 2009. ISCIT 2009. 9th International Symposium* (2009), IEEE, pp. 1223–1228.

[182] NOH, S., LEE, C., CHOI, K., AND JUNG, G. *Detecting Distributed Denial of Service (DDoS) Attacks through Inductive Learning*. Springer Berlin Haidelberg, 2003, pp. 286–295.

[183] NORTHCUTT, S., BEALE, J., BAKER, A. R., ESLER, J., AND KOHLENBERG, T. *Snort: IDS and IPS toolkit*. Syngress Press, 2007.

[184] O'BRIEN, D., SMITH, R., KAPPEL, T., AND BITZER, C. Intrusion tolerance via network layer controls. In *Proc. of the DARPA Information Survivability Conf. and Exposition (Discex), vol. 1* (IEEE Press, 2003), pp. 90–96.

[185] OSIRIS: HOST BASED INTRUSION DETECTION. http://itg.chem.indiana.edu/inc/wiki/software/osiris/222.html.

[186] PAL, P., RUBEL, P., ATIGHETCHI, M., AND ET AL. An architecture for an adaptive intrusion-tolerant applications. *Software Pract. Experience 36* (2006), 1331–1354.

[187] PAL, P., WEBBER, F., AND SCHANTZ, R. The DPASA survivable JBI-a High-Water Mark in intrusion-tolerant systems. In *Proc. 2007 Workshop Recent Advances in Intrusion Tolerant Systems (Wraits 07)* (2007).

[188] PAPADAKI, M., AND FURNELL, S. Achieving automated intrusion response: A prototype implementation. *Information Management & Computer Security 14*, 3 (2006), 235–251.

[189] PARK, K., AND LEE, H. On the effectiveness of route-based packet filtering for distributed dos attack prevention in power-law internets. In *ACM SIGCOMM Computer Communication Review* (2001), vol. 31, ACM, pp. 15–26.

[190] PAULO, S., BESSANI, A. N., AND OBELHEIRO, R. R. The FOREVER service for fault/intrusion removal. In *In the Proc of WRAITS 2008* (ACM, Glasgow, Scotland, 2008).

[191] PENG, T., LECKIE, C., AND RAMAMOHANARAO, K. Proactively detecting distributed denial of service attacks using source IP address monitoring. In *Networking 2004* (2004), Springer, pp. 771–782.

[192] PETERSON, W. W. *Error-correcting codes*, vol. 16. Wiley and Sons, 1961.

[193] PHPIDS. https://phpids.org/.

[194] PIETERSE, H., AND OLIVIER, M. S. Android botnets on the rise: Trends and characteristics. In *Information Security for South Africa (ISSA), 2012* (2012), IEEE, pp. 1–5.

[195] PORRAS, P. A., AND NEUMANN, P. G. Emerald: Event monitoring enabling response to anomalous live disturbances. In *Proceedings of the 20th national information systems security conference* (1997), pp. 353–365.

[196] PRAS, A., SPEROTTO, A., MOURA, G. C. M., DRAGO, I., BARBOSA, R., SADRE, R., SCHMIDT, R., AND HOFSTEDE, R. Attacks by anonymous? Wikileaks proponents not anonymous. Design and Analysis of Communication Systems Group (DACS) CTIT Technical Report, pp. 1–10.

[197] PRINCE, M. Technical details behind a 400 Gbps ntp amplification DDoS attack. *Cloudflare, Inc 13* (2014).

[198] QUINLAN, J. R. *C4.5: Programs for Machine Learning.* Morgan Kaufman publisher, 1993.

[199] RAGSDALE, D. J., CARVER, C., HUMPHRIES, J. W., POOCH, U. W., ET AL. Adaptation techniques for intrusion detection and intrusion response systems. In *Systems, Man, and Cybernetics, 2000 IEEE International Conference on* (2000), vol. 4, IEEE, pp. 2344–2349.

[200] RAMAMOORTHI, A., SUBBULAKSHMI, T., AND SHALINIE, S. M. Real-time detection and classification of DDoS attacks using enhanced SVM with string kernels. In *IEEE Int'nl Conference on Recent Trends in Information Technology (ICRTIT)* (IEEE Press, 2011), pp. 91–96.

[201] RANJAN, S., SWAMINATHAN, R., UYSAL, M., AND KNIGHTLY, E. DDoS-resilient scheduling to counter application layer attacks under imperfect detection. Proc. of IEEE INFOCOM, 2006, Barcelona, Spain, pp. 1–13.

[202] RATNASAMY, S., FRANCIS, P., HANDLEY, M., KARP, R., AND SHENKER, S. *A scalable content-addressable network*, vol. 31. ACM, 2001.

[203] RBOT. http://ruby-rbot.org/, 2003.

[204] RENYI, A. On measures of entropy and information. In *Proc. of the 4th Barkeley Symposium on Mathematics, Statistics and Probability* (1960), pp. 547–561.

[205] REYNOLDS, J. C., JUST, J., CLOUGH, L., AND MAGLICH, R. On-line intrusion detection and attack prevention using diversity, generate-and-test and generalization. In *Proc. of the 36th Int'nl Conference on System Sciences (HICSS'03)* (IEEE Press, 2003).

[206] ROESCH, M. Snort: Lightweight intrusion detection for networks. In *Proc. of the 13th USENIX Conference on System Administration* (Washington, DC, 1999), pp. 229–238.

[207] ROWSTRON, A., AND DRUSCHEL, P. Pastry: Scalable, decentralized object location, and routing for large-scale peer-to-peer systems. In *Middleware 2001* (2001), Springer, pp. 329–350.

[208] SAIFULLAH, A. Defending against Distributed Denial-of-Service Attacks with Weight-Fair Router Throttling. Technical Report no wucse-2009-7. Department of Computer Sc and Engineering, Washington University, 2009.

[209] SALTZER, J. H., REED, D. P., AND CLARK, D. D. End-to-end arguments in system design. *ACM Transactions on Computer Systems (TOCS) 2*, 4 (1984), 277–288.

[210] SAVAGE, S., WETHERALL, D., KARLIN, A. R., AND ANDERSON, T. Practical Network Support for IP Traceback. In *Proc. of the ACM SIGCOMM 2000 Conference on Applications, Technologies, Architectures, and Protocols for Computer Communication* (Stockholm, Sweden, August 28 September 1 2000), ACM, pp. 295–306.

[211] SCARFONE, K., AND MELL, P. Guide to intrusion detection and prevention systems (idps): Recommendations of the nist. *NIST Special Publication*, 800–94.

[212] SCHERRER, A., LARRIEU, N., OWEZARSKI, P., BORGNAT, P., AND ABRY, P. Non-Gaussian and long memory statistical characterizations for Internet traffic with anomalies. *IEEE Transactions on Dependable Secure Computing 4*, 1 (2007), 56–70.

[213] SCHNACKENGERG, D., HOLLIDAY, H., SMITH, R., DJAHANDARI, K., AND STERNE, D. Cooperative intrusion traceback and response architecture (CITRA). In *IEEE DARPA Information Survivability Conference and Exposition (DISCEX I), vol.1* (2001), IEEE, pp. 56 – 68.

[214] SCHNACKENGERG, D., HOLLIDAY, H., SMITH, R., DJAHAN-
      DARI, K., AND STERNE, D. Cooperative intrusion traceback and
      response architecture (CITRA). In *DARPA Information Surviv-
      ability Conference & Exposition II, 2001. DISCEX'01. Pro-
      ceedings* (2001), vol. 1, IEEE, pp. 56–68.

[215] SECURENET IDS/IPS. http://www.intrusion.com.

[216] SECURITY, I. P. D. E. http://www.ibm.com.

[217] SEKAR, V., DUFFIELD, N., SPATSCHECK, O., VAN DER MERWE,
      J., AND ZHANG, H. LADS: large-scale automated DDoS de-
      tection system. In *Proceedings of the Annual Conference on
      USENIX Annual Technical Conference* (Boston, MA, 30 May–
      3 June, USENIX Association, 2006), pp. 16–29.

[218] SHANNON, C. E. A mathematical theory of communication. *Bell
      System Technical Journal 27* (1948), 397–423.

[219] SHIAELES, S. N., KATOS, V., KARAKOS, A. S., AND PA-
      PADOPOULOS, B. K. Real-time DDoS detection using fuzzy es-
      timators. *Computers & Security 31*, 6 (2012), 782–790.

[220] SHON, T., AND MOON, J. A hybrid machine learning approach
      to network anomaly detection. *Information Sciences 177*, 18
      (2007), 3799–3821.

[221] SHUAI, W., XIANG, C., PENG, L., AND DAN, L. S-URL Flux:
      A novel C&C protocol for mobile botnets. In *Trustworthy Com-
      puting and Services*. Springer, 2013, pp. 412–419.

[222] SIATERLIS, C., AND MAGLARIS, V. Detecting incoming and
      outgoing DDoS attacks at the edge using a single set of net-
      work characteristics. In *10th IEEE Symposium on Computers
      and Communications (ISCC'05)* (IEEE Press, 2005), pp. 469–
      475.

[223] SNOEREN, A. C., PARTRIDGE, C., SANCHEZ, L. A., JONES,
      C. E., TCHAKOUNTIO, F., KENT, S. T., AND STRAYER, W. T.
      Hash-based IP traceback. In *ACM SIGCOMM Computer Com-
      munication Review* (2001), vol. 31, ACM, pp. 3–14.

[224] SOMAYAJI, A., AND FORREST, S. Automated response using system-call delay. In *Usenix Security Symposium* (2000), pp. 185–197.

[225] SORENSEN, S. Competitive overview of statistical anomaly detection. *White Paper, Juniper Networks* (2004).

[226] SPECHT, S. M., AND LEE, R. B. Distributed denial of service: Taxonomies of attacks, tools, and countermeasures. In *ISCA PDCS* (2004), pp. 543–550.

[227] SPEROTTO, A., SCHAFFRATH, G., SADRE, R., MORARIU, C., PRAS, A., AND STILLER, B. An overview of IP flow-based intrusion detection. *IEEE Communications Surveys & Tutorials 12*, 3 (2010), 343–356.

[228] STAKHANOVA, N., BASU, S., AND WONG, J. A cost-sensitive model for preemptive intrusion response systems. In *AINA* (2007), vol. 7, pp. 428–435.

[229] STAKHANOVA, N., BASU, S., AND WONG, J. A taxonomy of intrusion response systems. *International Journal of Information and Computer Security 1*, 1-2 (2007), 169–184.

[230] STEWART, J. Spam botnets to watch in 2009. *SecureWorks, http://www. secureworks. com/research/threats/botnets2009* (2009).

[231] STONE-GROSS, B., COVA, M., GILBERT, B., KEMMERER, R., KRUEGEL, C., AND VIGNA, G. Analysis of a botnet takeover. *Security & Privacy, IEEE 9*, 1 (2011), 64–72.

[232] STOVER, S., DITTRICH, D., HERNANDEZ, J., AND DIETRICH, S. Analysis of the Storm and Nugache trojans: P2P is here. *USENIX; login 32*, 6 (2007), 18–27.

[233] STRASBURG, C., STAKHANOVA, N., BASU, S., AND WONG, J. S. A framework for cost sensitive assessment of intrusion response selection. In *Computer Software and Applications Conference, 2009. COMPSAC'09. 33rd Annual IEEE International* (2009), vol. 1, IEEE, pp. 355–360.

[234] STRATA GUARD IPS. http://www.data-alliance.com.my.

[235] STUDER, A., AND PERRIG, A. The Coremelt attack. In *Computer Security ESORICS 2009, Lecture Notes in Computer Science, vol 5789* (2009), Springer, pp. 37–52.

[236] SU, M.-Y. Real-time anomaly detection systems for denial-of-service attacks by weighted k-nearest-neighbor classifiers. *Expert Systems with Applications 38*, 4 (2011), 3492–3498.

[237] TAN, Z., JAMDAGNI, A., HE, X., NANDA, P., AND LIU, R. P. A system for denial-of-service attack detection based on multivariate correlation analysis. *Parallel and Distributed Systems, IEEE Transactions on 25*, 2 (2014), 447–456.

[238] TANACHAIWIWAT, S., HWANG, K., AND CHEN, Y. Adaptive intrusion response to minimize risk over multiple network attacks. *ACM Trans on Information and System Security 19* (2002), 1–30.

[239] TAO, P., LECKIE, C., AND KOTAGIRI, R. Survey of network-based defense mechanisms countering the DoS and DDoS problems. *ACM Computing Surveys 39(1)* (2007).

[240] TAO, Y., AND YU, S. DDoS attack detection at local area networks using information theoretical metrics. In *Proc. of IEEE International Conference on Trust, Security and Privacy in Computing and Communications (TrustCom)* (2013), pp. 233–240.

[241] TESCH, D., AND ABELAR, G. *Security Threat Mitigation and Response: Understanding Cisco Security MARS*. Cisco Press, 2006.

[242] THOMAS, R., MARK, B., JOHNSON, T., AND CROALL, J. Netbouncer: Client-legitimacy-based high-performance DDoS filtering. In *DARPA Information Survivability Conference and Exposition, 2003. Proceedings* (2003), vol. 1, IEEE, pp. 14–25.

[243] THOTTAN, M., AND JI, C. Anomaly detection in IP networks. *IEEE Transactions on Signal Processing 51*, 8 (August 2003), 2191–2204.

[244] THOTTAN, M., LIU, G., AND JI, C. Anomaly detection approaches for communication networks. In *Algorithms for Next Generation Networks*. Springer, 2010, pp. 239–261.

[245] TOOSI, A. N., AND KAHANI, M. A new approach to intrusion detection based on an evolutionary soft computing model using neuro-fuzzy classifiers. *Computer communications 30*, 10 (2007), 2201–2212.

[246] TOTH, T., AND KRUEGEL, C. Evaluating the impact of automated intrusion response mechanisms. In *Computer Security Applications Conference, 2002. Proceedings. 18th Annual* (2002), IEEE, pp. 301–310.

[247] TREND MICRO. Worm Agobot. http://www.trendmicro.com/vinfo /virusencyclo /default5.asp?vname=wormagobot_ajc, 2004.

[248] TROLLE BORUP, L. *Peer-to-peer botnets: A case study on Waledac.* PhD thesis, Technical University of Denmark, DTU, DK-2800 Kgs. Lyngby, Denmark, 2009.

[249] UDHAYAN, J., AND HAMSAPRIYA, T. Statistical segregation method to minimize the false detections during DDoS attacks. *IJ Network Security 13*, 3 (2011), 152–160.

[250] VALDES, A., AND ET AL. An architecture for an adaptive intrusion-tolerant server. In *Security Protocols, LNCS 2845* (Springer, 2003), pp. 569–574.

[251] VANCE, F. Clustering and the continuous k-means algorithm.

[252] VAUGHN, R., AND EVRON, G. DNS Amplification Attacks. *http://www. isotf. org/news/DNS-Amplification-Attacks. pdf* (2006).

[253] VERSSIMO, P. E., NEVES, N. F., CACHIN, C., PORITZ, J., POWELL, D., DESWARTE, Y., STROUD, R., AND WELCH, I. Intrusion-tolerant middleware: The road to automatic security. *IEEE Security & Privacy 4*, 4 (2006), 54–62.

[254] VIJAYASARATHY, R., RAGHAVAN, S. V., AND RAVINDRAN, B. A system approach to network modeling for DDoS detection using a Naive Bayesian classifier. In *3rd International Conference on Communication Systems and Networks (COMSNETS'11)* (IEEE Press, 2011), pp. 1–10.

[255] WANG, D., MADAN, B. B., AND TRIVEDI, K. S. Security analysis of sitar intrusion tolerant system. In *Proc of ACM Int'nl Workshop on Survivable and Self-regenerative Systems* (Fairfax, Virginia, 2003).

[256] WANG, F., JOU, F., GONG, F., SARGOR, C GOSEVA-POPSTOJANOVA, K., AND TRIVEDI, K. Sitar: A scalable intrusion tolerant architecture for distributed services. In *Foundations of Intrusion Tolerant Systems* (2003), pp. 359–367.

[257] WANG, H., ZHANG, D., AND SHIN, K. G. Detecting SYN flooding attacks. vol. 3, IEEE INFOCOMM'02, pp. 1530–1539.

[258] WANG, J., PHAN, R.-W., WHITLEY, J. N., AND PARISH, D. J. Augmented attack tree modeling of distributed denial of services and tree based attack detection method. In *Computer and Information Technology (CIT), 2010 IEEE 10th International Conference on* (2010), IEEE, pp. 1009–1014.

[259] WANG, X., REEVES, D. S., AND WU, S. F. Tracing based active intrusion response. *Journal of Information Warfare 1*, 1 (2001), 50–61.

[260] WANG, X., REEVES, D. S., WU, S. F., AND YUILL, J. Sleepy watermark tracing: An active network-based intrusion response framework. In *Trusted Information*. Springer, 2001, pp. 369–384.

[261] WEI, W., CHEN, F., XIA, Y., AND JIN, G. A rank correlation based detection against distributed reflection dos attacks. *Communications Letters, IEEE 17*, 1 (2013), 173–175.

[262] WEISS, S. M., AND ZHANG, T. *The Handbook of Data Mining*. Lawrence Erlbaum Assoc. Inc., 2003, pp. 426–439.

[263] WHITE, G., FISCH, E., AND POOCH, U. Cooperating security manager: A peer-based intrusion detection system. *IEEE Networks 10* (1996), 20–23.

[264] WHITE, G. B., FISCH, E. A., AND POOCH, U. W. Cooperating security managers: A peer-based intrusion detection system. *Network, IEEE 10*, 1 (1996), 20–23.

[265] WU, Y.-C., TSENG, H.-R., YANG, W., AND JAN, R.-H. DDoS detection and traceback with decision tree and grey relational analysis. *International Journal of Ad Hoc and Ubiquitous Computing 7*, 2 (2011), 121–136.

[266] WWW.PHION.COM. Netfence gateways.

[267] XIA, Z., LU, S., LI, J., AND TANG, J. Enhancing DDoS flood attack detection via intelligent fuzzy logic. *Informatica (Slovenia) 34*, 4 (2010), 497–507.

[268] XIANG, Y., LI, K., AND ZHOU, W. Low-rate DDoS attacks detection and traceback by using new information metrics. *Information Forensics and Security, IEEE Transactions on 6*, 2 (2011), 426–437.

[269] XIANG, Y., LI, K., AND ZHOU, W. Low-rate DDoS attacks detection and traceback by using new information metrics. *IEEE Transactions on Information Forensics and Security 6* (2011), 426–437.

[270] XIANG, Y., ZHOU, W., AND GUO, M. Flexible deterministic packet marking: An IP traceback system to find the real source of attacks. *Parallel and Distributed Systems, IEEE Transactions on 20*, 4 (2009), 567–580.

[271] XIE, Y., AND YU, S.-Z. Monitoring the application-layer DDoS attacks for popular websites. *IEEE/ACM Transactions on Networking 17*, 1 (2009), 15–25.

[272] XU, X., LU, Y., TUNG, A. K., AND WANG, W. Mining shifting-and-scaling co-regulation patterns on gene expression profiles. In *null* (2006), IEEE, p. 89.

[273] YATAGAI, T., ISOHARA, T., AND SASASE, I. Detection of HTTP-get flood attack based on analysis of page access behavior. In *IEEE Pacific Rim Conference on Communications, Computers and Signal Processing* (2007), IEEE, pp. 232–235.

[274] YEN, T.-F., AND REITER, M. K. Traffic aggregation for malware detection. In *Detection of Intrusions and Malware, and Vulnerability Assessment*. Springer, 2008, pp. 207–227.

[275] YU, J., LEE, H., KIM, M.-S., AND PARK, D. Traffic flooding attack detection with SNMP MIB using SVM. *Computer Communications 31*, 17 (2008), 4212–4219.

[276] YU, J., LI, Z., CHEN, H., AND CHEN, X. A detection and offense mechanism to defend against application layer DDoS attacks. *Third Int'nl Conference on Networking and Services*, IEEE.

[277] YU, M. A nonparametric adaptive CUSUM method and its application in network anomaly detection. *Int'nl Journal of Advancements in Computing Technology 4*, 1 (2012), 280–288.

[278] YU, S., AND ZHOU, W. Entropy-based collaborative detection of DDoS attacks on community networks. In *Proc. of IEEE Int'nl Conference on Pervasive Computing and Communications* (IEEE Computer Society, 2008), pp. 566–571.

[279] YU, S., ZHOU, W., DOSS, R., AND JIA, W. Traceback of DDoS attacks using entropy variations. *Parallel and Distributed Systems, IEEE Transactions on 22*, 3 (2011), 412–425.

[280] YU, S., ZHOU, W., DOSS, R., AND JIA, W. Traceback of DDoS attacks using entropy variations. *IEEE Transactions on Parallel and Distributed Systems 22* (2011), 412–425.

[281] YU, S., ZHOU, W., JIA, W., GUO, S., XIANG, Y., AND TANG, F. Discriminating DDoS attacks from flash crowds using flow correlation coefficient. *IEEE Transactions on Parallel and Distributed Systems 23*, 6 (2012), 1073–1080.

[282] YUAN, J., AND MILLS, K. Monitoring the macroscopic effect of DDoS flooding attacks. *Dependable and Secure Computing, IEEE Transactions on 2*, 4 (2005), 324–335.

[283] ZANDER, S., NGUYEN, T., AND ARMITAGE, G. Automated traffic classification and application identification using machine learning. In *IEEE Conference on Local Computer Networks, 2005. 30th Anniversary* (IEEE Press, 2005), pp. 250–257.

[284] ZEIDANLOO, H. R., AND MANAF, A. A. Botnet command and control mechanisms. In *Computer and Electrical Engineering, 2009. ICCEE'09. Second International Conference on* (2009), vol. 1, IEEE, pp. 564–568.

[285] ZENG, Y., SHIN, K. G., AND HU, X. Design of SMS commanded-and-controlled and P2P-structured mobile botnets. In *Proceedings of the Fifth ACM Conference on Security and Privacy in Wireless and Mobile Networks* (2012), ACM, pp. 137–148.

[286] ZHANG, C., CAI, Z., CHEN, W., LUO, X., AND YIN, J. Flow level detection and filtering of low-rate DDoS. *Computer Networks 56*, 15 (2012), 3417–3431.

[287] ZHAO, B. Y., HUANG, L., STRIBLING, J., RHEA, S. C., JOSEPH, A. D., AND KUBIATOWICZ, J. D. Tapestry: A resilient global-scale overlay for service deployment. *Selected Areas in Communications, IEEE Journal on 22*, 1 (2004), 41–53.

[288] ZHONG, R., AND YUE, G. DDoS detection system based on data mining. In *Proc of ISNNS'10* (P. R. China, April, 2010), pp. 62–65.

[289] ZHOU, C. V., LECKIE, C., AND KARUNASEKERA, S. A survey of coordinated attacks and collaborative intrusion detection. *Computers & Security 29*, 1 (2010), 124–140.

Index

An environmentally friendly book printed and bound in England by www.printondemand-worldwide.com

PEFC Certified

This product is
from sustainably
managed forests
and controlled
sources

www.pefc.org

PEFC/16-33-415